Trevor Mostyn has been journalist, p
world, Iran and India. He wrote for
Revolution in Iran and on the civil wa
Times's deputy correspondent in (
correspondent for *The Tablet.* In 199
Union's Med Media Programme, runn ——————— ——ween the media of
Europe and the Middle East. His has published eight books on the Middle
East. His book *Censorship in Islamic Society* was published in 2002 and
he has just finished a romantic novel set in Palestine. He is deputy chair
of English PEN's Writers in Prison Committee.

'This is an enthralling account of a period in Egypt's history now too often forgotten. Trevor Mostyn brings to life a glittering near century which opened with the Suez Canal and launched Cairo as one of the world's great cities.'

Lisa Appignanesi

'*Egypt's Belle Epoque* has the immediacy of oral history. This narrative depicts with wit and elegance the grandeur and decadence of a not so distant past. Trevor Mostyn writes as if he was himself a witness to the extraordinary events.'

Moris Farhi

'A teeming, vivid portrait of the pomp, lasciviousness and blood-soaked cruelty of a great culture at the crossroads of history. It cries out to be made into a film.'

Terence Blacker

'. . .the remarkable story of how Cairo was transformed into a modern city.'

The Middle East Book Review

'. . .an entertaining and enlightening account of high life in Cairo between 1869 and 1952.'

South

'The stories are told with relish and style. . .'

Al Ahram Weekly

Tauris Parke Paperbacks is an imprint of I.B.Tauris. It is dedicated to publishing books in accessible paperback editions for the serious general reader within a wide range of categories, including biography, history, travel and the ancient world. The list includes select, critically acclaimed works of top quality writing by distinguished authors that continue to challenge, to inform and to inspire. These are books that possess those subtle but intrinsic elements that mark them out as something exceptional.

The Colophon of Tauris Parke Paperbacks is a representation of the ancient Egyptian ibis, sacred to the god Thoth, who was himself often depicted in the form of this most elegant of birds. Thoth was credited in antiquity as the scribe of the ancient Egyptian gods and as the inventor of writing and was associated with many aspects of wisdom and learning.

EGYPT'S BELLE EPOQUE

Cairo and the Age of the Hedonists

TREVOR MOSTYN

TPP

TAURIS PARKE
PAPERBACKS

Published in 2006 by Tauris Parke Paperbacks
An imprint of I.B.Tauris and Co Ltd
6 Salem Road, London W2 4BU
175 Fifth Avenue, New York NY 10010
www.ibtauris.com

In the United States of America and Canada distributed by
Palgrave Macmillan, a division of St. Martin's Press
175 Fifth Avenue, New York NY 10010

First published in 1989 by Quartet Books Limited
Copyright © 1989 and 2006 by Trevor Mostyn
Cover image *The Khabanija Fountain, Cairo* 1845 (oil on canvas)
by Tchernezov, Tver Art Gallery, Russia

ISBN 1 84511 240 7
EAN 978 1 84511 240 0

A full CIP record for this book is available from the British Library
A full CIP record is available from the Library of Congress

Library of Congress Catalog Card Number: available

Printed and bound in India by Replika Press Pvt. Ltd

Dedication

To my Cairene friends, Hani and Rosemary, Adel, Amy, Liz, Anna, Janey, Kate, Niazi, Jack and Catherine, Bob and Jenny, Raouf, Salah, Ken, Chris, Gary and others who shared those beautiful evenings on our Nileside balconies at Saray al-Gezira, our 'Glittering Triangle'.

Contents

Introduction   1

1   Chibuks and Lice in Ismail's Harem   5
2   Obsession for an Empress   9
3   Napoleon's Hated '*Mission Civilizatrice*'   14
4   Muhammad Ali – a Brutal Age of Development   21
5   A Cruel Princess   29
6   Rulers of the New Renaissance   35
7   Ismail – a Ruler Obsessed   42
8   Paris's *Belle Epoque* and the Great Exhibition   52
9   Ismail's Cairo – a Glitzy Age   61
10   The Finest Opera House in the World   72
11   The Palace of the Empress   83
12   The Cousin of the Empress   88
13   La Belle Eugénie   96
14   The Opening of the Accursed Canal   101
15   A Week of Hedonism   107
16   The Fall of Eugénie   114
17   The Fall of Ismail   119
18   Mr Cook and the Hotel Age   125
19   Cairo: the Englishman's Playground   129
20   Cairo's Sweet-scented Odalisques   141
21   The Age of the Great Hotels   149
22   Cairo's Last Flame   160
23   Setting Fire to Ismail's City   167

Epilogue: Ismail's Cairo Today   171
Notes   178
Bibliography   185
Index   191

Acknowledgements

The author wishes to offer his warmest thanks to Albert Hourani and Adel Sabet for reading the manuscript and advising on changes, to Amani Kamal al-Din for her collaboration on an earlier, related project and to Elke Pflughardt for advice on the German architects and designers of several Cairo buildings. He is grateful to Carolyn and Nolly Zervudachi for lending him *Twilight Memories*, the memoirs of Despina Zervudachi, and to Nadim Shehardi, Director of the Centre for Lebanese Studies at Oxford, Edward Swinglehurst of the Thomas Cook Archive in London and Nabila Harris for helping him with the illustrations. He would also like to thank Princess Lody Cordahi, Prince Hassan Hassan, Prince Abbas Hilmi and John Papasyan for their help and advice.

Introduction

In September 1869, at the height of the heady pleasures of France's Second Empire and four months after the opening of the *Folies Bergère* nightclub in Paris, the Empress Eugénie embarked on a voyage to Egypt to inaugurate the opening of the Suez Canal. The celebrations were to be a final explosion of hedonism before the collapse of both the French regime and that of her adoring host, the Khedive Ismail of Egypt. In Cairo, however, a new tone had been set by the France of Baron Haussmann's boulevards and by the decadence expressed by both the great courtesans and the cancan dancers that repelled yet obsessed writers like Emile Zola. The tone was set – for Egypt's small, ruthless élite – for a European-style opulence that was to endure until the revolution of 1952 swept it all away.

This book is the story of Cairo's two worlds – high life, low life – subsequent to Eugénie's trip. The glittering courtliness of this woman who obsessed Europe, and of her ladies-in-waiting, is set against the primitivism of the Egyptian and Ottoman royal courts. During the Empress's stopover at the Sultan's court the French ladies are lifted by their dainty waists like bundles of straw by the giant eunuchs of Istanbul's Beylerbey Palace. In Egypt, meanwhile, a crude violence lurks beneath the new order made cosmetically respectable by the European scientists, literati and palace governesses employed to create it. According to the Orientalist memoires of European governesses, Muhammad Ali's daughter, Princess Nazli, had slave girls who fell asleep on duty promptly disembowelled in her bedroom, while even the mother of the debonair Khedive Ismail was said by the same writers to have had her night's lovers slaughtered before dawn. Such grossness is

1

balanced by stories of the little princesses of the Khedival harem flinging off their veils and dresses and peering giggling out of the train window to the disapproval of their stern eunuchs.

Ismail, a nineteenth-century Medici and the founder of modern Egypt, reflected the dichotomies of the age. Perfectly happy to have his finance minister strangled to death in the palace he had built for his beloved Eugénie, he posed in Europe as the perfect gentleman. In Paris he probably shared the actress-courtesan, Hortense Schneider, as his mistress with Edward Prince of Wales. If Napoleon Bonaparte's short visit had resulted in Paris becoming Egypt's cultural focus, the writings of sensualist authors like Gustave Flaubert had already established it as a symbol of worldly delight. The Suez Canal celebrations were to act as a catalyst for a *belle époque* in Egypt which would endure until the soft decay of King Farouk's tired reign brought it all tumbling down, to be replaced by the stern new order of Gamal abd al-Nasser.

After the exile of Ismail the balls went on in his Nileside palaces and the great operas were performed in his lovely opera house, while the Italian prostitutes stood under the gas-lit arches of nearby Ezbekiyya, the famous square where tourists could buy a live tiger in a cage or a hooded cobra. Cairo by now had become an essential stop on the Grand Tour for figures like Anthony Trollope, Benjamin Disraeli, Theodor Herzl, Edward Prince of Wales and Cecil Beaton. While the terrace of Shepheard's Hotel became a prism for Europe's social intrigues and vanities, the Turf Club became a colonial mirror-image of London's Pall Mall clubland. Yet tucked away in the nearby alleyways were the dens of vice, not only the places where the exotic Ghawazee girls danced, but also the haunting world of the great pimp of Wasah, that 'repulsive pervert'... who 'sat like an ebony doll, occasionally holding out a bejewelled hand to be kissed by some passing admirer'.[1] Flaubert had revelled in the fleshpots but the British policeman Russell Pasha was horrified by the 'painted harlots sitting like beasts of prey behind the iron grills of their ground-floor brothels'.[2]

Mark Twain found Shepheard's (often called 'the' Shepheard's by locals and so referred to throughout this book) a bore while Mrs Evelyn Waugh admired the 'demi-mondaines in picture frocks' – one led her pet monkey from a silver harness – and Cecil Beaton noted that Egypt's sloth was Hitler's greatest ally. The inter-war and war years, when figures such as Duff Cooper and Malcolm Muggeridge tasted Cairo's mixed delights, bring the book to an end, an end concomitant with that of Farouk, the last, sad ruler of the line of Muhammad Ali. What remains of the *belle époque* is now more discreet. The great drawing-rooms in which French persiflage is murmured over caviar and fine wines are now hidden in penthouse apartments at the top of high-rise buildings, and decorated with seventeenth-century English paintings, Ottoman miniatures and Greek and Roman statues.

The vicissitudes of fate have rarely threatened Cairo's worldliness. 'No one,' noted Freya Stark as Rommel prepared to march on Alexandria, 'can forget the gaiety and the glitter of Cairo while the desert war went on.'

If you gaze across the Nile from Cairo's Gezira (the Island) at dawn and watch the orange glimmer of the sun spill among the buildings and mosques of old Boulaq, you can just imagine the splendour of Ismail's city. In the dawn haze in the distance to your right you can see the Muhammad Ali Mosque and the citadel dominating the city from Muqattam Hill. At this hour you could still mistake the buildings along the Boulaq corniche for the palaces of the Khedive, palaces at which the Empress Eugénie would have gazed as she awoke in the nearby Gezira Palace. But as the light brings the city into focus and the increasing roar of traffic reminds you that you are in a bustling twentieth-century city, the buildings reveal themselves as the concrete piles that characterize so much of the Third World today.

Until the early 1950s, Cairo was considered one of the most beautiful cities in the world, but because of demographic realities – its urban sprawl contains fifteen million people – it is now, sadly, one of the most tortured. Many of the grand old palaces have disappeared. The core of the Gezira Palace, built for the Empress, survives as the five-star Marriott Hotel, and part of the immense Abdin Palace as the offices of Egypt's president. Villas such as that of the late Adel Bey Sabet, in Garden City, also remain, but the stone mansion in Gezira of the worshipped singer Umm Kulthum has been bulldozed like so many others.

If you choose dawn to roam the lawns of the Gezira Club, or some of the little squares around it with their imposing banyan trees and rococo buildings, you can still smell the scents of flowering trees and delight in the flowers of the blood-red flame trees planted during that period, and you can almost see in your mind's eye horses, harnessed to the broughams and the *calèches,* trotting by with their tightly-dressed Edwardian passengers: dandified men and magnificent women who would not have been out of place in Second Empire Paris. But the inhabitants of that romantic Cairo have gone, and the Cairo that was planned according to the plan of Baron Haussmann's Paris is today but a shadow.

1 Chibuks and Lice in Ismail's Harem

The story of the Khedive Ismail's love affair with the Empress Eugénie of France when she inaugurated the opening of the Suez Canal in 1869 must clearly be apocryphal. If the philanderous ruler had hoped to woo her to his bed, he was almost certainly spurned. In any case, the elaborate protocol of her visit is most unlikely to have given her an intimate moment, nor would her prudish Catholicism have allowed her to entertain it. However, when she returned to Cairo several decades later as a still lovely, white-haired old lady, she cheerfully confided to Lord Cromer's Oriental Secretary, Henry Boyle, that Ismail had hoped to include her in his harem.[1] Little, perhaps, did the exiled Empress realize that the hot, cloying world of the harem represented all that the Egyptian ruler wished to discard in favour of the libertine Europe of which Eugénie was the most dazzling symbol.

European governesses to the Egyptian princesses in Cairo found it almost impossible to describe the boredom which these sometimes lovely women endured in their gilded prisons within the lavish apartments of the Khedive's 'abode of bliss'. The only excitement was the hatching of domestic plots, and each of the several English and German servants would take the precaution of checking that her food was not poisoned by a jealous slave woman. It was a world of extraordinary contrasts, a world in which the royal women were sealed away to protect their virtue in a place where the language was fit only for a brothel and disgusted even the hardiest European visitor. The jewels, the costumes, the furnishings were lavish, yet the hair of some of the princesses was so full of vermin that sores appeared all over their scalps. The beauty of the younger girls contrasted with the ravages of the

Abyssinian slaves who rolled about their divans like wild animals, puffed at their *chibuks* (pipes) or shrieked curses in Turkish, Arabic, Amharic or Nubian.

It was not a uniformly hellish existence, and a lighter side was witnessed by Emmeline Lott, the English governess to Ismail's son, Ibrahim. Lott remembered a train journey with the eunuchs sitting poker-faced as the child princesses flung off their *habarahs* (veils) with relief and piled their silk dresses in the corner of the carriage before running to the windows and poking their heads out to chatter and laugh in the wind.[2] The English governess to Ismail's daughter, Princess Zeinab, remembers her charge's slave girl pretending to try to drown herself in a garden pool because her mistress had scolded her and the princess thoroughly enjoying the practical joke.[3]

The relationship between the princesses and their slaves was always ambiguous. On the one hand it was extremely familiar – after endless hours dressing themselves up, not to go out but merely to show off to each other among the harem rooms, each princess would dress up her favourite slave like a porcelain doll. In happy moods they would laugh with their slaves as if they were sisters (they often were half-sisters) and exchange banter. However, their whims were subject to constant change and even a child princess would think nothing of turning on her slave and condemning her peremptorily to a horrible torture. Lott remembered one of her first meals when a slave dropped a small jug at table. Without any fuss the slave was immediately replaced and Lott soon heard her muffled screams from some distant room. When she enquired she was told that the clumsy girl was having her arm branded with a red-hot iron, the regular punishment for breakages.[4]

The harem consisted of Ismail's four wives, their daughters and an almost endless hierarchy of slave girls and eunuchs, some of whom enjoyed discreet conjugal relationships. Indeed, some of the girls bore large families from the 'eunuchs'. For the princesses the day would start at 4.00 a.m. when, still wearing the dirty, crumpled muslin dresses they slept in, they would get up and move to their damask-covered divans, take coffee and smoke cigarettes – then the height of fashion in all the Ottoman harems. Each princess had five slaves to produce each cigarette. One arranged the papers, one prepared the tobacco, one rolled the cigarette, one passed it to the princess on a silver tray and one handed her a piece of red-hot charcoal in silver tongs to light it with. The morning hours would be passed in a trancelike silence as the girls squatted on the floor in their Parisian shoes, puffing at their cigarettes. Later they would wash from silver ewers held by slaves and dry themselves with rags. They would comb their vermin-infested hair only once a week and while some of them had beautiful pearly teeth, others had allowed theirs to rot away by the time they were twenty. Later they would change into their day clothes. These were stored in boxes which contained virtually all their possessions, since their lifestyle was, in a sense, nomadic and they had to be ready to move from palace harem to palace harem at a moment's notice. Bathing was rare among the princesses. Ismail's wives rarely bathed unless they were cohabiting at that moment with the Khedive. The bath water 'actually boiled' as they entered it and they would leave it shampooed and highly perfumed in readiness for their master's pleasure.

Breakfast would be taken at noon and after this the princesses would return to their divans and sit before their *narguileh* pipes filled with tobacco and small pastilles of opium. The effects of the drug would depend on the girl and her mood that day. The face of one princess would take on the most hideous appearance and her eyes would flash with barbarous cruelty while another would become giggly or smile with a radiant if dreamy compassion. The slaves made sure to remain aloof during the opium period of the day, since the drug-induced whims of their young mistresses could incite them to the most ghastly and arbitrary punishments. The princesses' mealtime seemed barbaric to the few Europeans working in the harem, the girls tearing lumps of meat apart like cannibals in silence, then leaving the remants to be eaten by their slavewomen. It was unthinkable for the slaves to leave the girls out of sight and no place was free from their presence, so in the harem privacy was non-existent. The governesses found that slaves would come in and out during lesson-time without any thought of seeking permission.

Sometimes Ismail would appear unannounced in the harem but even his visit would not break the dreamlike silence of this gloomy 'Abode of Bliss'. His three or four wives would *salaam* in silence and sail out of the room. One might bring him a piece of red-hot charcoal in silver tongs to light his cheroot before departing for the bedchamber to await him. No wonder he spent so little time in a haunted place that could inspire only a melancholic insanity provoked by utter boredom, stupefying narcotics and the almost total lack of physical exercise. Despite the beauty of the gardens of the Haramlik Palace on Cairo's Gezira, the princesses rarely walked in them, preferring to immure themselves in their smoky salons. In the centre of a long marble tank of water was a wooden pagoda and the tank was surrounded by terraces with marble steps and, at each corner, large marble lions from whose mouths water shot in arcs. Pleasure boats lay on the water which was filled with swans, ducks and water fowl. Statues of Greek gods and goddesses were scattered among groves of orange trees, myrtle hedges, geraniums, jasmine, verbena trees and cacti. By the pool stood a life-size statue of the Greek goddess Ceres surrounded by four angels spitting water. At the end of the pool was a white marble kiosk in which yellow and crimson damask cushions lay about on the divans.

Such was the background to the life of the Ottoman Wali or Viceroy in Egypt, Ismail Pasha, when he attended the 1867 Exposition Internationale in Paris and immediately decided to transform his own primitive society into a copy of glamorous France.[5]

2 Obsession for an Empress

Ismail's preparations for Eugénie's visit had been extraordinary. He had had German architects build an exquisite palace for her on the banks of the Nile and when she sighed for the cherry blossoms of her beloved Spain, he is said to have had a spinney of them, in full pink blossom, planted beneath her window as she slept. Perhaps in order to malign him for his profligacy, Cairo's wits coined the vulgar tale that his farewell gift to the Empress was a solid gold chamber-pot with a ruby for an eye in its centre, around which these words were inscribed: 'My eye, at least, will admire you for evermore.' Today, such stories of an era when the Byzantine splendour of Ismail's Egypt met European society with an explosion of hedonism are still told by aristocrats in the salons of Cairo's crumbling palaces or among the shaded lilac groves of the Gezira Sporting Club.

The year of the opening of the Canal was also the last, wretched year of France's Second Empire, to which Eugénie had added such lustre. On her return from Egypt in 1869, the last of the great masked balls was held in Paris's Tuileries Palace. With an ominous symbolism the Empress appeared dressed as Queen Marie Antoinette. The fated Queen had become a cult figure for Eugénie; she assiduously collected her memorabilia. On her bedroom mantelpiece she kept a Sèvres bust of the Queen and a portrait of the Dauphin; by her bed Eugénie kept the Queen's biography and her *Registre des Toilettes*. Both Eugénie and her husband, the Emperor Louis Napoleon (Napoleon III), were to lose their thrones the following year with Count Otto Von Bismarck's ruthless Prussian troops camped around Paris and hysterical Communards storming through the gardens of the

Tuileries. Ironically, the two principal statues erected by Ismail in the Winter Garden of Cairo's Abdin Palace were of Marie Antoinette and Eugénie, a Queen and an Empress who had both ruled France in splendour before losing their crowns (and the former her head) in a tempest of revolution.

Eugénie was cold (some would say cruel), mean, church-obsessed and exquisitely beautiful; a hopelessly complex personality. When she was twenty-six, she dressed, like George Sand, in trousers, and lived economically with her mother at the Hôtel Baudard de Saint James in Paris's Place Vendôme. It appears to have been there, in her mother's salon, that the Emperor's lustful eye first fell on her. He began to visit her in secret and probably made his first advances there before his more formal – and promptly rejected – offer to make her his mistress at a ball at the Tuileries. This was the same hotel in which Chopin was to die on 17 October 1849, aged thirty-nine, in the arms of his beloved Polish mistress, Delphine Potocka. Ironically, it was also the hotel in which Ferdinand-Marie de Lesseps, Eugénie's cousin, was to set up his Compagnie Maritime de Suez in 1860. In that same year it also housed Théophile Gautier, whose correspondence with Princess Mathilde, the daughter of ex-King Jerome of Westphalia, a younger brother of Napoleon I, when he attended the inauguration of the Suez Canal, makes such lively reading. To add a final twist to a litany of coincidences, it was also the hotel which had lodged Claude Henri, Comte de Saint-Simon, whose followers were to be the first to survey the Suez Canal during the reign of Muhammad Ali, the founder of modern Egypt. Today, the hotel has retained its ties with the Near East, housing as it does the headquarters of the Banque Arabe d'Investissements Internationaux.

Born on 5 May 1826 in Granada, Eugénie Ignacia Augustina was the daughter of Dona Maria Manuela Kirkpatrick, whose father, William Kirkpatrick of Dumfries in Scotland, had fled Scotland after the 1745 Stuart rebellion and settled in Andalusia. Her father was almost certainly the Spanish Count of Teba, Don Cipriano de Guzman y Palafox y Portocarrero, the younger brother of Don Eugenio, Count of Montijo. Gossip, however, murmured that Eugénie's father was either Lord Palmerston or Lord Clarendon until her mother wryly pointed out to Louis

Napoleon, 'But Sire, the dates don't correspond.' Nevertheless, influenced by the rumours, Queen Victoria's self-righteous consort Prince Albert did not approve of Louis Napoleon's marriage to Eugénie, remarking to King Leopold of Belgium that 'she is said to be British on her father's as well as her mother's side' because 'Lord Clarendon is supposed to be her father.' But, morals apart, Manuela was, in the words of Eugénie's biographer Robert Sencourt, 'original and bewitching, with Andalusian grace, English gentleness, French facility; yet always a Spaniard ... She was one of those dauntless and glittering women who move as much by instinct as by stratagem towards the seats of power. She scattered pleasures about her and made joy an obligation.'[1] Significantly for the events that follow, Manuela was the niece of Mlle Catherine de Grivegnée, who married a young French diplomat, Mathieu de Lesseps, in 1801. Mathieu's son, Ferdinand, was to be the architect of the Suez Canal.

Eugénie, in contrast with her mother, grew up to be a terror to her governesses and, perhaps as a result of stern ethics acquired at a convent, was to be labelled by her many rejected suitors a 'notorious virgin'. 'Where,' the Emperor is said to have asked her, 'must one go to reach your bedroom?' The girl replied promptly: 'By the chapel, Sire.' She would give her body to Louis Napoleon for nothing less than marriage and, having failed to seduce her, he was obliged to marry her in 1853. Curiously, Wilfrid Blunt, always ready to debunk a myth, contradicts the story of Eugénie's modesty, maintaining that the Duke of Sesto was among her lovers and that when the Emperor married her she had recently been the mistress of the Marquis d'Aguado.[2]

Louis Napoleon had once asked Princess Mathilde to marry him but the engagement was broken off by a livid Jerome after Louis Napoleon's pitiful attempt to invade King Louis Philippe's France from England in 1831. When, as Emperor, he offered his hand to Mathilde again in 1852, she was no longer interested: she already had a lover to make up for her own disastrous marriage. Ironically, Louis Napoleon was to meet Eugénie in Princess Mathilde's drawing-room. He immediately began inviting her to every reception at the Elysée Palace and to hunting parties at Fontainebleau and at Compiègne. When he took up residence at Compiègne, actors were brought from Paris to delight the young woman. On 12 January 1853 Napoleon gave a ball at the Tuileries at which the Baron James de Rothschild led Eugénie to a sofa on the left of Napoleon's throne. At this, the wife of the French Foreign Secretary strode up to Eugénie and whispered that the sofa was reserved for Cabinet ministers. Deeply embarrassed, Eugénie rose at once to move away. No sooner had she done so, than Napoleon, who had been gazing at her all evening, approached her and, taking her arm, led her firmly to a far more important sofa reserved for the imperial family. Six days later, their betrothal was formally announced. Although the wedding inflamed the curiosity of Paris, Parisians had as little sympathy for it as the government. When the wedding cortège passed through the streets no flags flew from the windows and men did not uncover their heads. One wit shouted out, to laughter from the crowds that lined the roads, 'It's just like a young girl's funeral procession.'

But, for better or for worse, Eugénie was widely regarded as more emperor than the Emperor himself. In the portrait of her by Queen Victoria's court painter, Winterhalter, one can recognize from her bearing that she possessed far greater determination than her husband. The painting of Napoleon by Maguès shows a witty man twisting his moustaches, but there is no feeling of charisma about him. Returning from a visit to Germany in 1867, the Comtesse de Pourtales warned Napoleon that Germany was welding together a mighty army and that the Minister of the Prussian Royal Household had boasted to her that Alsace would belong to Prussia within eighteen months. The frivolous Napoleon is said to have replied, 'Comtesse, your beautiful blue eyes have seen things through the prism of your imaginings – things that don't exist. Believe me, we have nothing to fear from Prussia.'[3]

Louis Napoleon, whose mother Hortense was the Empress Josephine's daughter by her first marriage, seems to have inherited both the idealism of Napoleon Bonaparte and his dream of the unification as single nations of 'thirty million Frenchmen, fifteen million Spaniards, fifteen million Italians and thirty million Germans'. When Bismarck was accredited to the French Court in 1862, Louis confided these dreams to him but on his return to Prussia to become prime minister, the icy Prussian remarked cynically of the French Court, 'I met two amusing women, not a single nation.' The remark appears to have been ambiguously pointed both at Napoleon and Eugénie as well as at Eugénie and Princess Orloff, who had made a deep impression on him. 'Beside me,' he had written of his meeting with the Princess in a rare, human mood, 'is the most charming of women . . . gay, clever, amiable, pretty and young.'[4]

The inadequacies of Eugénie's marriage to Louis Napoleon did not help matters. She noted to her ladies-in-waiting that she regarded the physical act of love as disgusting. She seems to have been incapable of responding to the sensual advances of her husband, a flamboyant womanizer, and when she discovered that he had resumed his relationship with his English mistress, Miss Howard, she forbade him access to her rooms.[5] After the birth of the Prince Imperial in 1856, marital relations between them appear to have ceased entirely. Blunt maintains that her constant domestic scenes forced him into the arms of Marguerite Bellanger, a Paris courtesan whose father ran Voisin's Restaurant. However, Napoleon admitted to Princess Mathilde that he had been faithful to Eugénie for six months but had then needed his 'little distractions'. The French writer Prosper Mérimée, a bosom friend of Eugénie's mother Manuela, noted regretfully that 'there is no longer an Eugénie, there is only an empress. I complain and I admire . . .' But even Mérimée could not resist quipping that, whereas Louis Napoleon had become emperor by election, Eugénie had become empress by 'erection'.

Many admired Eugénie's iron will, one English observer of the period describing the Emperor as 'a very minor show' whereas the Empress struck 'a splendid figure, straight as a dart, and to my young eyes the most beautiful thing I had ever seen . . .' who 'dominated the whole group'. To others, she appeared cold, capricious, unpredictable, adventurous and aggressive, an altogether disastrous influence on the Emperor. Above all, they accused her of responsibility for the war and for France's catastrophic defeat by the Prussians at the Battle of Sedan.

3 Napoleon's Hated 'Mission Civilizatrice'

When Napoleon Bonaparte invaded Egypt in July 1798 the Egyptian writer Gabarti described it with remarkable hyperbole as an event of 'great battles, terrible events, disastrous facts, calamities, unhappiness, sufferings, persecutions, upsets in the order of things, terror, revolutions, disorders, devastations – in a word the beginning of a series of great misfortunes'.[1] But although Napoleon did, unintentionally, bring many of these things to Egypt, he also brought the influence of Europe and, in particular, of France. A hundred years after Napoleon's visit the British were to control Egypt for seventy years, but even then, and to this day, Egypt has looked towards France for its culture and for its language of manners.

Even Gabarti was impressed by the cultural and social influence of the French invasion, in particular the society club set up as a precursor of clubland, later to become the fulcrum of British high society in Egypt. 'Among other things,' wrote Gabarti, 'the French constructed near Ezbekiyya a building where ladies and gentlemen met at a certain hour to pass the time and amuse themselves. The spectator paid on going in and needed a ticket to enter.' The club was 'the first service club in history', named Le Tivoli after the club and gardens in Paris that had been one of the most popular amusement spots from the time of Napoleon Bonaparte until the end of Napoleon III's Second Empire. Cairo's Tivoli offered a dance band (though few partners), billiard tables and other games, a library, the two newspapers published by the army, coffee, European food, a pleasure garden and other similar comforts of the home. At the grand opening, the *Courier de L'Egypte* reported that what 'produced the most agreeable sensation . . . was the presence of fifteen or twenty women dressed with some splendour – an absolutely novel sight in Egypt'.[2]

However, society clubs and pretty women were only marginal recommendations; the French occupation was in almost every other way a colossal failure. According to Thiers, historian of the French Revolution, Napoleon's invasion of Egypt was even more rash than his disastrous march on Moscow in 1812. The Directory in Paris wanted him to attack England directly but Napoleon was reluctant, recognizing that British imperial power had to be broken before it could be conquered frontally. By taking Egypt and cutting off Britain's imperial supply lines, he reasoned that 'as soon as I have made England tremble for the safety of India, I shall return to Paris, and give the enemy its death-blow'. His vainglory was without limit. He told his beloved Josephine that he would return after six months or six years, 'perhaps never'. In reality, his heart remained with his new wife and former mistress whom he knew had many lovers (he had evidence that she had resumed her affair with Hippolyte Charles) and his eye was on France and on control of the Directory. Josephine had married this lugubrious egoist born for greatness, but dreaded having to follow him to Egypt. She was, perhaps, frightened of his passion for her. He was the conqueror of Italy and now had total authority over all who knew him. He appears, moreover, to have been less than dexterous in his passions, one of his mistresses in Paris, Ms Grassini, complaining that his 'caresses were on the furtive side and often left the ladies unsatisfied'.[3] The English pamphleteer, Lewis Goldsmith, hinted at other characteristics, remarking brutally: 'I should not wonder if he should, like his prototype Nero, marry a boy.'[4]

However, the men who followed him to Egypt, artists like Vivant Denon and mathematicians like Gaspard Monge, fell immediately under his spell. The new commander-in-chief of his Egyptian campaign, General Louis Desaix (who was to die heroically a year later at the Battle of Marengo against the Austrians), declared, 'I am persuaded that Bonaparte will achieve so immense a glory that it is impossible that it will not reflect on his lieutenants . . . He is proud, hidden, never forgives. He follows his enemy to the end of the world.' Desaix, only twenty-eight when he commanded the army on the Rhine, recognized Napoleon's

15

charisma immediately. Desaix himself was called the 'just sultan' by the Egyptians because of the story circulating that he had become so absorbed in admiring the Temple of Denderah that he had forgotten to put down a Mamluk uprising against the French.

Napoleon's hundred savants led by Monge and Denon were to produce the greatest work ever compiled on Egypt, the *Description d'Egypte*. Napoleon took over a new palace with excellent vineyards and owned by the Mamluk Muhammad Bey al-Elfi on the banks of Cairo's then Ezbekiyya lake and the site of the famous Shepheard's Hotel. He set up his *Institut d'Egypte* in the Nasiriya quarter where the savants and literati could start their great work. It was all, in those early days of idealism, intended to be a democratic form of France's Civilizing Mission. The French established a large library in a building belonging to the Mamluk Amir Hasan Kashif. 'The French,' wrote Gabarti, 'were particularly happy when a Muslim visitor showed himself interested in the sciences; they at once got into discussion with him and showed him all sorts of printed books, with pictures representing different regions of the world, as well as plants and animals.'[5]

On the day following his occupation of Alexandria, Napoleon issued a proclamation in Arabic which began: 'In the name of God, the Merciful, the Compassionate; there is no god but God, he has no offspring and no partner.' And he continued, speaking to the 'shaikhs, judges and imams, officers and notables of the land...tell your people that the French are also sincere Muslims.' The French had, he pointed out, occupied Rome and 'ruined the Papal See which was always urging the Christians to attack Islam' and had at all times 'been sincere friends of the Ottoman sultans and enemies of his enemies'. With what appears to have been a genuine ecstasy, he cried to the people: 'Glory to the Sultan ! Glory to the French Army ! Curses upon the Mamluks and wellbeing to the people of Egypt'.[6]

Although the story of the Empress Josephine's origins probably had little or no influence on Napoleon's apparent empathy with all things Islamic, it intriguingly showed how this period in Egypt and Asia Minor was characterized by extraordinary dynastic coincidences. It is believed that the Ottoman Sultan Abdul Hamid I received a beautiful blonde French girl, captured by Algerian pirates on the high seas between France and Martinique where her parents lived, as a slave. Her name was Aimée Dubucq de Rivery and her closest friend was her cousin, Josephine, also from Martinique. The pirates had taken her to Algiers where the Bey took immaculate care of her in order to perpare her as a bewitching gift for the Sultan, his nominal master. The gift was to be well received but Aimée must have had some difficulty in transferring from a French convent in Normandy to the Sultan's harem where the girls spent much of the day, writes Lesley Blanch, 'lolling in Turkish baths, naked and sleek, ladling perfumed water over each other, twisting pearls and peacock feathers in their thin long hair, nibbling sugary comfits, gossiping, idling away the hours, becalmed in the dreamy, steamy, limbo-land . . .'. However, she was soon taken to the Sultan's bed and, a year later in 1783, gave birth to a son, Mahmoud. From that moment she became Abdul Hamid's favourite and her influence in the court increased by the day. The Sultan was so delighted that he gave a festival for which a kiosk of spun sugar was built in the grounds of the seraglio. On the Sultan's death Aimée was to wield immense influence on his nephew and heir, Selim, who was soon to adopt liberal French ideas under her supervision. It seems most likely that she also became Selim's mistress.[7]

Although Napoleon's fascination with Islam was mainly born from genuine idealism, he also had excellent political reasons to demonstrate his respect for the Sultan, whose nominal authority spread from Tunisia in the west to Iraq in the east, Asia Minor in the north to Yemen in the south. He begged the Egyptians in lyrical language to trust and even love the French. 'Was there a beautiful slave, a beautiful horse, a beautiful house,' he asked them, 'which did not belong to the Mamluks?' No mosques, he assured them, would be violated, no Muslim clergy would be disturbed, no plunder would be taken, no woman would be molested. French officers were ordered to enforce the strictest discipline in their treatment of Egypt's civilian population. Perhaps, however, even the Egyptians realized that Napoleon's Islam was merely part of a personal, emotional vision. He himself seems to have nurtured it as a vision. 'I saw myself founding a religion,' he had written, 'marching into Asia, riding an elephant, a turban on my head and in my hand the new Qur'an that I would have composed to suit my needs.'[8]

In any case, his flamboyant attempts to fraternize fell on deaf ears. The Egyptians would have no truck with this eccentric and saw the French merely as a corrupting influence threatening their social environment, their women in particular. After the defeat of the French, the daughter of Shaikh al-Bakri, Egypt's most eminent clergyman, was executed for having mixed with the French and dressed up like a French lady of fashion. An Egyptian observer wrote somewhat prophetically: 'Cairo has become a second Paris; women go about shamelessly with the French; intoxicating drinks are publicly sold and things are committed of which the Lord of heaven would not approve.' Although women were forbidden to accompany Napoleon's expedition, some three hundred French women dressed as French soldiers had succeeded in secretly joining it. One, the wife of a Lieutenant Fourès, was called Marguerite Pauline Bellisle and was nicknamed Bellilote. Napoleon spotted her one day playing *vingt-et-un* at the officers' club. He quickly had the husband posted out of Cairo and made Bellilote his mistress, this being his first affair since his marriage to Josephine. Unfortunately for Napoleon, the British captured Fourès at sea and sent him back to Egypt to annoy 'Boney', as they nicknamed him. Napoleon installed Bellilote at his headquarters and outraged many of his officers by fondling her in public, humiliating Josephine's delightful and heroic son, Eugène, by kissing her passionately in front of him. To the Egyptians, Bellilote, in her white silk pantaloons that set off her boyish figure, was 'the Great Sultan's lady'. They seemed charmed by her although Napoleon himself soon began to tire of his new conquest, remarking to a friend that 'the little idiot does not know how to make a baby'.[9]

Noting the example of the great general, not only soldiers and sycophants but also debauchees who had left Paris in search of finer pleasures in Cairo were to join Napoleon's baggage train. However, if this added touches of charm and joyous colour to the early period of the occupation, they were short-lived. After the first major revolt against the French, fury turned the French soldiery from sympathetic comrades into vandals. Having torn down the barricades of the Egyptian mobs, they rode into the Mosque of al-Azhar, one of Islam's holiest buildings, and tethered their horses to the *mihrabs* (prayer-niches). They smashed and they looted, trampling the Qur'ans with their army boots and urinating on the mosque floor. Having quaffed gallons of wine – anathema to Islam – they smashed the bottles on the floor and stripped the Muslims praying in the mosque naked to steal their possessions.[10]

When Nelson destroyed the French fleet in the harbour of Abu Kir near Alexandria on 1 August 1798, Napoleon responded at first in a mood of despair, before reverting to his customary vainglory, but this no longer bore any relation to his now desperate situation. The Egyptians were overjoyed by the British action and even more so by Napoleon's secret return to France to fill the position of First Consul of the Directory. In Cairo he left poor General Kléber to hold the tottering fort and enjoy the questionable advantage of inheriting Bellilote as his mistress before falling to the dagger of a young Syrian Muslim, Sulaiman al-Halabi, on 14 June 1800. Three al-Azhar shaikhs who were unwittingly involved in the plot were beheaded. The revenge on al-Halabi, however, was horrific and a far cry from the philosophy that had introduced the supposedly humane guillotine. The brave young man was impaled on a *khazuk*, a sharpened stick, in Kléber's garden, later the garden of the Shepheard's Hotel. This form of execution was fairly common among the Ottomans and Mamluks; the French must have learnt it from them and used it in their panic-stricken fury. Victims could live in atrocious agony, suffering horrific thirst, for three days, but it appears that, in a gesture of compassion, Kléber's assassin was eventually given water, causing haemorrhage and instant death.

Reflecting Napoleon's own much-protested empathy with Islam, Kléber's successor General Menou at once tried to turn off the heat and appease the now threatening Cairene mobs by announcing his conversion to Islam, following this conciliatory gesture by decreeing that Egypt would now become a French protectorate. The French General Belliard backed up these carrot-and-stick tactics by begging the Egyptians 'to remain faithful to the French . . . otherwise their houses would be burned, their goods pillaged, children orphaned and women violated'.[11]

But the British, to whom the now desperate French army had to turn for rescue, were soon to see its pitiful remnants ignominiously out of Egypt. A British officer calling himself 'Carlos Bey' witnessed the embarkation of the French troops at Rosetta and watched what he derisively described as 'the enlightened spectacle

19

of the departing French soldiers and officers selling their women to the English for a few dollars each.'[12] The French had had their fill of this Egyptian inferno where any prisoners taken by the Mamluks became the victims of atrocities and "unnatural acts". If Napoleon's visit started in a flurry of idealism, it ended in chaotic trauma, but it did represent that early suggestion of French cultural influence which was, soon after his departure, to inspire Egypt's greatest modern ruler, Muhammad Ali.

4 *Muhammad Ali – a Brutal Age of Development*

The departure of the French left a vacuum: a country which had known countless periods of unparalleled splendour had plunged to ruin and anarchy. Egypt's population of eight million under the Pharaohs had dwindled to two and a half million impoverished *fellaheen* (rural peasants). Although Egypt is ninety-six per cent desert, a man-made country which depends for its survival on the constant irrigation of the Nile delta and the green strip of annually flooded agriculture along the banks of the Nile, it has always been a crossroads of the world. Napoleon had awoken the nation from a deep sleep and, breaking the power of the tyrannical Mamluks who had subdued Egypt with sword and whip, had left a void which Muhammad Ali, Ismail's grandfather, was soon to fill. Muhammad Ali was to play cat and mouse with the Mamluks before luring them to a terrible slaughter.

An Ottoman officer from Cavala in what is now Greek Macedonia, he had been sent by the Ottoman Sultan with three hundred troops collected by the Cavala merchants to help fight Napoleon's forces in Egypt. The Ottoman contingents were decimated at the Battle of Abu Kir near Alexandria, but the shipwrecked Muhammad Ali was rescued from the sea by the British admiral's gig. He returned to Cavala but was soon back in Egypt, where he became involved in the power struggle between the Ottoman Sublime Porte (the door to the Grand Vizir's palace which represented Ottoman rule in Istanbul) and the Mamluk beys, the heirs of Turkik slaves who had ruled Egypt until their formal deposition by the Ottomans in 1517 but had continued to govern with Ottoman blessing. Already a wily politician, Muhammad Ali started to build his own power base by first taking the side of the Mamluks and then that of the Sultan.

Muhammad Ali was a sober, uncompromising, ruthless man born for greatness. He had, noted the French writer John Ninet, 'a large thick nose, high cheekbones, small mouth, eyes small but bright as a hawk's and as keen, with a long white beard and shaggy white eyebrows'[1] and he wore a turban, a wide-sleeved Turkish gown and a curved Mamluk sword. He brought from Cavala a beautiful Roumeliot (from 'Turkey-in-Europe') wife, Emine, by whom he had five children – Ibrahim, Toussoun, Ismail, Tawhida and the sadistic Princess Nazli. By his twenty-seven concubines he is believed to have produced seventeen sons and thirteen daughters.

He brooked no opposition from any quarter. 'He may cause any one of his subjects to be put to death without the formality of a trial,' wrote Lane, 'or without assigning any cause; a single horizontal motion of his hand is sufficient to imply the sentence of decapitation.'[2] When he had a man decapitated the body would be flung on to a place below the Citadel where sterile Cairene women would plunge their hands into the corpse and smear the hot blood over their genital organs in the belief that this would help conception. Ninet saw Muhammad Ali as 'cruel, subject to caprice, and violent, but with occasional generous instincts'.[3] He was thought, however, to be the only person capable of restoring order in Egypt, and in 1805 the Shaikhs of Cairo proclaimed him Governor, a choice which the Sultan confirmed in 1806, making him a Pasha and Wali, or Viceroy, of Egypt, a title which he passed to his successors until Ismail managed to bribe the curiously insignificant Persian title of Khedive from the Sultan.

To the end Muhammad Ali remained a foreigner in outlook, and his attitude towards Egypt was to be more colonial and certainly more ruthless than that of the French. He told a European visitor: 'My history shall not commence till the period when, free from all restraint, I could arouse this land . . . from the sleep of ages.' Part of this distrust of indigenous Egyptians stemmed from his inability to speak Arabic. He surrounded himself with the most brilliant Europeans he could find. Many were Saint-Simonians, 'Christian socialists' whose patriarch, Claude Henri, Comte de Saint-Simon, called for the regeneration of mankind through the dignity of work. Others were mercenaries like Colonel Sèves, who was to convert to Islam and take the name of Sulaiman Pasha; sons of foreign officials like the Greek Paul Pavlides, who would become Draneht Bey; or doctors like Clot Bey, who founded Cairo's school of medicine. These were the men who helped the Wali rebuild Egypt, setting up institutions such as Cairo's Polytechnic School and the military academies at Giza and Tourah.

But first, in order to establish an impregnable power base, he had to deal with the haughty Mamluks. The Mamluks adored military pomp, which lifted them emotionally from their original slave status; the word *mamluk* is Arabic for 'owned', in other words 'slave', although the word is more closely associated with this marvellously creative dynasty. When, on 1 March 1811, Muhammad Ali invited five hundred of the Mamluk chiefs to a fête for his son Ahmed Toussoun, they arrived in splendid dress and shimmering armour on decorated war-horses. The fête was to celebrate the departure of Toussoun on an expedition to Arabia to recapture the holy cities of Mecca and Medina from the Wahhabis, more correctly the Muwahhidun (those who believe in the 'Oneness' of God), the ancestors of the present Saudi dynasty of Saudi Arabia. The Mamluks saw the invitation as a genuine attempt by Muhammad Ali at reconciliation when the Wali received each Mamluk in turn in his reception chamber. Coffee with cardamom, and sticky sweets were served and bubbling *narguileh* (hubble-bubble) pipes were passed around. At the end of the feast the Mamluks were placed in the central place of honour within a glittering procession of horsemen. First came a corps of Dehlis commanded by Uzoun-Ali, then the Aga of the Yeni Chehris (Janisseries), then the Ojaklis, then the Yoldashes, then the Albanians led by Saleh Kosh, then the Mamluks led by Sulaiman Bey al-Bawwab, then the Albanian infantry and cavalry of Muhammad Ali. But as they bade their farewells and rode swaggering out of the Citadel through a narrow defile towards the Azab Gate, the gate's huge doors closed before them and the Mamluks heard the champing of bits of the dreaded Albanian cavalry behind them. Then they heard Saleh Bey give his sudden, ghastly order: 'Exterminate them!' Responding to this command, the Albanians immediately galloped to the top of the rock on either side of the road from where they could have a surer aim.[4]

23

The Mamluks, aware of the horror that was to befall them, galloped frantically to and fro within the tight square. Then, quite suddenly, a fusillade poured down on them from the battlements on all sides and those who clambered up the walls tumbled down again as bullets rained upon them. Sulaiman Bey al-Bawwab ran half-naked to the *haremlik* (women's quarters) to implore protection but was at once dragged before Muhammad Ali and beheaded at his feet. Twelve- and fourteen-year-old Mamluk boys begged for mercy, promising to become slaves of the Wali, but each was dragged before him and executed.

Following their leader's hopeless example, other Mamluks rushed for the *haremlik*, crying out pathetically: 'Sanctuary in the ground of the harem!' But the girls would not open the harem doors. The wretched men, their jewelled costumes now torn and bloody, were dragged from before the doors, conducted to Muhammad Ali and beheaded one after another. 'The body of the brave leader Shahin,' wrote the Englishman James Webster, 'was exposed to every infamy. A rope was passed round the neck, and the bloody carcase dragged through various parts of the city, exposed all the while to the execrations and the contumely of the inflamed populace.'[5] Mamluks were slaughtered all over the city. Mamluk women who refused to hand over their bangles had their arms cut off. Hundreds of Mamluk heads were stuck along the walls of Bab Zouela, the great Mamluk gate near to the Azhar Mosque. 'The Citadel was one vast bloody arena,' wrote Walpole, 'the mutilated bodies of the dead encumbered the passages; on all sides were seen richly caparisoned horses stretched by the side of their masters . . . Not one of them [the Mamluks] escaped the massacre.'[6]

Webster was appalled by the scene of devastation at the end of that day.

The Citadel itself looked like like a hideous slaughterhouse, newly deluged with the blood of victims, and overstrewn with a multitude of reeking carcases. Dead steeds lay confusedly along the streets with their golden caparisons soiled in the filthy compound of dirt and gore; their knights, some with limbs hacked off, others without their heads, still clenching their scimitars with the last despairing, yet desperate grasp of death, were flung near their war-horses, prostrate in a black puddle of their own life-blood.[7]

A drawing by Comte A. de Forbin, in his *Voyage du Levant*, shows Muhammad Ali calmly smoking his *narguileh* pipe on finely carpeted steps as he gazes serenely at the grotesque slaughter taking place below him. The drawing is obviously apocryphal, however, because, according to contemporary writers, Muhammad Ali became increasingly anxious during the massacre lest the tide of battle turn against him and the Mamluks kill his family and himself. It was not until the Genoese Mendrici, one of his doctors, entered his apartment and shouted merrily, 'The affair is over; this must be a day of rejoicing to your highness', that he knew that his day was won and his new dynasty secure.

After half a millennium of rule under which both Egypt and Syria had reached the peak of architectural expression, the Mamluk dynasty was, in a few terrible moments, obliterated. The dynasty of Muhammad Ali and of his grandson, the master-builder Ismail Pasha, a dynasty that was to end with King Farouk, Egypt's last sad, royal ruler, had begun.

Completely indifferent to the high art that the Mamluks had bequeathed, Muhammad Ali was to rule Egypt like a modern sergeant-major. He had the power of his own new-found dynasty at heart rather than the interests of Egypt. He created a model army and ruled the country as if it were a personal estate, forcing taxes out of the people with the help of the *courbash* (the rhino-whip). Some 20,000 *fellaheen* died in the forced-labour gangs which built his canal linking the Nile with Alexandria. Lucie Duff Gordon wrote at the time: 'The distress here is frightful, in all classes, and no man's life is safe.'[8] Muhammad Ali built factories imported in kits from Europe and introduced long-staple cotton into the Nile Valley. He steeped himself in the high technology of the time and laughed merrily when the archaeologist Belzoni showed him how electricity worked by giving him a mild shock with a live wire. He ingratiated himself with the Western powers by offering them splendid gifts. To the French King Louis Philippe he sent a Rameses II obelisk which stands today on Paris's Place de La Concorde. To Queen Victoria he gave the obelisk which now stands as Cleopatra's Needle on the Thames Embankment.

He and his son Ibrahim conquered Arabia and Sudan, but when Ibrahim challenged Egypt's nominal Ottoman overlords by marching through Syria bound for Istanbul, the European powers decided that enough was enough, that a strong Ottoman Empire under Muhammad Ali was the last thing they wanted, so they forced the old man to command his son and his army back. To make up for this undignified pressure, however, Muhammad Ali's dynasty was given effective control of Egypt.

After his installation as Governor of Egypt in May 1805 and his confirmation as Wali by Ottoman decree in July, Muhammad Ali had made the Citadel on Cairo's Muqattam Hill his official residence. Within the confines of the Citadel he built palaces and offices where he found relief from the aggressive activities of his daylight hours. He lived in the largest palace and used the smallest, the Jawhar (Jewel) Palace, to offer hospitality in. During the summer he would move with his court to the domed Ras al-Tin Palace which he had built on the eastern end of Alexandria's harbour. As he grew older, however, he spent an increasing amount of time at Shoubra, today a sprawling slum to the north of central Cairo.

Within the grounds of his Shoubra estates, which rolled down to the riverside, he built the Shoubra Palace. The gardens were laid out in squares, parallelograms and triangles, each divided by long, straight alleys. Some were paved with mosaics of many-coloured pebbles. There were trellised arbours and marble fountains. The finest, sweet-scented plants were clustered around a tasteful alcove where Muhammad Ali would withdraw on calm summer nights. The air was filled with the perfume of lemon, orange, citron and pomegranates and the trees of the orchards were heavy with plump fruit. There were rows of cyprus and mimosa trees intersected by small canals. In these gardens Muhammad Ali kept deer, a kangaroo and four giraffes. An acre of the gardens was taken up by the baths, consisting of kiosks linked by colonnades with slender pillars of white stone or marble around a large, square basin. In the centre of the basin were the marble baths of the harem, adorned with the sculpted figures of crocodiles. The kiosks contained dressing-rooms with divans and other furniture, where Muhammad Ali and his family would take coffee after bathing. One, paved with alabaster, had a refreshingly cool interior and a ceiling dramatically painted with bright floral designs. The fountain kiosk, as another kiosk was called, was a rectangular colonnade surrounding a large marble pool. The water gushed from marble waterfalls and from the edges of a marble island which rose up in the centre. The daughter of the English King George V, the Princess Royal, attended a party in this lovely kiosk given by two princesses, Iffet Hasan and Behidja Toussoun, and recalled crossing the pool, fragrant with scents, in a rowing-boat.

During his 'Grand Tour' in 1831, Britain's future Prime Minister, Benjamin Disraeli (whose purchase of the Suez Canal shares was to lead Egypt into slavery), strolled in these gardens, where he met Muhammad Ali surrounded by black eunuchs in scarlet and gold and 'playing chess with his fool'. The talk turning on politics, the Wali told Disraeli with glee that he was going to have as many parliaments as the King of England himself. 'See here,' he cried as he produced two lists of names, 'here are my parliaments,' but added quickly 'but I have made up my mind, to prevent inconvenience, to elect them myself.'[9]

Muhammad Ali was to build upon the influence of France, laid by Napoleon Bonaparte, by taking a number of Frenchmen into his service. Accompanied by Ibrahim and Sulaiman Pasha, he had visited King Louis Philippe at the Tuileries, where he had forged strong ties with France, ties that he believed were severely threatened when the Kingdom was replaced by Louis Napoleon's Second Republic. 'The French *canaille* abroad is impressive – and, let me add, there is a lot of it,' wrote Flaubert to his mother.[10] Sulaiman Pasha, the ex-Colonel Octave-Joseph-Anthelme Sèves, whom Flaubert described as 'the most powerful man in Egypt, the terror of Constantinople', helped Ibrahim Pasha defeat the forces of the Sultan at the Battle of Nezib in 1839 and settled in Egypt, where he converted to Islam and married Mariam Hanim. Sulaiman Pasha made an eccentric figure, lounging among splendid cushions as he smoked his *narguileh* and watched pretty male slaves dressed as women dance before him. Born in Lyon in 1788, he lived to the age of seventy-two with his favourite Greek mistress, dying in Cairo on 12 March 1860. His daughter, Nazli Hanem, married Muhammad Sherif Pasha, who was to become an important prime minister under Ismail. Their granddaughter, the

27

beautiful, domineering Nazli Sabri, was to marry King Fouad and give birth to the last of the dynasty, King Farouk.

Other Frenchmen like Galis Bey; Princeteau Bey; Charles Lambert (Lambert Bey), a Saint-Simonian engineer; Mougel Bey, also an engineer; Antoine Clot (Clot Bey); the court chamberlain Lubbert Bey; and Bekir Bey, chief of the Egyptian *police des étrangers*, also joined the Wali's service. Another important foreigner whom the Wali took under his wing was the Greek Paul Pavlides, whom he sent to study at Paris University. There the young man explained to the Master of Chemistry Baron Thénard that the Wali had asked him to select a more oriental name. The quick-witted professor at once suggested that he take his own name and spell it backwards, giving it a somewhat Muslim sound. So, from that day onwards Paul Pavlides became Paul Draneht, later Draneht Pasha. He was to be appointed head of Ismail Pasha's Khedival Opera House and to become closely involved with Giuseppe Verdi and Claude Mariette (Mariette Pasha), the Keeper of the Boulaq Museum, in the performance of the première of *Aida* at the Khedival Opera House in 1871.

Visitors to Egypt bent over backwards to applaud Muhammad Ali's programme to develop Egypt, Lamartine calling him 'an adventurer of genius', but the manners of his court remained oriental and autocratic, and the break-neck grafting of European industry upon a traditional society did not hide the fact that this was a superficial grafting. In manners, Muhammad Ali retained the characteristics of brutishness and ruthlessness. It was said that a government official who had mistreated a baker was ordered to be baked in the baker's oven and a butcher who had sold underweight meat had the same weight of meat carved off his back. Not all such stories were true, for Cairo was and has remained a hotbed of rumour and gossip. But it was a cruel period and Muhammad Ali had taken Western technology without showing a proportionate curiosity about the moral evolution of Europe.

5 A Cruel Princess

But if Muhammad Ali was himself brutish and ruthless, the manners of his court remained positively primitive, with suggestions of *A Thousand and One Nights*. The cruelty of his daughter Nazli, the first of three charismatic Nazlis, illustrated this primitivism only too well. She had bright-blue eyes and clear, pale skin and the delicate and voluptuous figure of her mother Emine. Nazli lived in a palace copied from a Turkish *yali*, on the banks of the Nile. Foreign visitors found her charming and immensely witty, although they had heard many rumours of her passionate cruelty.

Princess Nazli adored her Turkish husband, Muhammad Bey Khusraw al-Darawalli, but was desperately jealous of his relationships – or suspected relationships – with other women. One day, goes the Cairene tale, a beautiful Circassion slave girl was serving the Prince when her curls fell into his plate. 'Don't worry, my sweetheart, my dearest,' he said, 'it doesn't matter.' The Princess gave him a chilling look but said nothing. At dinner that evening another slave girl served the meal and the Prince asked where the previous girl was. 'You wish to gaze upon the lovely eyes of "your sweetheart, your dearest"?' asked Nazli. 'Look, then!' and so saying she lifted the great silver dish cover to reveal the head of the poor girl, her golden curls scattered in the steaming sauce. The traumatized Prince leapt from the table and ran from the palace, never to return.[1]

Despair at having lost him is said to have turned Nazli into an hysterical ogre. Her cruelties increased by the day. Slave girls had to stand all night around her great bed, holding up her mosquito net, and it was summary execution for those who dropped it.

According to one story still told by some of Cairo's aristocrats, when one sleepy girl did drop a corner of the net, Princess Nazli's vengeance was ghastly. She leapt from her bed, ordered her eunuchs to pin the poor girl to the ground, then had burning coals placed between her breasts, on which she calmly boiled a pot of tea while the girl shrieked her way to death. Rumour had it that a maidservant who had eaten a bowl of yoghurt prepared for Nazli summarily had her stomach split open. Perhaps to show that Nazli was not entirely representative of the manners of the Muhammad Ali family, some of its members maintained that her brother Ibrahim, exasperated with her wantonness, visited her when she was in her late twenties and told her that if she did not die that night he would kill her himself the following morning. She obeyed him, they said, took poison and died that same night. Given Ibrahim's own reputation for cruelty, the story would have been unlikely even if it had not been clearly proved false. The end of the story of Princess Nazli was, in reality, more mundane. Nubar Pasha, who was to become Ismail's most important adviser, visited her in 1848 in the Citadel's harem where Ibrahim was dying, and English visitors to the court were to visit her as a frail and witty old lady before she died in Alexandria in 1860.[2]

Nubar was repelled by her, calling her 'sanguinary and lascivious'. When he visited the dying Ibrahim, Nazli was in the room hidden by a large black veil which two eunuchs held between her and the menfolk. 'They forgot that the mirrors, which covered the room's walls entirely, reflected her face with its nose bent like a bird of prey,' he wrote in his memoirs. Nubar and his companions ·had to lie down on ottomans, their faces turned to the ground, as the Princess left the room from behind her huge veil, little realizing that they were cynically watching her in a cubistic chiaroscuro through the myriad chinks of mirror.[3]

Emmeline Lott, the governess of Ismail's five-year-old son Ibrahim, had been told a swashbuckling story about Princess Nazli by one of Nazli's former French maids. Eager for adventure, the effeminate Count Luigi persuaded a Levantine lady-friend of the Princess to smuggle him into her harem. An appointment for the 'lady' to visit was made with the terrifying Princess, and according to the shockingly modern plan he dressed up in the Levantine lady's costliest clothing, which consisted of a merino velvet dress trimmed with Mechlin lace to give the appearance of breasts, and a white chip hat.

Having reached her palace he was led by ferocious-looking eunuchs through courtyards and into a hall, where he was delivered to six young white slave girls whose jet–black hair hung down their backs in ringlets. They wore wide blue-and-red silk trousers tied over their feet with rolls of muslin, thus creating the shuffling noise that is the one sound to be heard in Cairo's otherwise silent harems. They wore gold bracelets set with diamonds, their waists were tied with cashmere shawls, and jackets embroidered with gold thread and lace reached down to their hips. He was taken through hall after splendid hall until he reached a small room full of Abyssinian slaves, whose robes glimmered with diamonds in the shape of butterflies.

The appearance of the notorious Princess made a lasting impression on the eccentric Italian. In contrast with the image of terror created about her and with descriptions such as those of Nubar, she turned out to be small and beautifully made, with alabaster skin, and she glided rather than shuffled into the room. Her prescient eyes pierced through the Count, who wondered with horror whether she had penetrated his disguise. Over wide, brightly-coloured silk trousers she wore a copious white cashmere dress open at the front. A waistband of big pearls was attached by diamond clasps, and a child's satin slippers covered her tiny feet. Golden crêpe was wound around her head and her plaited black hair was gathered up behind with large diamond pins. Her wrists and neck were covered with pearls.

As is customary in the harem she greeted the Count in utter silence. He spent the long period waiting for her to break it – for only she could do so – admiring her 'sweet, pretty mouth' and 'pearly-white teeth' and 'fell desperately in love with her at first sight'. From her conversation he realized that as right-hand person to her father Muhammad Ali she had acquired a sharp political guile but, posing as a woman, he was cautious about discussing politics, a subject rarely touched upon by Ottomen women. Instead, he restricted himself to complimenting her on her jewellery, which she had promptly produced. She showed him pearls as big as pigeon's eggs, topazes as big as fowl's eggs and emeralds as big as pears. He was then given a guided tour of the

31

harem where, despite the gorgeous furniture and jewellery, he noted the 'ennui which those lovely beings must endure in these gilded cages'. He noted that the princesses had no toilet-tables but sat on divans where they spent much of the day lolling around performing their toilet.

When he returned to Nazli's apartment, singing girls were ushered in, but it only took the voice of Nazli's favourite singing girl to fail because of a cold for the Princess's horrible cruelty to surface. She immediately condemned the poor girl to lifelong dumbness and ordered her dragged away by two eunuchs, then turned back to her guest 'all radiant with smiles' as the Count heard the girl's distant screams vie with the sound of the lute.

The dancers had been sent from Constantinople, and wore red silk trousers trimmed with gold, and blue damask jackets open at the chest. The most beautiful one would throw back her head, her small mouth half-open and eyes half-closed, as she leapt about like a gazelle or admired her sensuous figure coquettishly in the mirror. Nazli, meanwhile, lay lazily on her divan, her red lips puffing perfumed smoke from her *chibuk*. Violet, jasmine and rose sherbet in large golden cups encrusted with diamonds were passed to the Count throughout by slave girls, some of whom were as young as six, or by a Circassian girl whom he had much admired.

After elaborate farewells the Count was led by Nazli into the garden, where he fretfully tried to shuffle like a woman and in the proper harem way. But his praise of the flowers incited a violent reaction from the Princess, who promptly revealed that she had not been duped at all by his disguise and that the Count would have been impaled had her husband, the ruthless Defterdar, been at home. As it was she praised him for his courage and asked him meaningfully to visit her the following night.

That night he was led by eunuchs through sweet-scented gardens which finally led him on to a thick carpet surrounded by a divan and silk hangings. Suddenly he felt the embrace of 'the two soft arms of a lovely woman'; this was to be the start of a night of unbridled passion. Nazli insisted he leave before dawn but not before begging him to return the following night. However, he soon realized that he was being led by the eunuchs in an uncertain direction towards the Nile, and recognized that his death was imminent. After some shooting and swordplay and all the gung-ho adventures of a Dumas novel, he managed to escape from the harem and return to his house. He hurriedly left for Jerusalem, but on returning to Cairo some weeks later was to discover that Nazli had made many 'gracious' enquiries about her 'amiable lady-friend', and clearly did not want the adventure to be publicized.[4]

European ladies of the day knew the stories told of Princess Nazli, but only experienced the hospitable side of this schizophrenic woman. Miss Chennells gives a curious account of a meeting which the Princess imposed on a Miss Selina Harris, a famous Egyptologist, and the daughter of a favourite of Muhammad Ali. Miss Harris was also an admired musician who lived near Princess Nazli's palace. One morning three eunuchs unceremoniously entered her room to tell her that she was wanted by the Princess. Knowing Nazli's reputation, Miss Harris shuddered at the invitation but, being a fearless woman, shooed them into her salon until she had completed her toilet. When she eventually entered the salon it was in chaos. The eunuchs had ordered pipes and coffee and the room was full of tobacco smoke. All her books had been turned over and her photographs had been handled. Ignoring her severe reprimands the eunuchs repeated the Princess's order but the tough Miss Harris resolutely refused to go.

The next day they came again with the same message. This time they remained below and Miss Harris ordered pipes and coffee for them. But annoyed by an aggressive repeat of the same order, she declined again. After a third message, and a consultation with her father, it was agreed that she should make the terrible visit. She and her lady-friend were ushered into a room were several slaves were standing. Princess Nazli was seated on cushions but there were no introductions and the traditional silence ensued. After a long pause the Princess made a slight movement of the head to tell them to be seated. However, Miss Harris's friend was a very fat woman for whom settling down on a cushion and subsequently getting up again would have represented a major challenge. She gazed about for a chair and, not seeing one, stayed put until the Princess eventually called for chairs for both her guests. After a while she said, 'I hear you play very well – there is a piano.'

'No, I cannot,' said Miss Harris.

'Why not?'

'Because I am not accustomed to being ordered.'

'Oh, please play.'

'That is a different thing. When I am asked politely I always do what I am asked.' Miss Harris sat down and played, but soon some women on the ground began, at a signal from their mistress, to play an Egyptian tune. Turning to Miss Harris, Nazli asked if she could play that. She had an excellent ear and she played it. Nazli then said, 'I want you to come every day for three or four hours and teach these girls to play as well as you do.'

'Oh, I cannot,' said Miss Harris, 'I have my father and my house to attend to; there's the master who taught me – send for him!' After this Nazli, impressed by her lack of fear, would regularly send for her.[5]

6 Rulers of the New Renaissance

By 1848, Muhammad Ali was incapacitated and virtually senile. Effective power was ceded to his eldest, some said adopted, son Ibrahim, whose energetic efforts to have the viceroyalty passed to him in a *firman*, or decree, by the Sultan, was to brand him a traitor in the Ottoman court. However Ibrahim, although brave, cruel and a general to the core, was afflicted by a pulmonary disease and was to die, violently spitting blood, a year before his father in 1848, at the age of fifty-nine.

According to John Ninet,[1] a journalist who knew all the rulers from Muhammad Ali to Ismail, Ibrahim was addicted to 'those grossest Turkish vices which caused his end'. He cruelly treated the *fellaheen*, says Ninet, and 'but for his early death his would have been a notable reign of terror'. The archaeologist, Giovanni Belzoni, thought Ibrahim a foul man, and maintained that he had two Bedouin roasted alive like rabbits on the spit of a slow fire, and had had a man blasted from one of his cannons. One of Ibrahim's whims was almost to lose Egypt its greatest statesman, Nubar Pasha, who was to become the amanuensis of Ismail. An Armenian from Smyrna, and a nephew of Muhammad Ali's secretary Boghoz Bey Youssoufian, Nubar was sent to be educated at a primary school in Geneva, and then at Sorèze near Toulouse by the Jesuits. As Ibrahim's interpreter on his European tour, he came to be completely at home in the political world of Paris and London.

In 1848, Nubar accompanied the Wali's heir to Istanbul, where Ibrahim made a very bad impression, boorishly demanding the *firman* which would officially make him Wali while his father was still alive. Unbeknown to Ibrahim, the *firman* was only confirmed when an astrologer at the Ottoman court announced that the existing ruler had only six months to live, and that there was, therefore, nothing to be lost in granting the man his treacherous request. When the Ottoman ministers came to say farewell to him, he ignored all court protocol and told them rudely: 'Look at these hills: they are denuded; my father and I have planted ten million trees in Egypt; you, on the contrary, have destroyed what God has given you.'[2] As he sailed away, Ibrahim became increasingly neurotic, his disease giving him little rest. Blood frothed from his mouth; he constantly sought reassurance from his advisers over the implications of his vulgar behaviour at the Ottoman court, and he was becoming increasingly terrified of his father's wrath, should the old man recover his health and discover his treachery. As usual Ibrahim sought relief from his own paranoia by turning to cruelty.

When he saw an Egyptian frigate anchored at Rhodes against his orders, he had its captain tied to a cannon and given three hundred lashes of the whip. It was only Nubar's pleas which saved the man from death. As they sailed on, Ibrahim took umbrage at his business representative in Istanbul who he maintained had cheated him over a purchase of furs. When he was informed that the man had remained at the Ottoman capital at Ibrahim's own orders, he refused to believe it and ordered the man to be thrown overboard. Nubar was well aware that Ibrahim was losing his sanity and might soon turn on anybody, including himself. Later that night Nubar's friend Chirin Bey calmly informed him that Ibrahim suspected Nubar of betraying him on behalf of his father, and intended to decapitate him, put his head between his legs, and throw him overboard.

Nubar saved himself in a typically Byzantine manner. He sought every opportunity to remain with Ibrahim, reminding him of his success in winning the investiture from the Sultan, and of the tales of his heroic campaigns against the Wahhabis. His vainglory tickled, Ibrahim could not resist the flattery and talked energetically all night of the battles he had fought. As dawn began to break over the sea, Nubar knew that he and his companions were safe from the ogre's wrath. The ship was entering Alexandria harbour, and even Ibrahim could not commit such an act of violence in the full glare of publicity. Ironically, when Ibrahim died in the harem of the Citadel later in the year, Nubar was the only courtier who wept. As he was to admit, he wept not in mourning, but in disgust over the expression of joy he saw on every face in the Citadel, high functionaries chatting calmly and calling for pipes to be produced by their slaves, as if this were the most ordinary and satisfactory day in the world. The funeral, wrote Nubar, was 'lugubrious with cynicism and indecency', officials and their assistants openly breaking away from the cortège until, by the time the coffin borne by *fellaheen* reached the mosque in which the great man was to be buried, there were virtually no mourners left.[3]

In his early days in Cairo, Henry Boyle met an old Albanian woman whose husband had been Ibrahim's foster-brother and head groom, and had, in both capacities, enjoyed a personal friendship with him. She told Boyle of the day when, helping Ibrahim mount a horse, her husband had gently explained that he had attached a softer bit to the horse, because of Ibrahim's habit of savagely curbing it in and cutting its mouth. Ibrahim said nothing, but as his foster-brother bent to arrange the stirrup, he raised his scimitar and slashed the poor man's head off from his shoulders in one savage blow. When the old lady recounted the tale to Boyle, she added the extraordinary comment: 'Ah, they were real men in those days, not miserable creatures like now.'[4]

To give Ibrahim some due, his passion for trees was responsible for many of the trees that decorate Cairo today. Roda Island, for example, was completely transformed by Ibrahim's English gardeners. The beautiful banyan trees that fill the gardens of the Manial Palace, now the Club Méditerranée, are a fitting testament to this passion.

Ibrahim was succeeded by his nephew Abbas, whom commentators have for long painted as a gloomy sensualist who loathed Europeans and cared nothing for reform. Although present-day scholars have tried to rehabilitate Abbas, few would deny that he was a recluse and a xenophobe who undid much of Muhammad Ali's achievement. He closed schools and factories, and expelled most foreigners, among them Sulaiman Pasha, Clot Bey, Champolian and Cerisy, although they were mostly to return after his death. He also expelled his father's foreign minister, Artin Bey Chakrian, because he was an Armenian and a Christian. MacCoan saw him as 'a Turk of the worst type, ignorant, cowardly, sensual, fanatic, and opposed to reforms of every sort.'[5] The American Consul General, Edwin de Leon, described Abbas as 'swarthy, with a scanty beard, short and stout of figure, with a bloated, sensual face and dull, cruel eyes'.[6] He was rumoured by his enemies to enjoy having women stitched into sacks filled with rats, and flung into the Nile. Boyle was once told by a Scottish engineer of a visit he made with Abbas to a sugar refinery some miles north of Cairo. The engineer pointed to an immense bunch of grapes hanging from a palm tree. Abbas assured the engineer that it was not a bunch of grapes, but a man. The poor engineer reasserted his opinion that it was a bunch of grapes, so Abbas took careful aim at the object with his rifle and fired. The man dropped from the tree and fell to the ground, dead.

Probably the only positive act of Abbas's reign was the construction of the Cairo–Alexandria railway by George Stephenson's son, Robert, and this was only undertaken at the behest of the British, who wanted to improve communications with their Indian Raj. Modern research, however, suggests that contemporary descriptions of Abbas were overcritical, influenced as they were by his successor, Said.

The circumstances surrounding Abbas's death and its sequel are rather more interesting than the events of his life. He died quite suddenly in July 1854, and it was popularly believed that he had been strangled in his sleep by two boy slaves, who had been sent to him by a jealous wife in Istanbul. The Governor of Cairo, Elfi Bey, who was immediately summoned to the Benha Palace, took the extraordinary measure of arranging the pretence that the Wali was still alive. The state carriage was brought to the palace's private entrance and, assisted by the chief eunuch, Elfi Bey placed the corpse inside the carriage in a seated position, and calmly sat down opposite it. Having reached the Citadel, he arranged for its guns to be pointed at the city, reinforced the garrison, and only then formally announced the death of Abbas, declaring meanwhile that Abbas's son, the more manageable Ilhami, should succeed rather than his brother, Said. However, the attempt was forestalled by the British Consul-General, Sir Frederick Bruce, who insisted that Said should take his rightful place, and Elfi Bey's plans were thwarted. What is particularly interesting about this incident is that it made clear, even then, that Britain already had considerable influence over the affairs of Egypt.

Said, like Muhammad Ali, looked unhesitatingly towards Europe for inspiration, and gave his childhood friend and a cousin of the Empress Eugénie, Ferdinand de Lesseps, the right to build a canal between the Mediterranean and the Red Sea. Born of a Georgian mother, Said had European features, and a red beard and hair. MacCoan compared him in personality with Henry VIII, but added that Said remained loyal to one wife. However, the debts which Said began to run up were to be the prelude to Egypt's eventual bankruptcy under his successor Ismail, and to Britain's fiscal and then complete control of Egypt until 1922. 'He was eager, even anxious to please,' writes David Landes in *Bankers and Pashas*, 'and his inability to say "no" made him the prey of as fine a pack of fawning, sycophantic jackals as ever prowled a despot's court.'[7] When the cavalier parasite Bravay, who hovered about the Egyptian court from 1858 to 1868, once complained to Said that an estimate in Italian lire should be raised, the Wali simply ordered him to switch the sum conveniently to English 'pounds'.

Said's reign signalled the beginning of Egypt's *belle époque*, which was to reach its height under Ismail. Said's first language was French, and he was highly educated, bright and witty. Although no philanderer in the mould of Ismail, Said was also no puritan. He once bought a slave girl for the mighty sum of £70,000, but the courageous girl took the unheard-of step of refusing adamantly to enter his harem, calling him a 'fat old man'. She was in love with Mayloum Pasha and, in an unusual gesture for one of his family, Said allowed her to marry Mayloum.

Said's wife, the red-haired Ingee Khanum, was charming and accomplished and took centre stage at the splendid parties and receptions to which the Khedive invited dazzling European society. Said and his guests would dine in the palace, seated on a dais, at a table whose entire service at each remove was made of solid gold. The princesses and their ladies would peer from their *mashrabiya* (screens of interlacing wood) boxes in the gallery above. Said provided Edward Prince of Wales with the lavishly furnished Giza Palace during his 1862 visit. But Said was by no means merely a *bon viveur*. He sought Robert Stephenson's aid to extend the railway system which had been started reluctantly by the lugubrious Abbas and was to be the first railway line in Africa. The Cairo to Alexandria line was opened in 1856, just twelve years after Switzerland and Denmark had opened their first lines. Said also installed a telegraph system and carried out new irrigation schemes. But the project that was to immortalize his name, and that of Ismail, was the granting to Ferdinand de Lesseps of a concession to build the Suez Canal. In January 1856, de Lesseps was officially given the concession, and two years later he launched his Compagnie Universelle du Canal Maritime de Suez, with a capital of £8 million, on almost every stock exchange in Europe. On 25 April, de Lesseps began cutting a preliminary trench between the Mediterranean and Lake Menzaleh. However, despite the aid of 20,000 *fellaheen*, little progress on the historic project was made during Said's lifetime.

Said himself died, pathetically crippled, on 18 January 1863, having made desperate visits to a Paris surgeon to cure a disease of the internal organs which was tearing him apart. A month before he died, he confided to Sir Henry Bulwer his bitter remorse over the chaos of the Egyptian economy. He was buried quite simply, not in one of the grandiose mausoleums in Cairo's Northern Cemetery ('The City of the Dead'), but in the burial ground of a little mosque in the centre of Alexandria where his mother had been buried.

Lord Cromer was to take a far severer view of Said's character than the idealistic De Leon, accusing him of a cruelty that could only be ignored if one compared it with the far greater excesses of Abbas. Cromer's reflections, however, also portrayed a brave eccentric rather than a venal barbarian. He related how on one occasion Said, annoyed by accusations of cowardice levelled at him by the European press, had one kilometre of road strewn a foot deep with gunpowder. Once this was done, Said, with lighted pipe in his mouth, coolly walked along the road, with his enormous suite forced to follow him in terror. Cromer related in another story that when the Wali's steamer became stuck in mud, Said ordered the steersman to receive a hundred blows of the *courbash*, and these were administered. The boat managed to move away again, but when it became stuck for the second time Said roared: 'Give him two hundred!' The horrified boatman promptly leapt into the Nile in terror. When he was brought back to the feet of the

Wali, Said asked him why he had jumped overboard. The man replied that the preferred to risk drowning than receive further strokes. 'Fool,' shouted Said, 'when I said two hundred I did not mean lashes, but sovereigns.' The astonished man was immediately handed the money.[8]

That Ismail succeeded Said was thanks to the curious death of his elder brother, Ahmed. The catastrophe surrounding Ahmed's death was a *cause célèbre* at the time. On 13 May 1858, Said gave one of his sumptuous parties, on this occasion to celebrate Ramadan. It was held at the Ras al-Tin Palace in Alexandria, and Said invited every member of the ruling family. Ismail was ill and unable to attend, but the special train which left Cairo station, filled with illustrious guests, included Ahmed and Halim, a younger brother of Said. When the train approached the Nile, which was turbulent at this point, its British driver suddenly noticed with horror that the swing bridge had been left open. He desperately tried to reverse the engine, but it was too late. The train and its carriages tumbled fifty feet into the river, killing nearly everybody aboard, including Ahmed. Some gossipers saw Ismail's hand in the catastrophe, but critical observers of the time found the accusation implausible.

MacCoan noted how parasitic some of the foreigners at Said's court were. Knowing that Said's death was imminent, the British director of Cairo's telegraph system had hoped to be the first to inform Ismail of his accession, and thus win promotion and reward. For days and nights he waited patiently at his post, telling his Coptic assistant to inform him as soon as news came. However, when the news did come, the director had fallen asleep, and the wily Copt carried the news to Ismail himself and was at once promoted. When the Englishman woke up and heard the news of the death from his assistant, he raced to the new Wali with it, only to be dismissed contemptuously for bringing old news.[9]

7 Ismail – a Ruler Obsessed

Ismail was soon to be compared with Louis XIV, but as the Egyptian historian Muhammed Sabry noted, 'in this court-life after the manner of Versailles, the nobles were notorious foreign adventurers'. According to Nubar, 'France, the Emperor, the Empress, haunted the imagination of Ismail as they had haunted that of Said.'[1] It was this fatal attraction that was to be Ismail's undoing. He was as obsessed with European manners – not to speak of European women – as he was with European money and European imperial adventures. In the view of English critics of the day, he failed to understand the subtleties and harsh realities of European accountancy, and was unable or unwilling to distinguish private from public expenditure. However, when Egypt was declared bankrupt by the European banks in 1871, Ismail himself and members of the Khedival family pawned their estates and possessions (the princesses their jewellery) in a desperate attempt to pay off Egypt's crippling debts.

From the moment of his accession in 1863, Ismail demonstrated a boundless energy and imagination. His first endeavours were aimed at freeing himself from control by the Sublime Porte in Istanbul. After three years of bribes and blandishments, he was granted the somewhat insignificant Persian title of Khedive in 1866, and seven years later, in 1873, he obtained a *firman* that settled the succession on the Khedive's eldest son. The aspects of the *firman*, however, which effectively made him an independent sovereign were the granting to him of unlimited authority to make internal laws and regulations, to enter into commercial or other treaties with foreign powers and to increase the strength of his army and navy.

Having established his authority and his autonomy, Ismail embarked on reform. His goal was a spontaneous rebirth of Egypt on European lines. In some ways he was a man ahead of his time, trying to achieve in the nineteenth century what Mustafa Kemal (Atatürk) in Turkey, and Reza Khan in Iran, successfully achieved at the beginning of the twentieth. Ismail was trying to build on the rough foundations laid down by Muhammad Ali, but these foundations had fallen into disrepair. He set up primary schools to which pupils from all religions were freely admitted and in which, in a gesture of early socialism, fees ranging from £26 downwards were paid, according to the wealth of parents. Most dramatic of all was his first wife's courageous decision to set up a school for the daughters of Cairo's leading ladies. At first the project was so novel that the school benches remained empty. Once the ice had broken, however, the school became so popular that there wasn't enough space for all the families fighting for admission. Ismail also set up an education system for the children of the *fellaheen* who would, under European moral pressure, later replace the slaves which he once claimed to a European friend 'were a great expense and a great nuisance'. The number of pupils in Egyptian schools, 6,000 in Muhammad Ali's time, had risen to 90,000 by 1873, more than a third of whom were girls.

Ismail reorganized the customs and excise system on Western lines, and was, as a result, lionized by traders who had suffered intolerably under the oppressive Ottoman system. In 1865 he took over the postal system, employing an official from London's St Martin-le-Grand to reorganize it on ultramodern lines. Towards the end of the century it was to win an international prize as one of the best postal systems in the world, a far cry from the present day, when it is one of the worst. American officers who had escaped from the vicissitudes of the American Civil War were employed to rebuild the army. Harbour works were undertaken at Suez, and new lighthouses gave increased safety to shipping. Ismail surrounded himself with a curious mixture of ministers, of whom the most important were the Ministers of Commerce, Foreign Affairs, Justice and Finance. By far the most important was the first, Nubar Pasha.

Ismail built himself countless palaces and idyllic gardens, and entertained the society figures of Europe with a reckless generosity. He was fascinated by people, and eccentrics like General Gordon (of Khartoum) greatly appealed to this streak in him. He extended the railways, roads, bridges and canals initiated by Said. He created a merchant fleet, set up a telegraph system and expanded the education system. Above all he oversaw the inauguration of the Suez Canal. But despite these successes it was all to end in disaster for Ismail and for Egypt. The treasury was bankrupted by Ismail's extravagance and by loans from European banks massively reduced by risk discounts. Ismail was then humiliatingly deposed and, after a brief interim, British rule was imposed under the towering figure of Evelyn Baring (later Lord Cromer).

'Egypt,' Ismail announced with passion in 1867, amid what was to be one of the most extravagant building booms in history, 'is no longer part of Africa. It is part of Europe.' Europeans themselves were to take a more cynical view of Egypt's identity. Following Ismail's abdication, the British Ambassador to the Ottoman Court, Sir Henry Drummond Wolff, was to tell the Ottoman Grand Vezir tersely in 1882: 'Turkey will retain her rights and we will keep Egypt.' A decade later the French writer Paul Ravaisse would describe Egypt as 'politically a part of Europe, and to a certain extent the common property of all nations'. Indeed, even many Egyptians saw Egypt as a sort of *grande cocotte*, whose carnal pleasures could be had by the highest bidder.

Ismail had taken one look at the Paris Exposition Universelle of 1867 and impetuously decided to turn Cairo into a copy of Baron George Haussmann's new Paris: a city of magnificent boulevards through which the Khedive and the sybarites of Europe would ride in gilded carriages; a city of palaces in which the crowned heads of Europe and its most beautiful women (in particular Eugénie) would be entertained in splendour. In a watercolour by Henri Barron of a soirée at the Tuileries, given in honour of the visit of the Tsar and the King of Prussia to the exhibition, you can see Ismail seated beside Eugénie and peering at her with an intensity bordering on obsession. The scene represented the height of Parisian Second Empire magnificence, and must have made a deep impression on Ismail. The women in the painting are all cosmetically beautiful, and tall marble pillars support baroque, gilded cornices. The hall looks out through trees at dusk towards a brightly lit kiosk in the Tuileries gardens. On a balcony in the foreground, elegant men in silk tail coats are dallying with nubile girls in flowing silk with an air of young Greek goddesses about them. Four years later, after the capitulation of Paris to the Prussians, thousands of unarmed Prussian soldiers were to visit the palace, escorted by detachments of French National Guards. It was a tidy occasion, despite the hissing and hooting of the French mobs – the very mobs who, as Communards, were to set fire to the palace, the Louvre, the Hôtel de Ville and the Ministry of Finance two months later.

The contradictions in the character of Ismail amounted, in the view of some observers, to virtual schizophrenia. He was a mixture of fine breeding and barbarism. He set up schools to fight illiteracy, but flogged the taxes out of the *fellaheen* who attended them. He used the *courbash* and forced-labour to build his new Egypt, but sent expeditions to Sudan under the command of quirky Englishmen to put down the slave trade – and, meanwhile, extend his empire. He could drink tea with Queen Victoria at Balmoral, and drink champagne with his beloved Eugénie at Versailles, then have his Minister of Finance, Ismail Sadiq, secretly strangled on his return to Egypt for fear that he would expose the corrupt chaos of the Khedival debt. Although loyal to him during his lifetime, Nubar was far from flattering of the Khedive in his memoirs, describing his jowl as that of an animal, and his subtle sea-green eyes as terrifying to all about him. To Nubar, it was to become apparent in his memoirs, Ismail was a despot and murderer, prone to fits of terrible rage.

But it would be unfair to condemn Ismail as an entirely irresponsible ruler. Indeed, there was genuine idealism bound up with the theatrical side of his character and, in a letter to his Prime Minister Sherif Pasha, he wrote at the beginning of his reign: 'As Chief of State and as an Egyptian, I consider it my sacred duty to follow the opinion of my country and to give complete satisfaction to its legitimate aspirations.' Adverse publicity in the European press worried him obsessively. When, at a ball at the Abdin Palace, he complained to an attractive young Englishwoman, Janet Ross, about an article criticizing him in the British press, the candid woman confessed that she had written the article, then promptly left the ball and took the boat to England.

According to the historian of the princesses, Aziz Hanki Bey, Ismail had fourteen wives. Each was given a splendid palace with ladies-in-waiting, slaves, musicians and dancers. They wore magnificent jewellery, and each had her own *dahabiyya* (Nile sailing boat) moored on the Nile. During Ismail's exile, while he was staying in Paris, Princess Mathilde Bonaparte visited the Khedival princesses and asked Despina Draneht (the daughter of Draneht Pasha) how many wives Ismail had. She replied truthfully that he had four. Ismail was greatly annoyed, determined as he was to pose as a conventional European aristocrat. 'Would Madame Draneht,' he admonished her, 'kindly remember that in Europe the ex-Khedive possessed only one wife?'[2]

Unsatisfied with his wives, Ismail was also an obsessive womanizer, and enjoyed the favours of a large number of Circassian odalisques. When the King of Italy sent him a woman and he was already occupied with another one, goes one somewhat far-fetched tale, he gave the second lady twenty-four locomotives to placate her; yet he was intensely mean over small things, and would spend hours arguing with a servant over a few piastres. His enemies accused him of every cruelty. Finding two of his harem intriguing with courtiers in the palace, it was said, he had them flogged to death and their lovers strangled in his presence. Some weeks later, the accusations continued, he found four other courtesans dallying with his guards in an ante-chamber to his bedroom. Having watched secretly and caught them *in flagrante delicto*, he stabbed his favourite concubine to death himself, and had the other three sacked and flung alive into the river. Some of these tales may only have possessed a grain of truth, but their telling reflected the disgust felt among many Egyptians over Ismail's profligacy and hedonism. This disgust was expressed by the contemporary Egyptian poet Salih Magdi:

> Your money is squandered on pimps and prostitutes.
> Normal men take a woman for a wife;
> He wants a million wives.
> Normal men take a house for living;
> He takes ninety.
> Oh, Egyptians, there is disgrace all around:
> Awake, Awake!

The Times correspondent shared this feeling of outrage. 'But Ismail,' he wrote, 'with a tyranny far greater than that of either Muhammad Ali or Ibrahim, seizes, without a show of pretence, the land and property of his subjects.' The fate of his Minister of Finance, Ismail Sadiq, who was married to his daughter Faika, was evidence of his cruelty, although Sadiq's method of obtaining taxes from the *fellaheen*, who would sell their women's jewellery to avoid the horrors of flogging, was itself cruel in the extreme. When the European tax consultants began to study Ismail's books in 1870, the Khedive was terrified that his Minister would expose some of the corruption and cooking of figures that had become prevalent. So the man was courteously brought by *calèche* to the Gezira Palace on the banks of the Nile and offered coffee. Sensing that the coffee was poisoned, he refused to drink it. The coffee was then, apparently, forced down his throat and he was strangled. The Khedive announced to the world that he had sent his Minister with all honours to the Sudan, and even produced forged letters from Sadiq saying how much he was enjoying himself. As time went by letters were received from Sadiq complaining that he was feeling unwell. Four months after his gruesome murder, the Governor of Dongola, scrupulously continuing the complicated pretence, sent a letter to the Khedive saying that the Minister had sadly passed away.

Ismail's mother, the Paramount Princess Khoshyar Hanem, the third Circassian wife of Ibrahim, was said to share the cruel, amorous traits of Princess Nazli, Muhammad Ali's daughter. Driving in her *calèche* through Cairo, she was said to have handsome young men picked up for her royal bed. None would ever return alive. One day a comely young gentleman received the invitation from her eunuchs, and determined to confront the macabre, erotic adventure. His friends begged him not to, but he was bent on discovering the secrets of the Paramount Princess's bedroom. After a sensual night with her a eunuch politely informed him that it was time to leave and led him down the corridor. As he followed the eunuch, the young Italian muttered that 'his friends', who included the Italian Vice-Consul, were awaiting him at the palace gates. The anxious eunuch at once ordered him to remain where he was and raced off for further instructions. He was told to cancel the usual reward for royal copulation – summary execution – and return to lead the young Don Juan to the safety of the palace gates.[3]

The Paramount Princess tried to inculcate similar cruelties into her servants, but failed to do so with her German maid, a fact that impressed Emmeline Lott, who found herself a victim otherwise of the rivalries between the British and Germans within the various harems. On many occasions Lott herself failed to stem the sadism of her own precocious charge, the Grand Pasha Ibrahim. In one of his temper tantrums, the five-year-old dug his fingers into the arm of his half-sister by a slave mother, then pushed his hand into the little girl's mouth and ripped its edges until the blood came frothing. When the second Princess, Ibrahim's mother, came running and heard his own tearful account, the little girl was promptly forced to kiss the ground, then the hem of the odious Prince's tunic. When Lott remonstrated at this injustice, the second Princess smiled at her, murmuring '*malesh, malesh*' ('It doesn't matter! It doesn't matter!'). Ibrahim was once so enraged with a slave who refused to stop talking, that he flung a shovel-full of burning charcoal in his face, setting himself briefly on fire at the same time. On another occasion he espied crocodiles from his *dahabiyya* and rushed to the captain to order the nearest slave flung overboard so that he could enjoy watching the kill. Luckily the compassionate captain flung the young man over the other side, from where he was able to swim to safety.[4]

As the expenses involved in building Ismail's new Egypt accumulated, and the day of the inauguration of the Suez Canal approached, life for the masses of Egyptians became intolerable. Lucie Duff Gordon wrote a year after the Canal celebrations:

> I cannot describe to you the misery here now . . . Every day some new tax. Now every beast, camel, cow, sheep, donkey, horse is made to pay. The *fellaheen* can no longer eat bread; they are now living on barley-meal mixed with water and raw green stuff, vetches, etc . . . Even here [in Cairo] the beating for the year's taxes is awful.[5]

Lucie Duff Gordon was almost certainly the only English person to live in the Egyptian countryside and describe in her diaries what was happening during this period. For some years she lived in a house in Luxor built by Salt, the English Consul-General, on top of the temple of Khem. During her visits to Cairo children would be heard chanting in the slums:

> MEN: We are all in rags,
> We are all in rags,
> That the shaikh may be dressed in cloth.
> BOYS: They starve us,
> They starve us
> GIRLS: They beat us,
> They beat us
> BOYS: But there's someone above,
> But there's someone above
> GIRLS: Who will punish them well,
> Who will punish them well.

Ismail, however, was intent less on improving the welfare of his people than on leaving behind him a testament of greatness. Overnight, between his visit to France in 1867 and the opening of the Suez Canal in 1869, he turned much of Cairo into a superficial copy of Paris, building an opera house, a racecourse and several palaces for the great event. Lord Milner wrote in 1892:

> Luxurious, voluptuous, ambitious, fond of display, devoid of principle, he was at the same time full of the most magnificent schemes for the material improvement of the country. Over and above the millions and millions wasted in entertainments, in largesse, in sensuality, in the erection of numerous palaces – structurally as rotten as they are aesthetically abominable – he threw away yet other millions upon a vast scheme of agricultural development, started with inadequate knowledge at inordinate cost.'[6]

Writers of the period differ radically in describing Ismail's personality. Butler, in his *Court Life of Egypt*, quotes Ismail's son Tewfik as telling him: 'People in Europe would be astonished if they knew Ismail Pasha's real character and history; but thank God! those barbarous times are over.' Fearful of conspiracies, Ismail kept his son under close and constant surveillance, and treated him, according to Butler, with such little respect that ministers were heard taunting him: 'You a prince? Why, your father will send you in irons to the Sudan tomorrow if you don't behave.' However, Tewfik clearly remained loyal to his father, rejecting outright all offers of intrigue against him.

But foreigners were impressed by Ismail's industriousness. At noon, announced by cannon from the Citadel, he would retire for an hour for breakfast, then he would be back at his post until seven at night. On rare days he would take the afternoon off, and take a brougham or barouche down the Shoubra or Abbasiyya roads. After the evening meal, he would sit out on his balcony in the lilac-scented Cairo night, smoking and chatting with ministers and others who might drop in on him. Sometimes he would work deep into the night, keeping a whole staff of secretaries, chamberlains and other officials at their posts until the work was completed. He would work a twelve- to fourteen-hour day throughout the year, and no detail of public business would pass him by. 'He is, in fact,' wrote MacCoan, 'both sovereign and minister in one – seeing everything, knowing everything, and ordering everything for himself: the titular heads of departments being merely so many *chefs de cabinet*, who do little more than register and execute his will.'[7] Ismail was accessible to all. 'The readiness with which His Highness receives almost everybody is one of the incidents of a visit to Cairo that most surprises and gratifies a stranger.'[8]

Visitors would inscribe their names in the visitors' book in the room of the Assistant-Master of Ceremonies, and if they had the remotest pretext for an audience, would be ushered up after a short delay. Speaking perfect Parisian French, the Khedive would receive his visitor,

> with a courtesy and affability that at once set him at his ease, rising as he approaches and motioning him to a seat on the divan or to a chair near his own . . . Be you engineer, merchant, journalist, politician, practical agriculturist, or almost no matter what else, you will soon feel you have met your match in special intelligence and information . . . How he has found time to acquire this encyclopaedic information is a marvel . . .[9]

After his retirement, the American Consul-General, Edwin de Leon wrote:

> The Khedive is an immense worker, and as it is one of the taxes on absolute power that its head must know and supervise everything, even to the minutest detail, he is compelled to get up early and sit up late at the labour he loves of directing the whole state machinery . . .[10]

8   *Paris's* Belle Epoque *and the Great Exhibition*

The influence upon Ismail of his visit to the Exposition Universelle, held in Paris's Champ de Mars in 1867, was to leave its mark on Egypt as only that of the Mamluk master-builders could have done. Cairo must be rebuilt according to the ruthless plans for Paris of the great French town planner. Haussmann himself seems to have been somewhat troubled by the Khedive's idealistic plans for the new Cairo, turning to Nubar to remark unkindly: 'The Viceroy asks me for gardeners and artists of every kind; that's fine, I can give him them; but have you a man in Egypt who can make these buffoons work?'[1]

Ismail was greeted in France with the pomp and ceremony that should properly have been accorded the Ottoman Sultan Abdul-Aziz, who arrived several days later to attend the exhibition, and whose vassal the Khedive nominally remained. Ismail sailed on the Khedival yacht, the *Mahroussa*, from Alexandria on 10 June, and landed five days later at Toulon, where he was greeted with a magnificent salvo of shore batteries. At the Gare de Lyons in Paris, he was received by Haussmann. An imperial *calèche* took the Khedive to the Louvre, where a splendid suite of rooms had been prepared for him and his immense retinue. His first act was to pay his respects to the Empress. Napoleon was ill with the gallstone that was to trouble him throughout the horrors of the Franco-Prussian War, but on 19 June he paid his respects to the Khedive, and took him to lunch at Versailles and to the steeplechases at Vincennes. Ismail, meanwhile, found time to order from his Paris tailor immense wardrobes of gentleman's clothing.

Invited to a soirée at the Tuileries, Ismail was delighted, and probably astonished, to be loudly introduced by the Swiss chamberlain as 'His Majesty the King of Egypt'. The unorthodox announcement must clearly have enraged the Sultan, and caused considerable protocol problems over how the two men should be treated – problems that the British press was to trumpet when the canal was inaugurated two years later. Although the Elysée Palace was converted to a fairyland of lights in the Sultan's honour, he was mortified when Louis-Napoleon dared to suggest that the two rulers were related through the Empress Josephine, in that her cousin, Aimée, was Abdul Hamid I's favourite odalisque, and probably his successor Selim's mistress. The Sultan clearly regarded Louis-Napoleon as a *parvenu*, which, in comparison with the Ottoman sultans, he was.

The new Paris designed by Haussmann – the very symbol of the salon life, balls and wild and sensual women that was the essence of Second Empire Paris – intoxicated Ismail, but shocked the writers who were its life force. Emile Zola wrote caustic articles in 1869 about Paris's lurid Théâtre des Variétés, 'where two years ago all the princes of this world went to pay homage before even visiting the Exposition Universelle'. The Parisian social diarist, Edmond de Goncourt, was fascinated by the women. He wrote on 21 October:

> At the English buffets in the Exhibition there is a fantastic quality about the women, with their splendid beauty, their crude pallor, their flaming hair; they are like whores of the Apocalypse, something terrifying, frightening, inhuman. Their eyes gaze unseeing into the distance. A cross between clowns and cattle, they are magnificent, alarming animals.[2]

Ismail himself, during a cure at Vichy the previous year, appears to have fallen in love with the actress Hortense Schneider who, wrote Zola as he made notes for *Nana*, hypnotized a stupid public with 'an obscenity underlined by a wiggle of the hips' but who was, with her sister and fellow Offenbach star, the toast of Paris. According to Despina Draneht, the Khedive, feeling bored one day, sent Hortense a telegram requesting her to join him as Les Ambassadeurs Restaurant. He was busy at his writing table when his valet announced the arrival of a M. Schneider. Absorbed, Ismail muttered, 'Let her take a bath and then pass her to me.'

'Monseiur says a bath!' stammered the valet. 'Does Monsieur want me to make M. Schneider of Creusot take a bath?'

Red in the face, Ismail roared, 'It's Mademoiselle of the Palais Royale – Hortense – I'm waiting for, imbecile! Why do you speak to me of M. Schneider of Creusot, what do you want me to do with M. Schneider of Creusot?' Ismail soon calmed down and realizing how stupidly he had behaved, and to avoid ridicule and gossip, he is said to have promptly given M. Schneider an important order for railway material to Egypt.[3]

The exhibition was held at the height of an era in which the cancan was the rage, an era in which prostitution became a glamorous obsession for writers like Zola and Flaubert, and an era which spawned courtesans like the Plymouth girl Cora Pearl, the notorious mistress of the unpleasant Plon-plon, Prince Napoleon Joseph, the son of Napoleon Bonaparte's brother, King Jerome. Cora Pearl's favourite joke was to award her later lovers with the honour of wearing the wretched Prince's nightshirt. She also enjoyed being revealed nude on huge silver salvers. 'Cora Pearl,' wrote Arsène Houssaye in his *Confessions*, 'passed like an unruly comet across the sky of the Bouffes-Parisiens, all starry with beautiful girls – not to mention all the beds to which she gave stardom.'[4] Although the principal model for Nana was Blanche d'Antigny, whom Caroline Letessier installed at the Grand Hotel, Zola also studied the life of Cora Pearl, alias Eliza Emma Crouch, for his courtesan heroine. Zola described the Paris of *Nana*'s ambience as a 'whole society clinging to those women's skirts . . . Old men debauching themselves and breathing their last away from home . . . Young fools ruining themselves, some to keep in with the fashion, some out of infatuation.'[5]

The cafés that lined Haussmann's splendid boulevards became the core of Parisian literary and artistic life. In 1878, Zola began his research for *Nana* in the Café Anglais, the main haunt of the elegant hedonists of the time. In the Café Guerbois near the Place de Clichy, the painters and writers would meet: Cézanne, Monet, Renoir, Degas, Pissarro, Sisley, Nadar, Zola and Manet. Manet would drink, too, with his friend Charles Baudelaire on the terrace of Tortini's.

Paris provided operas, such as Offenbach's *Belle Hélène* which topped the bill for Parisians, and bawdy shows in its *cafés chantants*. On 12 April 1867, twelve days after the opening of the exhibition, the Théâtre des Variétés in the Boulevard Montmartre put on Offenbach's *La Grande-Duchesse de Gerolstein* which was as popular as *La Belle Hélène*. The corridor to the dressing room of Hortense Schneider, its leading lady, became known as the 'Passage des Princes', a phrase with obvious sexual connotations. Zola was contemptuous of the young men of grand families who 'applaud the trite productions of Messrs Offenbach and Hervé and make queens of wretched tightrope dancers, who frolic on the boards like fairground artistes.'[6] But the applause for Schneider was genuine and she entranced Paris as she entranced Ismail who regularly trod 'Le Passage'. Louis-Napoleon of course attended the opera, returning some days later with Eugénie. Apart from Ismail, visitors to Schneider's dressing room included Tsar Alexander II and his sons the Grand Dukes; King William of Prussia and Crown Prince Frederick; and the Kings of Portugal, Sweden, Belgium and Bavaria. Ismail – and at least one other head of state – were entertained more intimately at her house in L'Avenue de Versailles. On his nocturnal visits Ismail would, like others, be obliged to brave the vengeance of Schneider's discarded lover Xavier Feuillant who had rented a flat across the road and would, shortly after the arrival of her lover, switch on a veritable blaze of lights to embarrass her guests.

The exhibitions in Europe and America from 1851 onwards were designed as magnificent occasions to impress even those who could not afford to visit them through catalogues and news coverage. London held its first great exhibition, for which the Crystal Palace was built, in 1851, and its second, at which 16,000 visitors showed their goods, in 1862. The German steelworks Krupp sent a piece of cast iron weighing twenty-one tons to the exhibition as a precursor to the terrible gun it was to exhibit in Paris in 1867. In 1853, New York held a similar exhibition, for which its own Crystal Palace was built. Paris held great exhibitions in 1855, 1862, 1867, 1889 (for which the Eiffel Tower was built) and 1900. A mock–up of an entire Cairo street – *La Rue du Caire* – was created for the 1889 exhibition when the belly dance suddenly became the vogue in Paris and was soon being practised in every drawing room and performed at every dance hall. Edmond de Goncourt was fascinated by one dancer, although wishing that she were naked, who 'when people applauded her, with her body completely immobile, seemed to make little salutations with her navel'.[7]

Paris's 1867 exhibition was to be Louis-Napoleon's great testament and was to eclipse the two others previous to it. It attracted nearly seven million visitors, covered 146,588 square yards, over 20,000 square yards more than London's 1862 exhibition, and cost twenty million francs, about five million francs more than London's. There were an amazing 52,000 exhibitors. The exhibition was the supreme statement of Europe's state-of-the-art. Visitors could see a wagon for 'carrying lengthy goods on railways with sharp curves', a speculum for obtaining a view of the larynx and, more ominously for France, Krupp's Great Gun, which was to be used to lay siege to Paris three years later.

The Egyptian stand, widely considered the most marvellous in the exhibition, won over twenty medals of which three were gold. It consisted of three sumptuous pavilions. The first was a Pharaonic temple designed by Claude Mariette, the Keeper of Cairo's Boulaq Museum, whereby, according to Mariette's guidebook, the visitor, in a few paces, could pass through forty centuries of history. The second was a *salamlik* (the men's equivalent of the *haramlik*) whose great hall was modelled like Istanbul's Hagia Sophia in the shape of a Greek cross. Light filtered intricately from holes in the roof and the interior was covered from top to bottom with inlaid stones, marquetry and silver filigree stalectites against gold and alabaster surrounds. This was the place to which Ismail would adjourn in private to find his peace. The third pavilion was a *wikala*, a simple brick bazaar comprising a courtyard surrounded by small shops, in which Egyptian artisans produced traditional wares. At anchor just off the Pont d'Iena was an authentic *dahabiyya* whose prow was carved as a crocodile. The *dahabiyya* had a fourteen-man crew in white uniforms and red *tarboushes*.

Among the leading guests to the exhibition were the Tsar, the King of Prussia and Bismarck, the Sultan, Ismail, the Prince of Wales, the Duke of Cambridge, Prince Umberto of Italy and the son of the Shogun of Japan. 'The season,' wrote Prosper Mérimée, 'is prolific in princes and archdukes.' Queen Victoria, forever mourning the death of her beloved Albert, refused to come, seeing the exhibition as a symbol of the very decadence which he had so condemned. She sent the Prince of Wales, but took the precaution of ordering him straight back to report to her if any 'oriental brothers' showed irritating signs of wishing to visit her at Windsor.[8]

As it turned out, two 'oriental brothers' did come. One, after weeks of tireless negotiation, was the Sultan, accompanied by his nephews, Murad and Abdul-Hamid. The other was Ismail, who was treated, according to protocol, as a subject of the Sultan. This snub greatly annoyed *The Times* correspondent, who noted that Ismail was invited to Buckingham Palace by a side door. The Queen did not even bother to mention him in her letters or her diary, referring only to an inundation of 'Turks and Egyptions'. The Sultan, on the other hand, was given a grand reception. He was not to know that the Queen had scribbled in her diary before he arrived the hope that 'the Sultan is not likely to come again'. She wrote from Frogmore Gardens to her daughter Vicky, the Crown Princess of Prussia: 'The Sultan's visit is no satisfaction and I wish he were not coming. It is also, politically speaking, a bad moment. He can't, moreover, speak a word of anything but Turkish.'[9] She was amazed at the excitement Londoners expressed as they waited for his arrival. 'Here people are half-mad about the Sultan and altogether in a state of feverish excitement about everything; and most absurd and unreasonable.'[10] The very thought of his visit tired the Queen, as she explained to Vicky: 'Alice has written to tell you all about the Turks and Egyptians of which we have a perfect inundation – and how worried and bustled about it we are.'[11]

However, the Queen, with her well-known facility for becoming obsessed by a new man, was soon mesmerized by Abdul-Aziz. As part of a naval review she accompanied him on a boat 'swarming with Turks'. It was a stormy day and he became seasick. 'I fastened the garter round him myself,' wrote the Queen, 'and he smiled and laughed and coloured and was very much pleased.' The Queen quickly began to marvel at the oriental glitter of the visit. 'The Sultan is a handsome man,' she wrote, 'broad and fat rather, but with the true, splendid, soft, brown oriental eyes – and a fine nose and a pleasant expression. He wears the usual, present Turkish dress – richly embroidered, with a low, broad fez, a good deal out from his face. He never touched wine . . . All the pages served in State Dress – Brown and his brother, and Ross, in full Highland dress – Cowley in his full uniform. Quantities of gold plate on the table."[12]

In Paris, meanwhile, the exhibition continued with its splendid balls and extravaganzas. Johann Strauss, himself, conducted the première of the *Blue Danube*, which was soon being hummed in all the streets. *Don Carlos* was performed at the Opera. Eugénie gave a ball at Versailles, while Haussmann spent £30,000 to entertain 8,000 guests at the Hôtel de Ville which had been converted to a green grotto with three waterfalls and flowering trees. The festivities were imbued with political drama as news arrived of the execution of the Emperor Maximilian of Mexico. In Paris there was an attempt on the Tsar's life. The bullet was fired by a young Pole crying '*Vive la Pologne*' but missed both the Tsar and the Emperor, giving Louis-Napoleon the opportunity to turn to his guest and say dramatically: 'Sire, we have been under fire together.'

However, the exhibition went on. A red-and-gold glass coach carried the Emperor and Empress at the head of a long procession from the Tuileries to the Palais de l'Industrie where 20,000 people were waiting. In the true Parisian fashion for irony, the dreaded Bismarck was made a kind of folk-hero, although when the crowds shouted '*Vive Bismarck*' the rough Prussian replied with rare modesty: 'No, no, they're only shouting "*V'là Bismarck*".' The *couturiers* gave the iron Chancellor the colour brown and soon, to illustrate their moods through the magic of the *couturier*, pretty Parisian women were wearing Bismarck '*malade*', Bismarck '*content*', Bismarck '*en colère*'. Every sort of clothing was given the Bismarck stamp. There were Bismarck silks, satins and velvets, woollen stuffs and cotton fabrics, Bismarck boots, Bismarck gloves, Bismarck parasols and Bismarck bonnets. Parisians only half-realized that Bismarck, as he gazed at Paris from his carriage, was preparing to devour them.[13]

The inspiration for the rebuilding of Paris had come from Louis-Napoleon who, from 1853, embarked on clearing away many of the old streets and replacing them with grand new boulevards (from the word bulwark) and squares. During the seventeenth and eighteenth centuries, several straight, wide streets had been opened up both within and beyond the medieval town walls. The new city plan, furiously attacked by conservationists who watched with horror as medieval buildings were demolished to make way for streets such as the new Rue des Ecoles, extended this feature by a system of radiating avenues linking important squares and public buildings. Napoleon's plan was twofold: to lessen the spread of cholera and to make it more difficult for revolutionaries to build barricades. Ironically, his plans worked against him, giving the Communards who destroyed the regime in 1870 the very access of fire that had been prepared for the army. The responsibility for supervising the plan at first fell to the Prefect of Paris, Beyer, but he was so pessimistic about its cost and efficacy that Napoleon dismissed him and appointed the Prefect of the Gironde, Baron Haussmann, instead. A civil servant, Haussmann had started service during the reign of Louis Philippe under the government of Casimir Perier.

The plan was to be a joint effort between the Emperor and Haussmann, and the major part of it took ten years. At first it was deeply unpopular, but slowly the new city became accepted and eventually even loved by many Parisians. The mesmerized historian Georges Duveau wrote: 'Paris is neither a great iron-works nor is it a wallpaper factory; it is a dream factory.' Even Prince Albert, ever shocked by France's fun-loving imperial upstarts, was impressed. During his 1855 visit to Paris, he wrote:

Paris is signally beautified by the Rue de Rivoli, the Boulevard de Strasbourg, the completion of the Louvre, the great open square in front of the Hôtel de Ville, the clearing away of all the small houses which surrounded Notre Dame, by the fine Napoleon barracks, the completion of the Palais de Justice, and restoration of the Sainte Chapelle, and especially by the laying out of the ornamental grounds in the Bois de Boulogne, which really may be said to vie with the finest English parks. How all this could have been done in so short a time no one comprehends.[14]

The changes, however, at first made Haussmann himself almost universally disliked in France and jokes were made about dinner-table gaffes made by his wife who was ridiculed as mad. The arrival of the Sultan and of Ismail in Paris made Ottoman titles familiar and Haussmann was soon to be cynically nicknamed 'Haussmann Pasha'. Lovers of Paris were traumatized by the destruction of the tight little alleys around the Châtelet and the Hôtel de Ville and in the Ile de la Cité and of the narrow Rue de la Ferronnerie where Ravaillac had assassinated Henri IV. Wide streets led to the great new railway stations which acted as gates to the new city. Bridges such as the Alma, the de Solferino and the Pont National spanned the Seine. Parks such as the Bois de Boulogne, the Bois de Vincennes, the Monceau, de Montsouris and Buttes Chaumont were laid out for the recreation of the people. Broad streets were laid out along the Seine's Left Bank and British-style squares were built. Magnificent shops such as Les Grands Magasins du Printemps on the Rue du Havre sprang up, selling all conceivable luxury goods. But it was at the cost of beautiful gardens such as those of Beaujon, which were destroyed, and by 1870 few traces of medieval Paris survived.

9 Ismail's Cairo – a Glitzy Age

When the British writer J.C. MacCoan visited Cairo in the early 1870s, he noted that on approaching the capital a 'complete transformation scene begins'. What had been cropped fields around a desolate railway station in Said's time were now enclosed ornamental gardens crowded with 'bijou country houses'. Cairo was quite suddenly a brand-new town of neatly laid-out streets, flanked by 'handsome European houses and busy second-class shops'.[1] From 'Ataba al-Khadra Square near the Ezbekiyya Gardens, a new street named after Muhammad Ali was ruthlessly cut through the labyrinthine alleys to the point of supreme power, the Citadel, which overlooks the city today. *Bawaki* or 'weeping arcades' were built alongside so that homes could jut out over them, thus saving some essential metres and increasing the price of the land. After the great bankruptcy of 1875 much of the glamour and glitter of Cairene social life disappeared for a while, only to reappear by 1879 where, riding through Shoubra, you would once again see sartorially elegant men on glittering horses, giggling princesses peeping out of their harem carriages and prostitutes in bright dresses revealing as much leg as possible at the street corners.

In Egypt the process of restructuring its great cities was inspired by Napoleon Bonaparte and was to begin in earnest with Muhammad Ali. The destruction of the old buildings was as insensitive as the destruction of parts of old Paris by Haussmann. Muhammad Ali had begun the process continued so aggressively by Ismail by the expedient method of demolishing irritating obstacles with blasts from his cannons. However, like almost no other city on earth, Cairo is one where each urban infrastructure has followed its predecessor without necessarily destroying it, thus leaving layer after layer of civilization virtually, if crumblingly, intact. Much had deteriorated since the travel writer Ibn Battuta described Cairo in 1325 as 'mother of cities and seat of the Pharaohs, the tyrant, mistress of broad provinces and fruitful lands, boundless in multitude of buildings . . . peerless in beauty and splendour . . .'[2] Plans made by Napoleon's engineers show that by 1800 the city was in a state of severe stagnation, as it largely had been since its incorporation into the Ottoman Empire in 1517. Indeed, Cairo's populated area had barely changed since the sixteenth century.

Muhammad Ali's Cairo was little more than a graft from the classical styles of the Ottoman Empire, giving rise to a duality in Egypt's architecture until the 1840s. Egyptian public life and urban forms of expression carried on as before, side by side with an Islamic urban plan that was not really Egyptian in style. During the early 1840s, however, a fusing of styles began. The third period, from 1863 to 1877, was the period of Ismail's master plan in which Western styles were transferred lock, stock and barrel without respect to the pattern of Egypt's architectural development. The new Italianate neo-baroque was soon to clash violently with the monumental buildings of the Mamluks, vulgar mouldings replacing their elegant, carved doorways and Italian-style stonework with their traditional yellow stucco. Once the Nile's embankments had been made secure, the new city was built in the former zone of annual flooding, with Abbasiyya to the north and Ezbekiyya to the south-west. Ismail's Cairo radiated from elegant squares such as the 'Ataba al-Khadra, Opera, Ezbekiyya, Abdin and Sultan Hassan squares.

In charge of the new city were Ismail's Minister of Public Works, Ali Pasha Mubarak, who produced a master-plan based on an efficient European-style cadastral survey, and the planner-designer of Cairo, Mahmoud al-Falaky Bey. Ismail was himself fascinated with building, telling an English visitor, 'I am obsessed by stone', and to obtain the money to finance the scheme he depended upon tough men like his Minister of Finance, Ismail Sadiq, who knew how to 'squeeze the *fellah*'.

As we have seen, when Ismail succeeded Said as Wali, Egypt was impoverished. Said's Suez Canal scheme was seen as a white elephant, and bankruptcy seemed to stare the new ruler in the face. What saved Ismail, indeed what allowed him to pose overnight as one of the world's great master-builders, was the American Civil War. Until the Union blockade of the Southern Confederacy ports, and the call-up of every able-bodied white male between fourteen and fifty-five in the eleven states which had seceded, America had supplied almost all of Europe's cotton. But the Civil War brought a sudden stop to exports of US cotton and India and Egypt immediately filled the void. Although India supplied Europe with over seventy per cent of its cotton needs, Egypt's high-grade long-staple cotton was immensely valued. Thanks to the stoppage of American cotton exports during the 1861–5 civil war in the US, the price of Egyptian cotton rose from $7\frac{1}{2}$d a pound in 1861 to $29\frac{3}{4}$d a pound by 1863. The boom money was there, as was a Khedive willing to spend it without stint. By 1879, Ismail had, for example, bought Egypt 450 bridges, sixty-four sugar mills and almost 1,000 miles of railway. He built telegraph wires down into Sudan and was one of the earliest signatories of the General Postal Union. Indeed, under Ismail, Egypt was to develop one of the most efficient postal services in the world.

Ismail rebuilt his army with the help of both Union and Confederate soldiers and sailors from West Point and the Annapolis Naval Academy respectively. The recruitment had to be done without any help from the US government, since Ismail, a nominal vassal of the Ottoman Empire, had no foreign representation. At the beginning of 1869, Ismail made contact with Colonel Thaddeus P. Mott, a member of a grand New York family whose sister had married Blacque Bey, the Ottoman Minister to Washington. Before the recruited officers left for Egypt they signed contracts which bound them to 'make, wage and vigorously prosecute war against any and all enemies of the party of the first part wheresoever they may be'. Ismail told one of the officers, Chaillé-Long: 'I count upon your discretion, devotion and zeal to aid me in the establishment of the independence of Egypt. When this will be accomplished, it will be, *Inshallah*! I shall bestow upon you the highest honours.'[3] At that time, the US was considered to be completely non-aligned so that the employment of US officers meant that Egypt had successfully broken the hegemony of France.

When Ismail became Wali, the familiar area of modern Cairo between the Boulaq banks of the Nile and the Ezbekiyya was a swampy wasteland. Following Haussmann's example, he built a lacework of magnificent boulevards, based on Paris's Rue de Rivoli, across the winding, stenching alleys of Cairo's slums and across the swamp. He laid the biggest boulevard, Qasr al-Nil Street, from Opera Square to the Qasr al-Nil Palace where the Hilton stands today. The palace had for long been the British Army's principal barracks when it was destroyed after the Second World War. Ismail built countless palaces, of which the Abdin with its Italianate façade became his official residence. He installed gas lighting at a time when Paris had only just acquired it and he began the process of building out into the desert, creating a health spa at Helwan with a grand Hôtel des Bains and its own railway from Cairo. To the delight of the royal visitors to the opening of the Suez Canal, he built a raised road, lined with sycamores and acacias, to the Pyramids. The sycamores were up to thirty feet in circumference with short trunks and branches that spread out almost horizontally like parasols. The fashionable Shoubra avenue, too, was lined with sycamores and beautiful evergreen acacias.

However, most new projects excite stormy protest and Ismail's city-scaping had as many critics as admirers. The contemporary writer, Stanley Lane-Poole, complained:

> ... and beyond the limits of the metropolis the names of these gorgeous mansions is legion. At Qasr al-Nil and all along the neighbouring banks of the Nile, on the islands of Roda and Gezira, at Giza, Abbasiyya, Shoubra – everywhere rise the unsightly and ill-built palaces in which viceregal extravagance and ostentation have found an outlet. Not one of these huge buildings is other than an eyesore. Not one is tastefully furnished. The Khedive's reception room at the Abdin Palace used to be a monument of the meretricious style which rejoices in gold and crimson and pier glasses.[4]

In the view of many, however, such indictments were less than just. The Gezira Palace and the Salamlik kiosk, built by the German architect-designers Carl Von Diebitch and Julius Franz (Bey), were extremely graceful. So, too, was the Sabil Kuttab (public fountain and Qur'anic school) which still stands at Cairo's Bab al-Hadid. Built by the Italian architect Pantanelli in about 1870, this splendid kiosk is fronted with imposing cast-iron arches, not unlike those of the Gezira and the Salamlik. Most of the surface is covered with Islamic motifs and above the two stone side doors are friezes of tiles with lines from the Qur'an. Franz Bey built an Arab villa near Ezbekiyya which he described as 'a two-storey country house surrounded by a garden'. Another fine palazzo of the period was the Villa St Maurice, which was built in 1874 and later became the French Legation. Unfortunately, the villa was demolished and its older decorations were moved to the new French Embassy building in Giza built by the French architects Parcq and Hardy in 1937. This lovely building survives and today houses a private-sector company which produces Egyptian jams. It boasts marvellous marble marquetry, stained-glass *lunettes* and carved wooden *mihrabs* which were not used for prayer but were purely decorative. A more curious experiment in the Arabic style was the Sakakini Palace, built in 1897. On the ground floor were splendid baroque reception rooms and on the first floor a Turkish-style salon surrounded by bedrooms. In 1907 the son of Omar Pasha Sultan rebuilt an ancient *salamlik*, while the mansion of the great feminist, Huda Shaarawi, was also in the Arabic style.

The same kind of building speculation was taking place throughout the French colonies, with Redon-Stuckle basing the new squares and boulevards of Algiers on Haussmann's decrees for Paris. The first street of the new Algiers, La Rue de la Lyre, with its rows of arcades, was completed in 1862. Meanwhile, Frederic Chasseriau in 1858 planned a Napoleon City on Algiers' Mustafa beach. But as one traveller to Algiers remarked ruefully, echoing the critics of Ismail's Cairo: 'Algiers wants to copy Paris but all it has succeeded in doing is to become a wretched Marseilles.'[5] In England, meanwhile, the developer John Carr and his architect Norman Shaw planned and built Bedford Park in West London. It was the forerunner of the Garden City movement inspired by Ebenezer Howard who created Letchworth and Welwyn Garden City. These, in turn, were to be influential in the building by the British of the garden cities in Cairo and Alexandria.

Until the 1870s the Shepheard's was considered the only hotel worthy of foreign visitors to Cairo but there was soon a burgeoning of hotels such as the Grand Continental, the Savoy, the New Hotel, the Hôtel du Nil, the Hôtel d'Orient and a number of small guesthouses adapted to every pocket and every national taste. Magnificent new villas had been built in Cairo's new Ismailiya quarter and palatial blocks were built on three sides of the Ezbekiyya as well as down the Fagala on the road to Abbasiyya. Carriage roads were built between Abbasiyya and Heliopolis to Old Cairo and the Pyramids. Cairo was an eclectic city. One drove through streets reminiscent of Paris, past soldiers and barracks reminiscent of London, to the Nile, which could be nowhere but Egypt.

MacCoan describes the drive along the avenue of acacias and sycamores on the Shoubra Road as being

> a hundred times more picturesque than Hyde Park in May or June – *fellah*-bestridden donkeys, Arabs of the Nejd and prancing English bloods ridden by dandy Beys and still dandier Jew bankers, jostling every variety of wheeled equipage, from street hackneys packed with Cook's tourists, to the smartest of London or Vienna-built broughams and Victorias, with eunuch-escorted ladies of the Khedive's harem . . . or Polish 'countesses' – last from Monaco – beguiling bachelor guests of Shepheard's or the 'New'.[6]

From Opera Square where the statue of Ibrahim Pasha, erected by Charles Cordier in 1872, still stands as a testament to the *belle époque*, Ibrahim Pasha Street led to the Abdin Palace. Ismail was the first of his line to move his royal residence from the Citadel from which Muhammad Ali had ruled, a move with bad portents. Muhammad Ali was reputed to have said: 'As long as my descendants occupy the Citadel their rule in Egypt will be supreme.' Ismail built the Abdin for official receptions but his descendants never felt much at home there. The Khedive Abbas Hilmi told de Guerville when he received him at the Koubbeh Palace: 'Charmed to see you in my real home for, you see, this is where I really live, never at Cairo. The Abdin serves for official receptions and I have never once slept there. Even after the annual ball which I give, in the middle of the night I return here.'[7] Cosy it might have been, but European visitors found the Koubbeh Palace, as they found so much else in Egypt, ugly from the exterior. Its real cachet derived from its sumptuous drawing rooms, luxuriously decorated corridors, its huge rooms richly carpeted and filled with plants that were so large as to give the impression of an in-house spinney. Although the vegetation of the gardens was not luxuriant, the sycamores and acacias with their huge twisted trunks ran in long rows, melting away into the distant sky. Innumerable flowering trees gave off their mixed scents. In the distance were exquisite sand dunes and, in the west, the Pyramids. The city of Cairo appeared far away, like a village huddled around the Muqattam Hill and the domes and minarets of the Muhammad Ali Mosque which still dominates the Citadel. Splendid receptions were given in the palace gardens whose trees glimmered with multi-coloured lights. Great marquees of multi-coloured materials stool among the trees beneath whose branches lovely Ghawazee girls (dancing girls) and *almehs* (singing girls), musicians and conjurers would group.

Both the Koubbeh and Abdin palaces have happily been preserved during an era when so much was destroyed of this short, great period of Cairo's history. The Abdin Palace is today the Ministry of Culture and National Guidance. From its huge reception hall a white marble staircase leads to a reception room where visitors would sign King Farouk's visitors' book. In Princess Fawzia's room hung portraits of Muhammad Ali, Ismail himself and King Fouad and in her Blue Room hung a portrait of herself by Maillart and another of Ismail. It was in the Ismail reception room, with its huge dais, that King Farouk and Queen Narriman were married, and there, too, that Princess Fawzia received her divorce from the Shah of Iran. In the Long Gallery is a portrait of the Empress Eugénie inaugurating the opening of the Suez Canal. One of the finest suites is the Royal Guest Apartments, commonly called the Belgian Suite because the King of Belgium was the first to stay there after it was redecorated in 1924.

Sharing Muhammad Ali's love of nature, Ismail laid out parks and gardens in Cairo's suburbs, building palaces in each one. The Insha Palace on Qasr al-Nil Street is now the Ministry of Commerce and Industry, while blocks of modern flats have replaced the Ismailiya Palace which faced the Midan Ismailiya (now Midan Tahrir). The larger Ismailiya Palace on the southern side of the square was burnt down in 1911. It had paths paved with coloured pebbles which wound among exotic trees and shrub-beries and led to the palace's *haramlik*. On the site of this palace today stands the Stalinesque, monolithically hideous Mugama 'a Building, erected by Nasser to house Egypt's byzantine bureau-cratic machine. The Cairo zoo now stands on the site of the Giza Palace whose park, the largest of all the palaces, is now divided between the zoo and the botanical gardens. East of Cairo Ismail built the Zaaferan Palace, the simplest of all the palaces, where finely woven matting covered the floor.

After the siesta was over, singing would be heard among the flowering trees and pergolas of Ezbekiyya. Military bands would tune up in the gloaming and the whole chiaroscuro of Cairo would slowly converge until the gardens were a mass of colour and boisterous living. Beautiful women in silks, their mules shod with silver, would ride delicately through the lanes escorted by massive eunuchs in flowing gowns, and at night the gardens would be given over to bacchanalia with promiscuous wooings in the grottos. On the terraces of the great hotels, society figures in their frock coats and straw hats sat drinking with all the social elegance that they would have adopted in Nice or Trieste. Rich, young Egyptians were not excluded. 'Why,' complained the Egyptian writer Hafiz Ibrahim, 'do the sons frequent the Ezbekiyya, whereas the fathers used to frequent the mosque?'

With perhaps uncharacteristic sensitivity, Ismail had decided that his new city should not be allowed to interfere with old Islamic Cairo. The heart of his new city was named after him, Ismailiya (known today as Qasr al-Nil – the Castle of the Nile), and he offered free sites to anyone who would erect, on each, a house worth at least 30,000 francs within eighteen months – in other words, in time for the canal celebrations. The focal point of the city was to be Ezbekiyya, named after the heroic Emir Ezbek, the general of Sultan Qait Bey (1468–96). A mosque, demolished in 1869, had been erected there in 1495 in honour of Ezbek's victory over the Turks. The Ezbekiyya Gardens, today but a shadow of what they once were, are on the site of Lake Rotli on whose banks the Ottomans had built magnificent palaces in the seventeenth century. Gabarti describes a Turkish mercenary building a kiosk beside the Ezbekiyya Canal where 'he led a life of pleasure and debauchery . . . Cairo then resembled a country of gazelles or a paradise peopled with houris and mignons and the inhabitants drank with avidity from the eye of delight.'[8]

When Napoleon arrived, the French destroyed many of the houses around the lake and Napoleon set up his home and his headquarters in the Mamluk Elfi Bey's house on its western bank. Until Muhammad Ali's son, Ibrahim, drained the area and planted it with sycamores, the lake was busy with torch-lit boats during the four months of the year when it was filled. For another four months it was gardens but during Cairo's four hottest months its dusty squares became putrid with garbage. Ezbekiyya was known to local Europeans as the Rosetta Quarter after the Italian merchant consul Rosetti. It was also sometimes known as the Muski after the area between Ezbekiyya and Islamic Cairo, named after Izz ad-Din Musk, a relative of that great Ayyubid, Saladin. Ibrahim drained the swamp by means of a circular canal and raised the enclosed area above the level of the annual flooding of the Nile.

If Flaubert's reflections in the 1840s are anything to go by, the area must have been pretty rough until its transformation by Ismail into the heart of Cairene social life. Under a diary heading 'Civilian Hospital of the Ezbekiyya' he wrote:

> Lunatics screaming in their cells. One old man weeping, begging to be beheaded. The black eunuch of the Grande Princesse came up and kissed my hands. One old woman begged me to fuck her – she uncovered her long, flat breasts that hung down to her umbilicus and stroked them; she had an exquisitely sweet smile . . .[9]

As part of his master-plan, Ismail cut down Ibrahim's forest of sycamores and had elegant, regulated gardens landscaped in 1870 by the former chief gardener to the City of Paris, Jean-Pierre Barillet-Deschamps. The new Ezbekiyya upset the conservationists who mourned the replacement of their much-loved sycamores under which the Cairenes would drink coffee in the shade by 'stone' houses and arcades based on those in the Rivoli Gardens in Paris. The gardens covered an area of twenty acres and were lit by

2,500 jets of gas in tulip-shaped glasses. The narrow canal was replaced by an ornamental lake and soon the whole area became a sort of miniature Parc Monceau in which green lawns, beautifully maintained shrubberies, shaded walks, intricate artificial grottos with cool fountains and cascades, cafés, open-air theatres and magnificent military bands made it one of the finest public gardens outside Europe. Dozens of exotic trees were planted by Deschamps and later, the beefwood and gum tree from Australia, the banyan and rubber tree from India, the Madagascan flame tree whose blood-red flowers appear in mid-April, the Cuba royal palm, the Brazilian paper tree, the African red kane rubber tree and the sausage Africa with its sausage-shaped fruit and big, red flowers. The Australian bottle tree, called *Boudret al-'afrit* (ghost powder) because of the itching caused by the inner hairs of its fruit, was also planted, as was the *Eugenia Jambolana*, named in honour of Prince Eugène of Savoy and loved in Egypt for its delicious berries. So, too, was the shaggy-trunked *Washingtonia Filfera*, named after George Washington. Some of these trees survive at Ezbekiyya and many can still be seen scattered in other parts of Cairo. There is still a row of red kane rubber trees in Garden City while flame trees still line the banks of the Nile beside the Gezira Palace and sausage Africas can still be seen south of the Fish Gardens in Zamalek, to which Cairo's urban poor flock on Fridays for a few piastres.

Ezbekiyya was a central park, around which sprang up new streets, broad boulevards and public buildings. Arthur Rowlatt, who regularly visited Cairo on banking business, wrote to his family at the time: 'The new gardens are open in Cairo and every evening there is music, and plays are acted in a small theatre. I went twice and was much amused.' MacCoan was astonished by the changes, writing:

... The old has everywhere given way to the new, and where, twenty years ago, stretched the Esbekiyya of those days with its huge sycamores, its stagnant canal, and its fringe of tumble-down native houses, [the visitor] now sees piles of imposing stone buildings, broad macadamized streets, and – enclosed within half its former dimensions – a new Esbekiyya, so transformed, that if the ghost of Muhammad Ali could revisit glimpses of the Cairene moon, it would be hard to recognize the old *meidan* in the new public garden that now occupies its site.[10]

10 The Finest Opera House in the World

The jewel of Ezbekiyya was the little wooden opera house built by the Italian architects Fasciottoi and Rossi for the Canal opening. The first performance of Verdi's *Aida* was performed in the 'Italian Opera House', as it was known, on Christmas Eve of 1871. Tragically, the building, together with the original costumes, scenery and accessories of that incredible première, was burnt down under suspicious circumstances exactly a century later in 1971. Until that night, the visitor lucky enough to be invited backstage could see the gilded chairs, upholstered in red damask, on which the Empress Eugénie sat on the historic opening night. Also to be seen were the original scores of *Aida*, and the letters and contracts signed between Verdi and the Khedive. The building's treasures also included miniature replicas of the original set, jewels and costumes worn by the cast on the opening night, and the silk-covered chairs used in lavish productions such as *La Dame aux Camelias*.

Cairo bubbled with rumours the day after the building's destruction that the auditors were planning to visit it on the following day, and that its owners were frightened that frauds in its books might be revealed. Such gossip need not be believed, but the outstanding irony of that night was that Cairo's main fire station stands a few hundred metres away in Ataba Square. Despite this, the following morning nothing but ashes remained of this exquisite building.

The opera house, modelled on Milan's La Scala, was built in a hurry, like so much else of Ismail's Cairo, by gangs of forced labour and at a cost of fifteen million francs. Given the urgency, it was only built in stone and mortar up to a certain level. Above that level, as if its builders were in a panic to have it completed in time, it was made of plaster and wood from Lebanon. The inside hangings were of crimson and gold brocade and the boxes were scrolled with gilt. Silken screens hid the women in their harem boxes and in the interval you could see, between the screens, the flash of pretty eyes and the sparkle of tiaras. The front of the harem boxes was covered with metal lettice, painted white and covered with gold flowers. This intricate ironwork made it difficult to distinguish the lady behind it. The women entered the box via steps leading from a small garden. Nubar was dazzled by the building:

> It was a jewel, all white, with light golden lines running around the three levels of circles; and those earmarked for the palace women thoroughly spacious, covered by a fine tissue of metal, giving the impression of light lace-work, through which they could watch the spectacle without being seen themselves, but perceived like white apparitions with all the charm of the uncertain and the unknown. And the material! And the decor! Veritable works of art; and the costumes! And the choice of casts! Certainly the Paris and London opera houses were bigger; but there is nothing as harmonious, as perfect, as the orchestra, the decor, the artists and the interior of the house.[1]

Watching a ballet at the opera house before the First World War, Ronald Storrs remembered snoozing Egyptian ministers leap awake when the performance began and eagerly rake the ballerinas with their powerful binoculars. Coquelin considered the acoustics of the opera house as good as any in the world. It was certainly one of the loveliest landmarks left of Ismail's Cairo although it suffered from one irritating drawback: it had no wings and very little dressing-room space so that the conductor and the orchestra had to walk down the main aisle of the theatre to reach the pit.

Draneht, who, as we have seen, had had an admiring patron in Muhammad Ali, was appointed superintendant of the opera house by Ismail because of his close contacts with the great opera houses of Europe. Under his guidance, the Cairo opera house soon became one of the finest in the world, attracting celebrities from the great European opera houses such as La Scala, the Opéra de Paris, La Monnaie de Bruxelles and the Comédie Française. Offenbach's opera *La Belle Hélène* by de Meilhac and Halévy, then the rage of Paris, was performed on the building's opening night on 4 January 1869 to some 300 spectators. During the first three weeks of that month, Ismail's staff translated *La Belle Hélène, Oeil Greve* and *Mariée de Mardi Gras* into Arabic for the use of harem ladies who were forbidden to attend even from behind screens. Edward Prince of Wales attended an Offenbach opera there during his 1876 visit.

Shortly before the opening of the Canal, Ismail commissioned the French Egyptologist Auguste Ferdinand François Mariette to write a libretto on an Egyptian theme, which would be performed as a *post hoc* commemoration of the inauguration. A giant of a man who wore a red *tarboush* and black spectacles, Mariette had been sent by the French government to acquire ancient manuscripts for French museums. Once in Egypt, he became interested in archaeology and helped to discover the Serapeum at Memphis to the south of Cairo. His discoveries were later to lead to his appointment as Assistant Director of Egyptology at the Louvre. Ismail awarded him the titles of Bey and Pasha and after the Franco-Prussian War had ended he became Ismail's curator of ancient monuments and founded the museum at Boulaq where he was to die. Mariette, something of a poet and writer, wrote the story of *Aida* on the basis of his archaeological research and used a book he had written, *La Fiancée du Nil*, as his source material. Describing the commission to his brother in Paris, he wrote somewhat disloyally of his patron: 'The Viceroy is spending a million. Don't laugh; it is perfectly serious.'

The invitation, signed by Draneht, 'to write an opera for a very distant country' went to Giuseppe Verdi in the summer of 1869, a few months before the Cairo opera house was opened and the Suez Canal inaugurated. Verdi promptly turned it down although his *Rigoletto* was performed on 1 November 1869 as part of the Canal celebrations. The orchestra of sixty-one La Scala musicians was conducted by Emanuele Muzio, Verdi's adoring former pupil who was, at that time, chief conductor to Bagier, the Director of the Opéra Italien in Paris. The performance was preceded by a solemn and pompously vainglorious recital of

Ismail's achievements for his country. On the same night some forty young Italian girls, housed in the local police station to protect their virtue, performed a lightly erotic ballet. There was a fire on stage during the second performance and the actors had to leap into the pit until it was extinguished, while the Khedive tried to calm the panic of his illustrious audience.

But Verdi was adamant that he would write nothing for the Canal opening. 'Although I deeply appreciate that you wanted to give me the honour of writing a hymn to mark the date of the opening, I regret that I must decline this honour, because of the number of my current activities, and because it is not my custom to compose occasional pieces.'[2] Little did he realize that this 'hymn', this 'occasional piece' – *Aida* – was to be his great memorial and one of the greatest operatic *tours de force* in history. In mid-1870, while visiting Paris, Verdi was again approached by Draneht, through his friend Camille du Locle, with the offer of 150,000 lire in gold, a considerable sum of money, to write the opera. The offer appears to have thrown him into a depression and he refused again with even more vigour. In his reply to du Locle he ignored the issue, merely reminding him that he had failed to send him translations of the literary writings of Wagner, which he needed in order to study the mind of a man whom he was always to regard as an insidious competitor, a symbol of the harsh culture of the Goths as against the heady passion of Italy. However, soon after this he seems to have discovered that Ismail had authorized du Locle, via Mariette, to approach Wagner or Gounod if Verdi refused. Clearly this would have riled him considerably. In any case, a while later du Locle sent Verdi a four-page précis of the libretto of *Aida*, which immediately fired the composer's curiosity. His previous scepticism may well have been based on his belief that the author of the libretto was Ismail himself, whose musical flair he clearly did not value.

Draneht had passed on a letter from Ismail to Verdi: 'In choosing you, dear Maestro, to be the composer of an opera whose action revolves in my state, I have realized my wish to create a national production which may become one of the most glorious memories of my reign.'[3] It is unlikely that Verdi cared two figs for the Khedive's wishes and far more probable that his sudden change of mind was influenced by his reading of the libretto. In any case, he quickly saw the potential for a heroic *tour de force*. 'Now,' he told du Locle, 'let us hear the pecuniary conditions of Egypt and then we shall decide.' On 2 June 1869, he formally accepted the commission. Possibly on the advice of Muzio, he asked for the 150,000 lire to be paid as a straight fee. Although he reserved his own rights for all countries outside Egypt, he honourably agreed to send someone to Egypt to produce the opera, and agreed to pay the expenses of the libretto. Burdened with a terror of the sea, he refused to visit Egypt himself. Ironically, he still seemed unaware that Mariette was the author of *Aida*.

By May 1870, Verdi and du Locle began working on a text in French prose. The final scene of the opera, in which the lovers Aida and Amneris are entombed together in a cave, was suggested by Verdi himself. Verdi's Italian editor, Ricordi, suggested the Italian poet Antonio Ghislanzoni as librettist for setting du Locle's French prose into Italian verse. Verdi agreed to Ghislanzoni and suggested Muzio as conductor, but when he discovered that Bagier had offered Muzio the post of conductor at Paris's Théâtre-Italien he withdrew the offer, explaining to his loyal pupil that he did not wish him to forego this excellent career opportunity. Meanwhile, Verdi soon discovered the identity of Mariette, with whom he quickly began a valuable correspondence. He became increasingly obsessed with the project and began working on the music in tandem with Ghislanzoni's libretto, although as letters between the two showed, Verdi demanded tiresome and frequent revisons, and often tried to dictate the very words to be used by the poet. In many ways Verdi was *Aida*'s real librettist, undertaking his own research into the manners and customs of Pharaonic Egypt. In a reply to one of his litanies of queries on the subject, he was told by Mariette, via du Locle, that:

> They performed in long robes and to a slow and solemn rhythm. The music that accompanied it was probably a kind of plainsong, which constituted the bass part, with a very high upper part performed by young sopranos (boys). The instruments that accompanied these dances were twenty-four stringed harps, double flutes, trumpets, timpani, and smaller drums, enormous castanets (rattles), and cymbals.[4]

Verdi spent the entire period at his Villa Sant' Agata, a villa with a river in front near Busseto, which he had bought in 1848. In order to attempt to meet the Khedive's January 1871 deadline for the opera's first production in Cairo, composer and poet had to work in a hurry, but the start of the Franco-Prussian War on 14 July 1870 soon completely destroyed the schedule agreed upon. Verdi's mistrust of France, 'the world's greatest nation, it is true, but one I cannot bear for long', gave way to sympathy as it crumbled under the Prussian advance, and he arranged for 2,000 francs from his advance on *Aida* to be given to the French wounded. He wrote to his old friend the Comptesse de Maffei:

> This French disaster fills my heart with despair as it does yours. It's true that the blague, the impertinence, the presumption of the French was, and is, despite all their misfortunes, insupportable. Nevertheless, France gave liberty and civilization to the modern world; and, if she falls, let us not delude ourselves, the liberty and civilization of us all will fall.[5]

He mourned for 'poor Paris, which I saw looking so gay, so beautiful, so splendid last April'. But what really scotched any chance of *Aida* being completed in time was the fact that Mariette himself was in Paris, besieged by Bismarck's army and by the hysterical Communards raging through streets which had, until so recently, been the glory of Haussmann's new Paris. All of the costumes and scenery were being produced in Paris. Communications with the outside world were restricted to the hot-air-balloon post, but because of the prevailing westerly winds, the balloons could carry letters out of Paris but not back again. This meant that Mariette, in charge of the opera's negotiations but besieged within the city, remained completely incommunicado. Evoking the war-torn period in France, Verdi would write to Draneht with expressions such as: 'The costumiers and decorators have written to me by balloon, they are seeing to all ...' In view of this, Draneht decided to make direct contact with Verdi at Sant' Agata. In particular, he was anxious, given the delay, that *Aida*'s première at least be performed at Milan's La Scala, since Verdi had written into his contract with Mariette that it would be performed there in February, immediately after its première in Cairo.

However, Verdi was a deeply honourable man, and determined not to take advantage of what was a case of *force majeure*. Whatever happened, *Aida*'s première would be in Cairo.

Draneht's problems were not only restricted to the date of the performance. He came up against considerable opposition from the great Italian singers, who seemed to regard it as beneath their dignity to perform outside Europe, or to accept the fairly large fees offered. Draneht wanted to engage Niccolini, considered the best tenor in existence, as Radames, but the singer refused 180,000 lire. Finally Draneht reluctantly agreed to give the part to the far lesser known Pietro Mongini, who turned out to be an unexpected and triumphant success. Antonietta Pozzoni played Aida, a role that the marvellous Bohemian soprano, Teresa Stolz, refused at a fee of 100,000 francs, although she had already been engaged for the Venice carnival season of 1870–71 so would not have been free in any case. As it turned out, Mongini was actually paid 125,000 lire. Italy's finest conductor, Angelo Mariani, strongly suggested the voluptuous Isabella Galleti-Gianoli for Aida, and she might well have been given the part had it not been for the postponement of the première because of the war. Rossini had once remarked of this wild woman: 'Execute my commission, Sig. Menghino, with lowered eyes, for I'm told Signora Galleti is too seductive!!!'

Eleonora Grossi was Amneris, Francesco Steller was Amonasro, and Paolo Medini was the High Priest Ramphis. Verdi asked Mariani to conduct the opera, but this invitation came to nothing for personal reasons. Teresa Stolz lived as natural wife with Mariani. After watching him conduct at the Genoa opera house, Verdi developed a respect for, and friendship with, the man. However, a split eventually developed between Stolz and Mariani at a time when it was rumoured that Verdi was having an affair with her. Despite the consequent deterioration of their friendship, the ever-honourable Verdi continued to admire Mariani's skill, and begged him to conduct *Aida* in Cairo. However, Mariani, who had committed the double sin of deserting Verdi for the hated Wagnerian camp, firmly refused. His refusal may well have reflected that contempt for performing in 'second-rate' countries that had obviously influenced Italy's other opera giants. So Verdi had to look around again, and eventually gave the honour to

Giovani Bottesini. To add a further sting to Verdi's relationship with Mariani, on 1 November 1871, just two months before the première of *Aida* in Cairo on Christmas Eve, Mariani conducted a performance of Wagner's *Lohengrin* at Bologna's Teatro Comunale that delighted the composer, who sent him his portrait inscribed 'Evviva Mariani!!!'. This, for Verdi, was the last straw, although he did, in fact, discreetly attend a performance on 19 November and when he was spotted by the audience he was solidly applauded for a quarter of an hour. Although Verdi had found the music of *Lohengrin* 'beautiful', his impression of the opera was otherwise mediocre. If Verdi symbolized Italian liberty, he saw Wagner as the representative of the dreadful revival of the Goths. His sympathies had gone out to the French after the humiliation of Sedan, and for him the Prussian victory was the victory of barbarism over the great civilization which France and Italy shared. Two years later poor Mariani was to die miserably of cancer in Genoa, and although Verdi, who found it hard to forgive on a personal level, sent his condolences, he resolutely refused to attend the funeral.

As an indication of the greed prevailing among the great Italian singers, Teresa Stolz had asked three times as much to perform in Cairo as she had asked to perform at La Scala. Mariani had asked for 30,000 to 35,000 francs for the season; she had asked for 120,000 to 125,000 as Aida for the season, an extraordinary sum given that she would normally only expect to earn 5,000 francs from a benefit night in Italy. She and the other singers clearly regarded an Egyptian visit as a potential gold mine. In a letter to Lampugnani from Venice on 13 March 1871, Stolz wrote:

> Now I beg you, dearest friend, to keep these negotiations of ours secret, because there are people in Milan who don't look favourably on my giving preference to theatres outside Italy !! ... Please do me the favour of telegraphing at once to Cairo to let them know my final demand and that of Mariani.[6]

After Draneht had visited Verdi at Sant' Agata, Bottesini was sent to Cairo where *Aida* was at last performed, with Egyptian trumpeters, a Cairene military band and 300 people on the stage by the end of Act Two, to immense acclaim on 24 December 1871, almost a year after the surrender of Paris in the previous January. Draneht cabled Verdi immediately after the first performance: 'Maestro Verdi, Genoa: First performance *Aida* triumphant success. First, second finales, two duets soprano and tenor, grand march, council scene, total fanaticism. Enthusiastic audience applauded absent Maestro. Congratulations, thanks. Draneht.'[7] It was indeed an incredible performance. Amneris wore a coronet of real gold and precious stones, and Radames was armed with weapons and a shield of solid silver. In Paris Mariette had had the costumes made at the *atelier* of Madame Delphine Baron, and the scenery and accessories executed by Lublin Granger. Mariette's son Alfred presented the original designs as a gift to the Paris National Library, and they are now on display in the French Opera Museum.

The myriad music critics invited to the performance were housed in the splendid Khedival Buildings, which still stand in Cairo's Emad al-Din Street. The opera's second performance lasted from seven o'clock at night until three thirty in the morning and Ismail attended it in rapture from beginning to end. The Milanese critic Filippo Filippi was obsessed by the exoticism of the theatre, by the harem ladies peering through their screens in the boxes and by the multi-coloured dress of the Jewish and Coptic merchants, but his report was restricted to a general impression with little comment on the performance itself. The reason was probably not far to seek. In advance of the performance Filippi had offered to be at Verdi's service, implicitly agreeing to write whatever Verdi wanted him to write. Verdi, however, detested sychophancy, and wrote to Ricordi that he felt 'so disgusted, so revolted, so irritated' by Filippi's offer that he 'would a thousand times set fire to the score of *Aida* without a sigh'. He tried to discourage Filippi and the Parisian music critic Reyer from attending in a cryptically cynical letter:

You at Cairo? Why, nothing could be more important for *Aida* in the way of publicity. To me it seems that art practised in this manner is no longer art but a trade, a diversion, a sport, something to be run after, to be made, if not successful, at least notorious at any cost! . . . Journalists, singers, players, choristers and directors, etc., etc., all have to contribute their stone to the edifice of publicity, to make in this way a cornice of nonsensical trifles that add nothing to the merit of an opera and may quite possibly detract from its real value. It is deplorable, absolutely deplorable . . .[8]

Reyer did not particularly like *Aida*, as Verdi may have foreseen, but he wrote with some fairness: 'If Verdi persists in his new orientation, he may lose some enthusiasts but he will make many converts and will find followers in circles in which he has never hitherto been received.'

Filippi, meanwhile, revelled in his contempt for the Egyptians:

The curiosity, the frenzy of the Egyptian public to attend the première of *Aida* were such that, for a fortnight, all the seats had been bought up and at the last moment the speculators sold boxes and stalls for their weight in gold. When I say the Egyptian public, I speak especially of the Europeans; for the Arabs, even the rich, do not care for our kind of theatre: they prefer the miaouing of their own chants, the monotonous beatings of their tambourines, to all the melodies of the past, the present and the future. It is a perfect miracle to see a fez in the theatre of Cairo. On Sunday night the theatre was crowded from top to bottom long before the performance began. Ladies occupied the boxes in great numbers, and one's attention was distracted by their unseasonable chattering or by the rustling of their garments. Speaking generally, I found much beauty and elegance, particularly among the Greeks and foreigners of high extraction who are numerous in Cairo. I ought also to say, from love of truth, that by the side of the handsomest and the best dressed were to be seen every evening the faces of Copts and Jews, with strange headgear, impossible costumes, colours which clashed so violently that nothing worse could be imagined. As to the ladies of the harem of the Court, no one could see them; they occupied the first three boxes to the right, on the second tier, and a thick white muslin hid their faces from indiscreet looks. For this splendid Italian creation, the Khedive had the satisfaction not only of the excellent outcome, but also of seeing how all the public which crowded into the theatre on Sunday evening recognized immediately what a debt of gratitude art and civilization owe to this rare prince, unique in his intelligent munificence. The applause for him, universal, long and frenzied, soon exploded. At the end, the soft, high last notes of the violins had hardly died away when a cry of 'Long live the Khedive' was heard re-echoing throughout the theatre . . .'

On 8 February 1872, *Aida* was performed with equal success at La Scala (where Teresa Stolz agreed to sing the title role) although one critic couldn't resist reflecting popular current opinion by accusing Verdi of following the 'strange erratic paths of Wagner'. This hurt Verdi, ever-neurotic to competition from the dreaded Wagner, to the core. Many critics accused Verdi of Wagnerianism because of his use of leitmotifs to suggest characteristics of the protagonists, such as the jealousy of Amneris or the sinister qualities of the Pharaonic priest. After *Aida* was performed again at La Scala, he wrote: 'Let's not discuss *Aida* any more; it brought me a lot of money but it also brought me a great many worries and the greatest artistic disappointment possible.'

Soon *Aida* was to be performed to increasing popularity throughout the world. Adelina Patti played the role of Aida at the Chicago Opera Festival in 1885, when 500 extras acted the Ethiopian captives. There were said to have been 2000 extras in all, so many that Patti had to be ushered on to the stage by the police.

11   The Palace of the Empress

While the opera house was being built at Ezbekiyya, other high-technology buildings were rising up all over the city. The Gezira Palace, built to receive the Empress and other crowned heads attending the Canal celebrations, was completed in 1867 and still stands today as a five-star hotel on the banks of the Nile in the northern, Zamalek end of Cairo's Gezira ('Island'). 'Of all the palaces built by the Muhammad Ali dynasty,' wrote Ellen Chennells, 'that of the Gezira is the finest . . .'[1] On 18 January 1869, nine months before the inauguration of the Canal, the Khedive gave the first ball of an extravagant social season in this controversial pile, whose imposing wrought-iron arches were assembled from numbered kits forged in the foundries of Lauchhammer near Dresden.

Two weeks later, on 3 February, Edward Prince of Wales and his wife Alexandra spent several nights in the palace, which the Prince described as uselessly extravagant. The bedroom, he complained, was over 150 feet long, the huge double beds were made of solid silver, and the chairs, covered in beaten gold, were too heavy to move. However, to make up for such 'annoyances' beautiful young dancing girls and harlequin acrobats performed for the couple among the flowers and glimmering fountains of the palace's botanical gardens.[2]

The palace was one of three buildings on the island which Ismail turned, overnight, into an immense botanical garden. Containing a zoo and elaborate fish gardens, it was landscaped by the gardener of the city of Paris, Delchevalerie. The Haramlik had been built in the 1840s by Muhammad Ali, while the third building, the Salamlik Kiosk, was built at the same time as the Gezira Palace by the same German architects. Although the traditional *haramlik* was the ladies' quarters and the *salamlik* the men's, the names were used loosely for these palaces, the Salamlik representing a lyrical garden refuge for Man's fantasies. Magnificent royal weddings were held in both the Gezira and the Salamlik, but many writers of the period confused the two buildings when they described events. As part of the month-long wedding celebrations of four of Ismail's children (Tewfik, Husain, Hasan and his second daughter Princess Fatma), a magnificent ball was given in the Palace on the third day of the festivities, 18 January 1872. The illuminated gardens overflowed with guests.

During the Canal celebrations, Nubar was responsible for the welfare of the Emperor of Austria who was housed in the Salamlik, while Austrian government officials were housed in the Haramlik. Among them was the Austrian Ambassador to the Sublime Porte, the Baron de Prokesch, who was bitterly disappointed not to be housed in the same palace as the Emperor, given his status as the Emperor's representative in Istanbul. However, Nubar placated him with his usual subtle charm, explaining that there was no apartment in the Salamlik that would offer as much comfort to the Baron as the First Princess's apartment in the Haramlik. At the words 'harem' and 'First Princess' the Ambassador's mood changed and when he was introduced into the princess's rose-tinted bedroom his contentment was complete. 'Nothing,' mused Nubar philosophically, 'cheers up an old man so much as a lady's bedroom, even when the bed is empty and the room deserted.'[3]

The task of the building and interior design of the Gezira Palace and the Salamlik went to the German architects Carl Wilhelm Valentin Von Diebitch and Julius Franz, to whom was attached the title Bey. A French magazine of the time, *L'Illustration*, gives us a captivating guided tour of the Palace:

> Let us enter into this palace of *One Thousand and One Nights* ... apologies, into this Gezira Palace, which the Empress occupied and which the Khedive wanted to make a very marvel ... let us go inside. Here is the Louis XV-style bedroom; all the wealth of luxury of our era. A bed in gilded metal, entirely enveloped in a mosquito net of blue satin and whitened gauze; lace coverings ... and in the middle the silver statue of the Prince Imperial

[Eugénie's son] and the bust of the Emperor [Louis Napoleon]. Let us go further and enter the bathroom. What wealth! How well the Egyptians do things! Here it is the Louis-XIV style with some details of Turkish and Arab ornamentation. The ceiling, the curtains and the door coverings are of blue satin and in the lavatory it is rose-coloured satin . . . which pleases the eye. Each piece of furniture is a marvel of luxury and workmanship.[4]

The Gezira Palace was known by many at the time as 'Ismail's folly' but European doctors encouraged patients to stay there, as its then rural surroundings and accessibility were considered beneficial. Ismail lent Edward Prince of Wales the Gezira Palace for his 1876 visit, just as his predecessor Said had lent the Prince the Giza Palace for his previous trip in 1862. An English writer of the day, Mrs E.L. Butcher, remembered being introduced to Ismail, 'a little, waddling elderly man', by his son Tewfik amid a glittering circle of socialites at a Gezira Palace ball in 1878, then settling down to a dinner set for 1,000 guests. After the Great Debt and Ismail's abdication, the Palace became a hotel, and its Swiss manager Luigi Steinschneider advertised it in a popular guide book as 'the most comfortable and luxurious hotel in the world – eight minutes drive from the opera'. It was in the Salamlik that the Princess of Wales stayed in 1893 and it is described by Ellen Chennells:

There is a beautiful kiosk in the grounds where the Princess of Wales stayed when in Egypt. It is a perfect gem . . . The building is in two divisions, connected by a large marble vestibule, open two sides, one on to the garden, the other on to a lake with a pleasure-boat close by, and opposite to the chief Haram[lik] entrance.[5]

The Salamlik was entered through a huge open hall of delicate mosaic, with a cast-iron fountain in its centre which cooled the air. All around it were the Von Diebitch wrought-iron arches similar to those to be seen today at the front and back of the Gezira Palace. German craftsmen assembled the Salamlik in less than three months. The Germans were entirely influenced by the architecture of the Alhambra in Spain, and in neither palace are there any

Egyptian influences. Julius Franz, responsible for the interior decor of both palaces, wrote of the kiosk: 'In the centre of the garden is the long kiosk, probably the finest modern Arabian structure of its kind.'

The Gezira Palace was built as a baroque three-winged palace, with a wall alongside the court of honour parallel with the Nile. The Prussian cast-iron porticos were stretched out between two wings of the palace. It was a two-storeyed building decorated with yellow and red horizontal stripes like those of the Alhambra, although today a third storey has been added and the building has been painted salmon pink. Chennells was fascinated by the furniture of the palace, in particular by two exquisite marble tables in mosaic, one from Florence, the other a gift from the Pope to the Khedive. On the other side of the hall was a drawing-room filled with a beautiful Aubusson carpet. A second drawing-room was fitted out as a bedroom for the Princess of Wales during her visit.

The immense gardens surrounding the palace and the kiosk were landscaped by the Frenchman Delchevalerie, with some influence of Repton but more, perhaps, of the German landscape gardener and adventurer Prince Pückler-Muskau. They were laid in a regular formation around the two palaces to avoid the direct confrontation of architecture and landscape garden. The immediate view had to be an ornamental rather than a natural landscape. Ismail wrote '. . . First the eyes of the onlooker will be pleased by colourful surroundings, the jewellery of exotic plants and the plain, emerald carpet of the garden, decorated very carefully; but beyond will be the "free" landscape with its imposing groups.'

In the north of the gardens was a long, straight avenue which struck across the natural arrangement of the landscape. Today, this avenue is bustling 26th July Street with its new flyover, and in place of lawns and copses are modern concrete tenement blocks. The boulevard extended across the island, through Giza and in a straight line to the Pyramids. The entire arrangement, reflecting the metamorphosis of Cairo into a copy of Paris, was designed to give the Empress and the other crowned heads a direct and elegant access to the Pyramids.

In 1871, seventy-five species of exotic animals and 150 species of rare birds were installed in the gardens. On Ismail's abdication these were transferred to Giza where they can still be seen amid the rich gardens of Cairo's zoo. Today, nothing remains of the Gezira gardens apart from the Gezira Club, the small gardens of the Marriott Hotel and pockets of garden scattered about the island. Nothing remains there of the wild animals, although some must have escaped from the gardens as an English family, the Rowlatts, remembered a large mongoose appearing in their garden nearby in the 1940s. They were also warned of a cobra who lurked in one of the bushes and remembered some parakeets that had been allowed to escape from the zoo to see if they would breed.

The bulbul, the 'nightingale' of Persian poetry, can still be heard in the gardens, and the bright and darting little bee-eaters can still be seen. Sitting today in a wicker chair beside the lawns of the Marriott Hotel and hearing the doves moaning in the tall palm trees, or watching the crested hoopoe bird spearing insects in the moist grass, is a reminder that these are the last few acres of some of the most magnificent tropical gardens in the world. Banyan trees still stand in Zamalek but little else remains of Ismail's magnificent gardens.

12　The Cousin of the Empress

The man who had justified the rebuilding of Cairo was also the cousin of Eugénie, the woman whose beauty would bless the birth of the new city. However, little could Ferdinand de Lesseps guess that his canal would bring suffering and tragedy to almost everyone involved in its inauguration.

Napoleon Bonaparte had carried an order from the Directory to the Army of the East to 'drive the English from all their Eastern possessions, wherever it goes, and in particular it will destroy all the trading stations of the Red Sea'. He was also ordered to 'arrange for the cutting of the Isthmus of Suez'. On 24 December 1798 Napoleon, accompanied by members of his Institut d'Egypte, travelled from Cairo to Suez to make an exploratory survey. On his return he instructed his Chief Engineer, Jean-Baptiste Le Père, to carry out a complete survey of the Isthmus which he finished in January of the following year, retracing Napoleon's steps along the ancient canal down to the Bitter Lakes. In February 1801, Napoleon wrote to Tsar Paul I asking for his support in cutting a canal:

> The English are attempting a landing in Egypt. It is in the interest of all the Mediterranean and Black Sea powers that Egypt remain French. The Suez Canal, which will join the Indian seas to the Mediterranean, has already been traced: it is an easy enterprise which will require little time and which will bring incalculable advantages to Russian commerce.[1]

But there was a curious flaw in Le Père's survey: it maintained, quite wrongly, that the Red Sea level at high tide was more than thirty feet higher than that of the Mediterranean, thus ruling out the possibility of a direct canal. In this it reflected the mistaken beliefs of the ancient surveyors from Darius onwards. In any case Napoleon was soon defeated by the British, Le Père's report was forgotten and the canal project was shelved.

The next serious attempt was made by Muhammad Ali's Chief Engineer, Linant de Bellefonds, one of the many Frenchmen whom, like Colonel Sèves, the Wali gathered around him. Linant was one of the great oriental legends of his time. He had a Syrian wife who wore splendid Damascene-silk clothing and he sat in majesty on an ottoman strewn with oriental carpets and cushions. He was surrounded by young girls whom the fascinated Gerard de Nerval thought were his harem until he was disappointed to discover that they were merely Linant's own daughters and daughters of friends in Cairo.

According to de Lesseps, on his accession Muhammad Ali had told the American Consul-General, Edwin de Leon, 'I shall queen the pawn against you Americans. The Isthmus of Suez will be pierced before yours.'[2] Linant's research attracted the interest of Arthur Anderson, a founder of P & O, who placed the project before Lord Palmerston, but the British Prime Minister wanted nothing to do with it, reflecting continued British fears that it would be a French canal and would interfere with Britain's trade route to India. Perhaps he was not far wrong, because French popular opinion was suddenly inflamed with the project, and it became a source of inspiration for a host of French visionaries and literati. In particular, it inspired Claude Henri, Comte de Saint-Simon, a descendant of Louis, Duc de Saint-Simon, a key figure at the court of Louis XIV. The patriarch of 'Christian Socialism' which called for the regeneration of mankind through the dignity of work, the Comte de Saint-Simon saw the Suez and Panama Canal projects as the two jewels in the crown of his scientific philosophy. When he died in 1825 he passed on his idealistic mission to his successor, Prosper Enfantin.

The story goes that one day a disciple ran into Enfantin's bedroom and cried out in a state of trance: 'Jesus lives in Enfantin! Thou art one half of the couple of revelation!' Enfantin looked up and replied coolly: '*Homo sum*' ('I am He'). Enfantin soon saw himself as the leader of a bloodless revolution which would abolish every form of property. His community of Saint-Simonians institutionalized a series of castes, the highest of which was the Elect. Sex was the sect's sacrament and its first article of faith was the belief that one half of Jesus Christ was incarnate in Enfantin himself. The other half was in the body of a woman who, when recognized, would become his bride and constitute a new godhead.

These eccentric Saint-Simonians wore skirt-like tunics of graded hues over tight trousers, with a sash of embroidered silk on the left side. Enfantin, the 'Supreme Father', wore light blue, while his leading disciples wore dark blue and the lowest ranks royal blue. To further his messianic message, Enfantin mingled with the great men and the high politics of the world. However, both Church and State in France quickly saw him as a dangerous heretic and he was imprisoned for some time in the Sainte-Pelagie Prison, ostensibly for his advocacy of free love. He made an extraordinary impression at court, appearing in a flowing velvet coat bordered with ermine, and wearing tall hessian boots. He made no effort to defend himself, but cried out ecstatic verses such as this:

> Because if Jesus has been sent
> to teach the world
> the wisdom of the Father
> I have been sent by my God,
> Father and Mother, for all men and women,
> to make the World desire his maternal tenderness...

In 1832, Ferdinand de Lesseps had been posted to Alexandria as French Vice Consul, his father, Mathieu, having long been a respected Consul-General there before him. When, therefore, a year later, twenty Saint-Simonians led by Enfantin arrived there, the French Consul Mimaut handed reponsibility for the eccentrics over to him. De Lesseps was to be a useful ally for, on taking up his new post, Muhammad Ali had drawn him aside and reminded him that he owed his father Mathieu a debt which he intended to repay through the son. He was referring to an incident when, as a young Ottoman officer, he had been accused of stealing some silver at a dinner given by Mathieu. Mathieu, who had been convinced of the young man's innocence, had at once stood up for him, and as a result the charge was dropped.

From his prison cell the previous year Enfantin had sent some of his disciples to Istanbul to seek out his bride, the essential second half of the godhead whom he believed would reveal herself in the Orient. This meeting of East and West must have been bizarre. E.M. Butler wrote:

Behold them, therefore, disembarking in full costume, saluting all women, rich and poor, high and low, according to Enfantin's instructions; and experiencing at the sight of the veiled ladies more than the usual sense of glamour, since it was extremely likely that the 'free woman' was at that moment in a harem. The Grand Turk prevented possible complications at this point by transporting them to Smyrna . . . In the meantime the fame of Lady Hester Stanhope had reached the *compagnons de la femme*, and they hastened to visit her, a tremulous hope in their hearts, for had she not seen visions of a woman messiah? But this strange prophetess refused to play the part that was all ready for her. The great lady gave them money but would not further their schemes.[3]

Rejected by France and suspect in Istanbul, the Saint-Simonians won a grudging agreement from Muhammad Ali to survey the Suez isthmus. As it turned out, however, Enfantin only spent a short time on the survey and, increasingly suspect in the eyes of the Egyptian court, only managed to stay in Egypt thanks to the help offered by friends such as de Lesseps. His return to France in 1846 saw the end of his project and of his dream, but for de Lesseps himself it was to be the beginning of a great inspiration. Influenced by the surveys of the Saint-Simonians, and temporarily eclipsed by a political event which had damaged his position, Ferdinand retired to France to the family château at La Chenaie, near Gilly in the Indre, and settled down to study the whole question for himself.

Born in Versailles on 19 November 1805, de Lesseps had left school at the age of seventeen to study law before joining the French army commissariat. Three years later he joined the French Consulate in Lisbon. In 1829 he was transferred to Tunis to serve under Mathieu, who was Consul-General there. Three years later he was posted to Alexandria, then to Cairo. This was an interesting period, coinciding with Ibrahim Pasha's march on Istanbul and his turning back at the bidding of his father and the Western powers.

Muhammad Ali welcomed Ferdinand as the son of Mathieu, and at once took a personal liking to this bright and amusing young man. Worried about the somewhat grotesque eating habits of his son Said, the Wali asked Ferdinand to look after the boy whose movements were, otherwise, severely restricted. De Lesseps wrote:

> I was at that time the only person authorized to receive him. When he came to me he would throw himself on my divan quite worn out. He had come to an understanding with my servants, as he confessed to me later, to obtain from them secretly meals of macaroni, to make up for the fasting imposed on him.[4]

Said developed a strong affection for the Vice Consul, and this affection was later to pay Ferdinand splendid dividends. Said worshipped de Lesseps for his sophisticated French culture, his social grace, his excellent horsemanship and his extreme conscientiousness. During the great plague of 1834 which killed about thirty per cent of the native populations of Cairo and Alexandria, de Lesseps turned the French Consulate into a hospital, visiting the afflicted and drawing them into lazarettos.

When Abbas died in September 1854, Ferdinand was immediately invited to Egypt by the new Wali, Said. He wrote to his mother-in-law Madame Delamalle:

> The Messagerie steamer, the *Lycurgue*, landed me at eight this morning at Alexandria, my good friend Ruyssenaers [the Dutch Consul-General] and Hafouz Pasha, the Minister of Marine, came to meet me on behalf of the Viceroy, and I proceeded in a court carriage to one of His Highness's villas . . .[5]

Within a week of his arrival Said had approved of his project to cut the Suez Canal and by the end of November he was authorized by Act of Concession to begin preparatory work. It was to be the beginning of a period of great difficulties for Ferdinand and for the whole project which was by and large supported by France but strongly criticized by the British. Lord Palmerston was quite unimpressed. De Lesseps wrote of his interview with the British Prime Minister on 7 April 1855:

> He spoke to me with regard to the Suez Canal in the most contradictory, incoherent, and, I will even add, the most senseless fashion imaginable . . . He is firmly convinced that France has long pursued the most Machiavellian policy in Egypt against England, and that the fortfications of Alexandria were paid for by Louis-Philippe or his government.[6]

However, Queen Victoria was personally sympathetic and Albert was beginning to soften his critical views of the French imperial couple. The Queen, always ready to be swayed by little feminine things, had been delighted with the exquisite curtsy Eugénie had made when they first met. Meanwhile, in France, de Lesseps' key supporter was the clever, tubby Prince Napoleon (Plon Plon) whom few liked and one wit had commented was 'a good copy of the first emperor dipped in German grease'.

However, Said himself was soon surrounded by jealous cliques, and it began to emerge that, for one reason or another, almost every courtier and leading community figure in Egypt was against the Canal project. Alexandrian traders feared for their trade, but even the French community, so positive about the project until it threatened to become reality, was riven with jealousies. Alphonse Daudet makes his Nabob, Edmond About say:

> The isthmus is a witch who seduces the capital of imbeciles; but we Alexandrians have things just the way we want them. There are fifty or sixty amateurs down there who have nothing to do but to lunch by day and dine and drink champagne by night. When they have reached their last centime, M. de Lesseps gets hold of his gold mattock and *crac*! 100 million francs falls into their laps from heaven.

When even Louis-Napoleon's support seemed lukewarm and Palmerston's invective filled the pages of *The Times*, Said lost his nerve and ordered the project to be abandoned, although this was only to be a temporary measure.

For de Lesseps the next important phase was to agitate for popular support in Britain, leading to further discord with Palmerston and criticism of the project even from experts on Egypt such as Robert Stephenson, who was to make himself look foolish by announcing that the project would never be commercially viable. Despite all the odds, however, de Lesseps pushed ahead and floated the 400,000 shares of his new company on 15 October 1858. Of these France took 207,111 and the Ottoman empire, including Said's personal subscription, took 96,517.

On 19 April of the following year de Lesseps carried out his survey of the freshwater canal, and on 20 April Port Said was founded. However, the European war – Austria invaded Piedmont on 29 April – and increased British opposition were once again to put a stop to all progress. The shareholders were soon becoming desperate and bankruptcy seemed to stare de Lesseps in the face. Between this period and the death of Said in January 1863, the project oscillated between periods of optimism and despair. With the coming to power of Ismail, however, everything was to change. Ismail was, almost from the start, a *canaliste* but he was also determined that this canal would be an Egyptian canal and not a foreign one. Little was he to know that it was to become the Trojan Horse that would destroy him and make Egypt a European preserve for almost a century.

However, even on Ismail's accession, every party continued to take advantage of the situation. The British wanted no canal until they had established their own political authority in the area; the Sultan did not want his Egyptian vassal to upstage him by taking the credit for building it; Nubar was seeking British support for his own dominant role in Egypt; and Louis Napoleon wanted to satisfy the British so that they would, in return, support his European adventures. When the legality of the project was challenged in the French courts, de Lesseps won his case, but the desperately complicated manoeuvres that surrounded the project led to the famous arbitration by Napoleon called for by the Sultan. At first it seemed that even de Lesseps' pleas to his cousin could not save him from a plan aimed by his enemies to pass the project on to the French Government, in the person of the pro-British Duc de Morny. However, the arbitration decision that was signed on 2 August 1864, after byzantine wrangling, was almost entirely in de Lesseps' favour. From that moment the Canal was a reality, de Lesseps was saved and the great project began in earnest, working its way up to the magnificent celebrations of 1869.

13   La Belle Eugénie

The Empress Eugénie was deeply religious, but also headstrong and not, perhaps, particularly intelligent, and her own determined political decisions were usually hopelessly awry, eventually contributing to the collapse of France's Second Empire. On 23 September 1862, Bismarck became Minister-President and Foreign Minister of Prussia. What Bismarck shared with the idealistic Napoleon, but for very different reasons, was the dream of a united Germany. In 1850, Louis Napoleon had told the Prussian Minister to Paris: 'Have France and Prussia not the same culture, the same ideals of enlightened liberalism, the same reasons to free and unite nations and races?'

Ever the naïve idealist, Louis Napoleon encouraged the unification of Italy under Cavour and Victor-Emmanuel, thus weakening Austria and strengthening Bismarck's hand. In contrast, Eugénie herself favoured Austria against Italy, which largely explains the cool meeting she was to have with him in Rome when she was *en route* for Istanbul and Cairo.

By 1869, when the war clouds that were to burst the following year into the Franco-Prussian War were already gathering, there were many forces in Europe who wanted Eugénie to be as far away as possible from affairs of state. Bismarck, in particular, saw her as a threat to his plans for German unification and European adventure. But in Paris, too, her popularity was waning. Her open support of Austria, her apparent responsibility for the collapse of the Bourbon monarchy in Mexico, and her wild extravagance had lost her many friends at court and outside. The last straw for her was the advice given to the Emperor in a letter by the retired politician Persigny, that she no longer attend the Council meetings. She was embittered when she saw the letter and petulantly agreed to forgo her attendance henceforth. So when Ismail invited her to inaugurate the opening of the Suez Canal in that year it seemed both to her and to some of her enemies an ideal opportunity. Eugénie and Napoleon both had personal reasons for supporting the Canal project, she because she was a cousin of its architect for whom she felt a respect mingled with passion and he because of the survey that Napoleon Bonaparte had already carried out.

However, France's republican press railed against her trip, claiming that it was going to cost one million francs and that it was unbecoming to send a woman to a Muslim country where women were thought to enjoy little respect. However, both Emperor and Empress were determined that she accept the invitation and the voyage was eventually arranged. Some sixty dresses were made for her and for her ladies by the Paris *couturier* Worth who sent his own packers to the Tuileries to fold them in massive trunks. The reverence which Eugénie dedicated to the journey reveals the luxury of the Canal opening. Louis Napoleon's cousin, Princess Mathilde, bitterly told the writer and diarist Edmond de Goncourt after Eugénie's departure:

> The last time I was at Saint-Cloud she showed me all her dresses for the trip to Suez. And that was all! The whole journey is nothing to her but an opportunity to make eyes at some Eastern prince from her steamboat. Because she always needs men around her to pay court to her and talk smut to her without rumpling her dress. You see, she carries flirtation as far as it will go. Why, the other day she actually said to me that a woman could yield almost everything except the *main thing*. And she's so dry in her coquetry. A trollop without any temperament . . . She never shows any sign of tenderness, never even kisses her son![1]

The Empress embarked on her historic trip surrounded by a glittering party of her Paris élite, her two nieces, the Comtesse de la Poëze, Madame de Nadaillac, Prince Murat, General Douay, Commander de Reffye, Monsieur Rainbeaux, Compte Davillier, Comte de Brissac, Comte Clary and Eugénie's pretty young maid of honour, the Comtesse des Garets. She made the great Egyptologist, Maspero, lecture her on the Pharaonic sites before she left Paris, showing him the attentiveness that was characteristic of her insatiable intellectual curiosity.

The party left Paris on 30 September. It was to be a rapid journey as the date for the opening of the Canal was fixed for 15 November. The group were to visit Venice, Piraeus, Athens and Istanbul before reaching Egypt, where they were scheduled to visit Alexandria, Cairo, Upper Egypt and Suez prior to the Canal opening. The train took them to Venice, where they spent two days before embarking on the Empress's yacht *L'Aigle*. The Empress had an interview with Victor-Emmanuel after mass at St Mark's, but the visit was short. Eugénie had never liked the man since his visit to Paris with Cavour in 1855. His crude behaviour had repelled her. He had left behind him a bad feeling in Paris where, meeting a lady at the Tuileries, he had announced at the top of his voice that he nad made love with her in Turin. He had also asked Eugénie whether it was true that French ballerinas did not wear knickers, adding that if that were so 'it will be absolute heaven for me'. 'The King,' wrote the Comtesse des Garets, 'had an impertinent manner and could never remain very long with a woman without asking the most outrageous questions.'[2] Politically, moreover, Victor Emmanual was embittered over Eugénie's opposition to Cavour's policy for the unification of Italy.

At Piraeus, Eugénie was received by the King of Greece, who escorted the party to the palace and to the Acropolis and other sites. From Piraeus to Athens the journey was characterized by general sea-sickness by all except the Empress, who spent most of her time on deck. It was only tactful that, before reaching Egypt, Eugénie first visit the Sultan in Istanbul who should by rights have been the host at the Canal celebrations but was in fact not invited at all. Ismail had justified this manifest lack of tact with the curious comment that a vassal could not invite his overlord. In reality, of course, he knew perfectly well that had the Sultan come the whole fiesta would inevitably have become the Sultan's show.

On Friday 13 October, the party reached Istanbul. Raouf Pasha, the Sultan's chamberlain, took them first in Imperial caiques to the Beylerbey Palace then on to a dinner with the Sultan which astonished his guests with its mixture of formality and oriental confusion. The table of dainty French women and plump, *tarboushed* Ottomans sat about fifty. The Comtesse des Garets kept as a souvenir the menu of 'this wretched dinner' which included *Potage Princesses, Ananas à l'Impératrice* and *Kaimackli Ekmek Cadaif,* a splendid Turkish attempt to satisfy both the Empress and the Sultan. 'The Sultan had a fine head,' wrote the Comtesse, 'but his glance resembled that of a wild beast; and his palace was very beautiful but there was too much gold about!'[3] In this somewhat demonic atmosphere, the usually garrulous Empress spoke little and the Sultan even less.

They then embarked on the Sultan's personal caique which was upholstered in purple velvet with gold fringes and was rowed by twelve men. The Empress wore a white dress embroidered with gold and a tiara of diamonds. Exquisite stones glimmered all over her arms and neck, and a long tulle veil covered her head. 'She was ravishingly beautiful,' wrote the Comtesse, 'as beautiful as the wonderful night; as we saw her approaching over the water, she might have been an apparition from another world.'[4] The caique returned them to the Beylerbey Palace, whose rooms, as far as the eye could see, glimmered with lamps placed on the floor. The corridors were enveloped with strange half-shadows that threw patterns on the long, thick carpets.

On the following day the Sultana Valide (the Sultan's mother), a 'really terrible woman ... accompanied by a dozen utter savages', returned the Empress's visit.[5] The Comtesse was horrified. Eugénie awaited her guests with imperial formality at the top of the stairs, but the Turkish women poured into the bedrooms, howling with ribald laughter as they opened drawers and cupboards, 'crying out like delirious parrots'. The black eunuch Moussa had failed to leave the harem in time and the women went wild with delight when they found the terrified man hidden in one of the rooms. Eventually Eugénie came to his aid, assuring him that he would come to no harm. The following evening the party strolled in the beautiful Palace gardens, where the Sultan's tame lions and tigers, who followed him about like dogs, roared.

Sent to visit the wife of Ali Pasha, the Grand Vezir, the Empress's ladies descended from their *fiacres* only to be seized and carried under the arms of two eunuchs with huge black hands. All the way up the stairs of the Palace Circassian girls played strange musical instruments. The ladies of Ali Pasha's wife proved pleasant, however, caressing the hands and faces of the French ladies and murmuring endearments. The girls danced for them while they were served with violet water, rose jam, and Turkish coffee served in glasses embedded with diamonds or tiny cups of gold filigree.

Two further incidents made the visit somewhat alarming. When the Sultan accompanied Eugénie to his harem, they met the Sultan Valide in a long dark corridor. Infuriated to see her son arm in arm with an unveiled woman, this ferocious lady assaulted her. In exile in England the following year, Eugénie told Queen Victoria that she had given her a violent punch in the stomach, that this had led to a furious argument between son and mother, but that all had ended in laughter. Luckily, the story never reached the French press for whom it would have been dynamite. An even more serious incident involved her American dentist, Doctor Evans, who was to help her to exile from Paris. Accompanying the Sultan on his caique, she spotted a small boat in the way in which a European gentleman was happily snoozing. A rule which she probably did not know was that the royal boat gave way to nobody and would happily run down whoever stood in its way. The poor dentist had simply gone fishing on the Bosphorus and fallen asleep. Eugénie desperately grabbed the Sultan's arm and his unique order to change course was given promptly and just in time.

After a week of festivities, Eugénie and her dainty ladies sailed away to Alexandria, breathing sighs of relief once they were back on board the cosy security of *L'Aigle*.

14 The Opening of the Accursed Canal

> Ah! It is true that the Canal has proved highly remunerative to the company which exploits it; but Egypt has never obtained the smallest advantage; on the contrary, the Canal has been the principal cause of Egypt's miseries.
>
> (A few words on the Anglo-Egyptian Settlement, by ex-Khedive Abbas Hilmi)

On her arrival at Port Said from Istanbul on 22 October, Eugénie wrote to her husband: 'I have just arrived at Port Said in good health. Magnificent reception. I've never seen anything like it in my life.' From Port Said she sailed to Alexandria where she was greeted by the Khedive and accompanied by train to Cairo. In Cairo she was treated to a reception by the 5,000-strong French community beneath an Arc de Triomphe erected in front of the French Consulate, and from there she was driven to the Gezira Palace. She wrote again to the Emperor, comparing Cairo with her beloved Spain, although this mood of nostalgia was probably influenced by the Andalusian arches and gardens of the palace. Mass was said for her by the Pères de Terre Sainte and the great Mariette gave her a lecture on Pharaonic history.

As the inspiration for the libretto of *Aida*, Mariette held a curiously important position in the celebrations. During the Exposition Universelle in Paris, Napoleon had asked his wife to use her charms on the Khedive to persuade him to bequeath to the Louvre the replica of the Philae Temple, which represented the heart of the Egyptian stand. Over-confident in the admiration she had instilled in Ismail, she couldn't resist going a step further and asking for more. She asked that the temple should go to the

Louvre and the jewels that were on show to her. The Khedive is said to have replied to her with dignity: 'Alas! Madame, I have no power to grant you your request. There is a man in Boulaq who is far greater than I and he alone can decide on such matters.' The man was Mariette, the Empress's request was politely refused and the temple was shipped safely back to Cairo after the exhibition had ended.

Few Egyptians realize that the Statue of Liberty, a feature of New York Harbour since 1871, was originally to have been erected at the opening of the Suez Canal at Port Said. It was to have symbolized Middle East progress – 'Egypt carrying the light of Asia', in the words of its thirty-three-year-old sculptor Frederic Auguste Bartholdi who was said to have a 'lust for the colossal'. Fired with enthusiasm for the statues of Abu Simbel, this French Alsacian sculptor put his project to Ismail during the latter's visit to the Exposition Internationale. Ismail encouraged Bartholdi to spend two years making sketches and models, but eventually decided that the project was too expensive, so the sculptor turned for his new vision towards America.

In the final model that he produced for New York, he copied the arms and body of his mistress and the face of his domineering and intolerant mother. He chose Bedloe's Island, opposite New York Harbour's narrows, as 'the gateway to America'. With the encouragement of the French politician Edouard Lefèbre he raised funds with all the fanfare of a modern election tour and appeared at the US Centennial Exhibition beside a full-size replica of the arm and torch, both of which he had transferred from left to right after his rebuff by Ismail. Gustave Eiffel worked on the prefabricated structure which Bartholdi unveiled.

Despite his penny-pinching over the statue, Ismail's celebrations to inaugurate the opening of the Canal are thought to have cost some £2 million, several billion pounds by today's standards, on top of the £20 million spent on the construction of the Canal itself. Five hundred cooks and a thousand servants from Trieste, Genoa, Leghorn and Marseilles were imported to prepare the feasts. Yet, although nothing that money could buy was neglected by the Khedive, he felt in true oriental fashion that he had fallen short in the hospitality he was offering his guests, and wrote anxiously to Nubar, '. . . I will not be able to have more than eight palaces available for the sovereigns and princes who are honouring me by coming for the occasion of the opening of the Suez Canal.'[1]

Six years later, hemmed in by debts to European banking houses in which risk discounts and interest repayments represented some forty per cent of the loans, Ismail was 'persuaded' by the British Prime Minister, Disraeli, to sell his 176,602 out of a total of 400,000 shares for a mere £4 million. But the sale did not save him, and his abdication in 1879 was to be the prelude to a century of effective British rule in Egypt.

However, he had judged correctly that a flamboyant opening of the Canal, by far the most important waterway in the world, would give Egypt a special status in the eyes of the Europe he craved to impress. When he came to power in 1859, he assured Ferdinand de Lesseps that 'he would not be worthy of being Viceroy if he wasn't more *canaliste* than himself [de Lesseps]'. The Canal would add charisma to his own rule and it would increase his independence from the Sublime Porte in Constantinople. This last ambition represented an endemic irony in the relationship between Egyptian rulers and the Ottoman Sultans, for only a decade later Ismail would be begging his titular sovereign in Constantinople to protect his rule and his country from the British. It was a question of perpetually wanting to have one's cake and eat it. As Nubar points out in his memoirs, even de Lesseps was to cause some embarrassment over this issue. When all the guests had arrived in Egypt for the inauguration, he had asked Nubar via M. Ruyssenaers, the Dutch Consul-General, to obtain for him the title of Prince of Suez, 'a title, and an unknown title in a Turkish country, and that [i.e. – asking for the title] at a time when we were in full conflict with the Porte!' Instead Ismail offered de Lesseps the title of 'Pasha', which originally meant 'the Sultan's foot' and which he refused, probably regarding it as too mundane.

In July 1869, Ismail set out on a tour of European capitals, a venture which infuriated the Sultan who had not been informed of the trip and who was, astonishingly, not included on Ismail's itinerary. Ismail was visiting Europe as Head of State, rather than as a 'Vice-roy' who theoretically owed his position to Istanbul. He had come to invite the crowned heads of Europe to the dazzling festival. The invitation embarrassed many of the monarchs of Europe, who did not wish to offend the Porte whose technical

right it was to represent Egypt abroad. As *The Times* put it on 25
November: 'Before the fêtes, as you know, the Sultan, who has an
abundantly exalted idea of his own dignity and power, was hard to
hold . . .' Vicky, the Crown Princess of Prussia, wrote to her
mother Queen Victoria:

> May I ask a question in confidence? What do you think of the
> opening of the Suez Canal – and the quarrel of the Viceroy and
> the Sultan? Do you think Fritz [her husband Frederick] ought
> to go to the opening? For my part I should think not for many
> reasons. First on account of the expense of such a journey – it
> does not seem fair to spend so much money on a journey when
> money is so scarce as it is here at present.[2]

The Queen replied severely:

> You ask about Fritz's going to the opening of the Suez Canal. I
> should say certainly he should not go; and I do not intend any of
> our sons should go. It would only make matters worse between
> the Sultan and the Viceroy or Khedive as he is now called, and
> they are bad enough.[3]

However, the Prussian Crown Prince did go, and enjoyed the
festivities thoroughly. *The Times*, however, covered the events with
a patronizing pessimism, harping on the likelihood that the Canal
would not work, that the banks would cave in and that the whole
project would prove to be a disastrous waste of money. On 17
November, the day of the inauguration, its correspondent wrote:
'The Suez Canal is to be opened today . . . a ship – possibly the
imperial yacht *L'Aigle* with the Empress Eugénie on board – will
this day pass through the Canal even if it may be necessary to close
it again immediately after the festivities.'

At that stage the Canal was, of course, a French affair, and the
British press saw it as a grievous threat to Britain's imperial
interests. *Punch* echoed this frenzied francophobia: 'Great Britain
will, indeed, become Little Britain; her Eastern commerce will be
annihilated . . . the sun of England will set forever . . .' It even put its
criticisms into poetry:

What of this piercing of the sands?
What of this union of the seas
This grasp of unfamiliar hands
This blending of strange litanies?
This pot-pourri of East and West
Pilau and potage *à la bisque*
Circassian belles whom Worth has drest
And Parisiennes *à l'odalisque!*[4]

Queen Victoria allowed the Prince and Princess of Wales to visit Egypt in the February before the inauguration but, with her full backing, the British Cabinet prevented them from attending the celebrations themselves, only allowing the British Ambassador to the Sublime Porte to attend.

The Prince was surrounded by friends such as Prince Louis of Battenberg, as well as relatives of an eminent Cairo figure, the Duke of Sutherland. Having justified his huge entourage to his mother on the grounds that Eastern custom made 'show' a necessity, the Prince and his party steamed up the Nile in six blue-and-gold steamers provided with 3,000 bottles of champagne and 4,000 bottles of claret. Four French chefs worked around the clock preparing seemingly endless feasts. On the way back from Wadi Halfa, Edward shot a nine-foot crocodile with an expanding bullet. As soon as he was back in Cairo he scrambled up the Great Pyramid, but was white with fear when he reached the bottom again. The Princess, meanwhile, was visiting the royal harems, and spent much of the rest of the visit teasing her husband over the lovely unveiled faces she had seen behind harem doors.[5]

The King of Prussia declined the invitation to attend the Canal celebrations on the grounds of old age, but agreed to send Frederick instead. The Emperor of Austria decided to come in person, taking the precaution of visiting the Sultan *en route*. The Kings of Greece and of Sweden and Norway refused, fearing offence to the Sultan. The King of the Netherlands sent his brother, Prince Henry. Russia was represented by its ambassador to Constantinople, General Ignatieff. The US President, General Grant, was neither able to come nor even to send a representative, since Congress, who would have to appoint one, was not in session. The King of Italy was to have been represented by the

Duke of Aosta but he was obliged to leave with his naval aquadron before the inauguration.

From Paris Ismail went to London where the British bent over backwards to entertain him and make up for his 1867 visit which had coincided with that of the Sultan. *The Times* published a leader urging that he should be offered every honour in return for his own hospitality towards the Prince and Princess of Wales during their recent visit to Egypt. On the second day of Ismail's visit, the *Pall Mall Gazette* ran an article entitled 'How not to honour him', revealing that he had been shown into Buckingham Palace by a side door. The article added with incredulity 'that diplomatic representations have been made to the effect that the Viceroy must not be allowed to sleep in the bed occupied by the Sultan'.[6] However, Ismail was well looked after, staying at Windsor Castle as a guest of Queen Victoria and being entertained by the Prince of Wales to a magnificent firework display at the Crystal Palace.

By the time of Ismail's return from Europe some 1,000 guests had been invited to the Canal celebrations, all expenses paid. It was almost as if the Khedive was trying to emulate Napoleon's Institut d'Egypte, inviting brilliant guests from every sector of the European community. Among the literati were Emile Zola, Alexandre Dumas and Théophile Gautier. Guests were distributed in hotels and lodgings according to their rank, a grading system that led to embarrassments. Kinross describes the plight of Louise Colet, the Romantic French poet, muse of Victor Hugo, mistress of Flaubert and confidante of Madame Recamier, who was consigned to an inferior hotel in Cairo and sent up the Nile on a 'rat-ridden boat and the most obstreperous donkeys. On one excursion, too tired to move a step further, she was placed in a sack and carried back to the boat by a team of *fellaheen*, to the keen amusement of all.'[7]

Eugénie was the glittering cult figure of Cairo during those magical days, of which Tugay would write: 'Her presence plunged Cairo into a vortex of gaiety. Illuminations lit up the city, while fireworks sent up from rafts on the Nile drew fairylike patterns against the velvety sky.'[8]

15 A Week of Hedonism

On November 17th, the greatest engineering feat of the present century is to have its success celebrated by a magnificent inauguration fête, at which nearly every European family will have its special representative. Truly the occasion will be an exceptional one. The formation of a line of water communications between Europe and the East has been the thought of centuries, occupying in turn the minds of Greek, Roman, Saxon and Gaul . . .

(Thomas Cook in his *Excursionist and Tourist Advertiser*, 1 July 1869)

The inauguration celebrations must have been among the most exotic of the century. For one month before the great day itself the steamers of hundreds of nations arrived at Port Said on the Mediterranean, the northern end of the Canal. Some of the hundreds of passengers were guests of the Khedive; some had come to arrange the extravaganza, and others had come merely as pioneer tourists to visit Pharaonic Egypt. It was still a difficult trip for individual travellers – Thomas Cook had not yet started his 'grand tours' – taxing intrepid travellers like the sensualist Gustave Flaubert and Maxime du Camp who had visited Egypt in the 1840s.

During the long period of the Canal's excavation, de Lesseps was to stay at the Hotel d'Orient, the favoured hotel of these two wild Frenchmen. He made a special point of introducing his engineers and contractors to famous French residents of Cairo such as Mariette, the doctor Clot Bey, and the legendary Sulaiman Pasha, whose vitality and gaiety made him extremely popular with visiting foreigners. Sulaiman was pleasantly cynical about the conversion which had won him the title of Pasha, merrily cursing at the feast of Ramadan and drinking flagons of wine with all the gusto of a Frenchman.

In contrast with gloomy editorials about the viability of the Canal itself, *The Times* correspondent waxed lyrical over the festivities on 16 November. He wrote,

> The illuminations of the ships and streets, the rockets and fireworks, produced an immense effect, and when a moon of intense brightness rose high over the scene and blanched the water of the harbour into a polished mirror, in which every vessel and every ray of light was reflected, it was like fairyland – a fairyland in which steamers and men-of-war and blue, green and red lights are admissible.

But by 22 November he was once again obediently reflecting British petulance over this French success story with a terse report: 'A P & O steamer traversed the Canal from Port Said to Ismailiya and touched ground several times. The Egyptian *Fayoum* was stranded several times. The *Latif* was grounded and had to return. The *Mahroussa* could not proceed beyond Azidieh. The banks are much damaged.' But he clearly enjoyed himself because he could not help adding: 'The fêtes have been magnificent.'

The first to arrive at Port Said was the Khedive himself, accompanied by Sherif Pasha and Nubar on board the Khedival yacht, the *Mahroussa*. On 13 November the Prince and Princess of Holland arrived, followed, the next day, by Ferdinand de Lesseps and his family. On 15 November Franz-Josef, Emperor of Austria, entered the port to a roar of artillery, escorted by a war frigate.

The names of the guests on the now constantly arriving ships read like a litany of figures from a Heroic age: Crown Prince Frederick; Prince Ernest-Auguste of Hanover; the Algerian Amir abd al-Qader; Prince Joachim Murat; the British Ambassador to the Porte, Sir Henry Elliot and his wife; Baron Porkosh-Osten, the Austro-Hungarian Ambassador to the Ottoman Court; Count Ignatieff; the Duke of Huescar; the Count of Cosse-Brissac; Count Jules Andrassy; Baron Frederick de Beust; Admiral

Teghetoff; M. and Mme. Charles de Lesseps; M. Jules de Lesseps; Auguste Mariette and many, many others.

Some of the guests, hoping for lascivious festivities and glittering dancing girls, were disappointed in what the Western-looking Khedive had prepared for them. 'Almost all the monuments have been painted red and white,' complained one French guest, 'all the original delicate traceries and arabesques have disappeared under a thick coating of colour . . .' After one of Ismail's magnificent receptions at the Qasr al-Nil Palace, there was a performance of *Caprice* by Alfred de Musset which disheartened many of the guests who were expecting an oriental orgy of Ghawazee girls and belly dancers.

The French writer Fromentin was more interested in the fantastic medley of orientals he saw everywhere:

> People from Asia Minor, Ukranians, men of Bokhara, Turks, Tartars, men in caftans, shaikhs with green turbans, women, children, old men, the sick, the paralysed. Bashibazouks with their high hats and cummerbunds swathed from chin to crutch, their weapons within the folds, their leggings partly covering down-at-heel shoes . . . A few veiled, white-robed women, whose long, less bold eyes do not suggest the Egyptian; they must be Turkish.[1]

When Eugénie's yacht *L'Aigle* arrived at Port Said on 16 November, there were 160 vessels of many nationalities in the harbour. French, British, Austro-Hungarian, Russian, Italian, Prussian, Turkish and Egyptian warships thundered out a welcome with their cannons, and the princes of the world put off in gilded state barges to pay homage to her and to the Khedive. At Port Said Eugénie held court. Sir Ian Malcolm wrote of the day:

> It was a gorgeous and glittering scene at the doorway of the desert . . . whilst the sandy littoral was covered with tented Arabs and Bedouin from far and near who had come with their families, on horseback and camel, to join in the greatest festival that Egypt had seen since the days of the Ptolemies. On the foreground were erected three large pavilions or enclosed terraces; in the centre one were amassed the illustrious guests of

the Khedive; on the right was the Muhammadan hierarchy supported by its faithful; and on the left, an altar for Christian worship and thanksgiving.[2]

On the next morning, to the booming of naval cannon, the royal visitors assembled to form a magnificent procession to the pavilions erected for the curious performance of Christian and Islamic religious rites that were to open the day's programme. An eye-witness described the occasion thus:

The heir apparent of Egypt came first with the Princess of Holland on his arm. The Empress of the French took the arm of the Emperor of Austria, and the Khedive and the Crown Prince of Prussia walked on either side. The Grand Duke Michael of Russia and the young Prince of Holland accompanied them; and a brilliant staff of French, Prussian, Austrian and Egyptian officers, all in uniform and decorations, followed in procession. There was much cheering all along the line for the Empress, and the Kaiser [meaning Franz-Josef] was warmly welcomed, there being many Austrian subjects at Port Said. The Emperor of Austria wore his uniform of white tunic, scarlet pantaloons, and a cocked hat and green feather; the Prince of Prussia [wore] the uniform of the Prussian Guard. The Viceroy's [Khedive's] uniform was blue, with gold lace, and with a broad green ribbon, the hilt of his scimitar blazing with jewels.[3]

And to think that just one year later so many of these figures would be involved in the ferocious Franco-Prussian War, that Eugénie would have slipped away to a humiliating exile in England, and that the army of the Prussian Crown Prince, backed by the ruthless nation-building aspirations of Count Bismarck, would be using Krupp's big new guns to besiege a starving Paris – the very guns that had been so magnificently displayed at the Exposition Universelle.

The eye-witness continued:

. . . entering the pavilion, the Empress took the central seat, having the Emperor of Austria upon her right and the Khedive upon her left . . . After a short pause the religious ceremonies began. The Ulamah or chief ecclesiastic of the Mohammedan faith, a venerable personage with a flowing white beard, read from his scroll of parchment a prayer to Allah to bestow a blessing on the multitude assembled there, and on the enterprise they had come to dedicate to the service of mankind. This part of the ceremony was very brief, but the scene was a striking one. The Mussulman having concluded, the Archbishop of Jerusalem, in full robes, ascended the steps of the high altar in the Christian kiosque and, with the attending priest, said mass. This over, the Archbishop retired, and a handsome priest, clothed in purple, who was Monsignor Bauer (Archbishop of Syracuse and Chaplain-General to the Imperial French Navy), the Empress's Confessor, came forward and, standing a few steps below the altar, proceeded to deliver an eloquent discourse on the Suez Canal, M. de Lesseps, the Khedive, the Empress and all the illustrious visitors present.[4]

That night Port Said was illuminated and filled with festivities and the day ended with a brilliant display of fireworks. The brothels, gambling houses and night clubs 'to which', quipped one reporter, 'people come to lose at night the money they have made during the day', did a vibrant trade. However, the day was not without bad omens or malicious tongues. It was suddenly spread about that the inauguration on the following day had been postponed, that a huge boulder was obstructing the Canal, that Eugénie had left petulantly for France, that the principal contractor had committed suicide, that the Austrian Emperor had become bored and left for Trieste and, finally, that Ferdinand de Lesseps had suddenly gone completely crazy!

None of this was true, although there had been a small incident when the *Latif*, one of the two Egyptian ships sent ahead to check the route, missed a line of buoys and ran aground. The Khedive, using all his resources, managed to get his engineers to set the ship afloat again. The *Latif*'s captain was the British Captain McKillop, and *The Times* correspondent noted that 'the fact that Captain McKillop was a British officer would afford ground for sinister rumours' (that the British were trying to abort the project and embarrass the French).

On the night before the complete crossing of the Canal set for the 18th, the Khedive lay awake asking himself fretfully: '... Will *L'Aigle* pass through the Canal? If it does, the Canal is open; if it does not – disaster!' On the morning of the 18th the procession of vessels began to move through the Canal, led by *L'Aigle*. Behind *L'Aigle* came the frigate carrying the Emperor of Austria, then the Crown Prince of Prussia in *Grille*, then the Prussian gunboat *Dolphin*, then *Walk* with the Prince and Princess of Holland, then General Ignatieff in the Russian corvette *Yachut*, then the British Ambassador in the *Psyche*. Salvoes of artillery and the stutter of small arms hailed the fact that the Canal was now technically open. Eugénie wrote:

> The ceremonial opening of the Canal was fixed for eight o'clock in the morning, in the waters of Ismailiya. There was a real Egyptian sky, a light of enchantment, a dreamlike resplendence. I was awaited by fifty vessels, all beflagged, at the entrance to Lake Timsa. My yacht, *L'Aigle*, at once took the head of the procession, and the yachts of the Khedive, the Emperor Francis Joseph, the Prince Royal of Prussia, Prince Henry of the Netherlands, followed at less than a cable's length. The spectacle was so supremely magnificent, and proclaimed so proudly the greatness of the French regime, that I could contain myself no longer: I was exultant.[5]

Ismailiya was in feast and thousands flocked to the celebrations. The Khedive's first official act was to go aboard *L'Aigle* to greet Eugénie and, with tears flowing from his eyes, congratulate de Lesseps. On the evening of 18 November, Ismail gave a magnificent fête at the Palace in honour of Eugénie and the other crowned heads.

It was a glittering display of uniforms, varied costumes, medals and jewels and pale shoulders glimmering beneath immense chandeliers. At ten o'clock a great crowd assembled under the peristyle. The Austrian national anthem was followed by the favourite song of Queen Hortense, 'Partant pour La Syrie'. Then came the national anthems of Prussia and the Netherlands. Eugénie wore a toilette of cerise satin veiled by priceless lace, while her long train was fastened to her shoulders by large diamond clasps. Around her forehead was a magnificent diadem from whose back hung a lace veil that fell among the folds of her robes. Supper was served in a large hall hung with cloth of gold and decorated with hot-house flowers and rare, exotic plants. Facing Ismail, the Emperor of Austria and Eugénie sat before a table decorated with cut crystal, flowers and gold plate. Fromentin wrote:

> Fireworks in front of the Viceroy's Palace. Open house everywhere. In one marquee there was a dinner party for five hundred guests, in another for two or three hundred . . . Luxurious dinners, vintage wines, exquisite fish, partridge, wild duck. Seven or eight thousand people sitting down to dinner in the middle of the desert. It was like something out of the *Arabian Nights*. An extraordinary mixture of sumptuosity and barrenness. After dinner, an amazing variety of entertainment. Dancers, jugglers and singers . . . outside it was like a huge fair. Everywhere, deafening music of fifes and drums.[6]

16 *The Fall of Eugénie*

While its crowned heads were celebrating in Egypt, Europe itself
was trembling in its anticipation of a tempest. By the time
Napoleon realized that he had opened a Pandora's box by
espousing the Prussian cause, it was too late to divert the storm.
Barely six months after the Canal celebrations, the Comtesse des
Garets, Eugénie's beautiful young maid of honour, was writing to
her mother: 'Everyone here, and the Empress most of all, desire
war so intensely that it seems to me that it must be a foregone
conclusion . . .'[1] The extravagant charm of the Canal celebrations,
at which the Prussian Crown Prince Frederick had paid homage to
Eugénie, was but a deceptive respite as the nations of Europe
geared themselves up for a terrible blood-letting.

The offer of the Spanish throne to a Hohenzollern prince in
June 1870, backed by the Prussian King and Bismarck, outraged
the French populace. Indeed, France's response was promptly to
call for war, with the French Foreign Minister, the Duc de
Gramont, loudly proclaiming that a Hohenzollern prince on the
Spanish throne would be a *casus belli*. Napoleon himself was only
too aware of France's military weakness, but the impetuous
Eugénie and the court at Saint-Cloud spoke with the voice of the
French people, the voice of dotty bravado and of vengeance. The
French Ambassador to Berlin, Benedetti, was immediately
instructed to place before the Prussian King the French demand
that the Hohenzollern candidate be withdrawn without further
ado.

Eugénie was probably trying to satisfy French wounded pride
and shore up her husband's regime, rather than express any real
confidence in France's preparedness for a war with a nation whom

the French military attaché in Berlin had described as 'not a country with an army, but an army that has a country'. She and the court were displaying a chilling ignorance of Prussian designs and capabilities. Bismarck had been waiting for the slightest opportunity of a war with France, a country he knew to be incapable of matching Prussia's model army. His response to the haughty demand of the French court was the Ems Telegram, a scoffing statement to the press, almost insulting in its patronage, rejecting the French ultimatum. With cavalier planning Bismarck had edited the telegram to enhance its sting. The telegram was greeted in France with the wave of hysterical emotion that the old warrior had been waiting for. France was immediately mobilized, and on 19 July 1870, war was formally declared on Prussia. Pasted all over the billboards of Baron Haussmann's shimmering new Paris were the gung-ho words '*A Berlin*', as *La Volonté Nationale*, the newspaper of Prince Napoleon (Plon Plon — the son of Napoleon Bonaparte's brother Jerome), quoted the Empress as crying out ecstatically: 'It is my war, at last!'

For France, it was to end quickly in a disastrous defeat. When the French army collapsed before Bismarck's counter-advance at the Battle of Sedan late in 1870, she flew into a fury, then retired to her room to weep, unimpressed by her husband's miserable telegram after his capture by the Prussians: 'The army is defeated and made prisoner; not having been able to get myself killed among my troops I have had to become a prisoner in order to save the army.' Eugénie's determination that he should not leave the battlefield had been chilling in its heartlessness. 'That he, a Napoleon, should abandon his troops on the eve of battle! ... He would be ashamed for ever in the eye of history! I would rather that he had killed himself!' Englishmen such as the Egyptophile Wilfrid Blunt were repelled by the accusations of cowardice that she hurled at her wretched husband, who had clearly met defeat with courage and with dignity.

Eugénie's own humiliations began with her dramatic exile from the Tuileries on the night of 4 September, when the Communards were already in the palace grounds. At midday her cousin, Ferdinand de Lesseps, had insisted on visiting her in order to persuade her to escape from the palace before she became a victim of the blood-hungry mob, but she remained in her room when he

115

arrived for lunch. Unbeknown to him, however, she soon slipped away through the public galleries of the Louvre with Madame Lebreton in attendance. Unaware that she had gone, de Lesseps desperately tried to keep the crowd back, and even recognized among the National Guard two loyal faces of guardsmen who were pretending to lead the mob while trying to gain enough time to allow for the Empress's escape. In the meantime, she found refuge with her American dentist, Dr Evans, who lived in Malakoff Street. It was he and a friend of hers called Crane who were to smuggle her out of Paris and to Deauville, disguised as a poor woman on her way to the lunatic asylum. Ironically, Dr Evans was repaying a long-owed debt, since she had saved his life when the Sultan's caique had borne down on the poor man.

From Deauville Eugénie was secretly taken to Cowes on the Isle of Wight in the yacht of the Englishman Sir John Burgoyne. Meanwhile, the Paris mob, enraged with a regime it considered responsible for France's humiliations, poured into the Tuileries and effaced every reference to it, chiselling away the Ns (for Napoleon) and the imperial eagles. In a letter to her daughter, the Crown Princess of Prussia, Queen Victoria wrote from Balmoral in 1870, shortly after Eugénie's arrival: 'She [Eugénie] looks dreadfully ill and altered, coughs very much and was very poorly dressed in black . . . She is in an uncomfortable, smelling hotel [the Marine Hotel] at Hastings with hot, disagreeable rooms.'[2]

After her escape, Eugénie was tormented by brutally unjust newspaper headlines in the Paris press such as: 'The Napoleon woman; her lovers, her orgies.' She was cartooned naked, being sketched by King Louis Philippe's son, the Prince de Joinville, or dancing the cancan with her petticoats floating above her head for the pleasure of the King of Prussia (whose son had just attended the Suez Canal celebrations) while the King lay back on a sofa drinking champagne and Louis-Napoleon hung in a cage from the wall. Eugénie was to live the rest of her days in England, first at Camden Palace, Chislehurst, and later at Farnborough Hill, although it was in her beloved Spain that she was to die in 1920, forty-seven years after the death of her husband.

As a delightfully witty and still lovely old lady, Eugénie in her old age made several visits to Cairo, where she became a friend of

Henry Boyle, although she took an instant dislike to Cromer when she met him in Cairo in 1902. According to Boyle's wife, Clare, the French Legation found it politic to ignore her, although the French Minister could not resist the temptation to pay her his personal respects in secret. Cairo's French-language press referred to her contemptuously as 'Madame Bonaparte' or 'La Veuve' ('The Widow') but the British community supported her ecstatically. During her exile of almost forty years she had become a popular figure in England. Boyle was deeply moved to witness her meeting with the Duke of Connaught. When the Duke bent to kiss the old lady's hand, the ex-Empress leant forward spontaneously and kissed his cheek. This was the woman who had once been the toast of Europe, and had been a Pharaonic goddess figure during that magical year of 1869.

In 1905 Eugénie made what appears to have been her last visit to Egypt, where de Guerville describes the lonely sight of her standing on her *dahabiyya* near the temples of Abu Simbel:

It was the hour of sunset, when a short distance above Abu Simbel, our boat passed a large *dahabiyya* covered with green plants. In the midst of these, on the deck, a lady with white hair gazed dreamily across this land of Nubia which she had once before looked on thirty-six years earlier. It was the Empress. Who can explain the desire which had urged this woman to come at the close of her life, almost unknown and unrecognized, to revisit those places which were witnesses of her beauty and her power, of the adoration of the thousand flatterers who surrounded her? Who can explain the state of mind which had led her, robbed of all of which she was proud, to these scenes which had witnessed her days of triumph? . . . Suez, Ismailiya, Cairo, Abu Simbel, Paris! Have you ever seen her at the window of the 'Continental' [Hotel], regarding the site of the palace where she once reigned?[3]

In December 1919, aged ninety-three, Eugénie set out from Farnborough Hill for France and Spain. In Paris she visited Les Invalides where, wrote Blythe in *Skittles*: 'A frail but formidable old woman was seen to stump her way down to the tomb of Napoleon [Bonaparte]. On reaching it, she took a newspaper from her bag and slowly read out the terms which the allies had laid down for the German surrender.'

In April 1920, against her doctor's orders, she sailed to Gibraltar and returned to Spain. Her brother-in-law (the widowed husband of her sister Paca), the Duke of Alba, drove her to Seville where she was visited by King Alfonso and Queen Ena, who entertained her as if she was still Empress of France. Amid the beautiful, tumbling flowers of the Alba Palace she once again gave the glittering dinner parties which reflected her past glory. At the beginning of May she went with the Duke to Madrid's Liria Palace where she was surrounded by relations and was at long last formally visited by the French Ambassador, signifying that all was now forgiven by France. Duff wrote of the visit:

> Their meeting joined her great memories – driving up the hill to Windsor Castle and Queen Victoria waiting to receive her . . . the cheering of the crowds at the christening of the Prince Imperial at Notre Dame . . . Napoleon riding into Paris at the head of his troops after the victory at Solferino . . . drifting across the torch-lit lake at Annecy, scarlet burnous about her shoulders, and the cry of '*Vive l'Impératrice*' echoing from shore to shore . . . on the bridge of *L'Aigle* as she led the ships of all nations at the opening of the Suez Canal . . .[4]

On 9 July the Duke of Alba went to England to arrange his marriage at Farnborough Hill. Eugénie was to follow three days later. On the 10th, however, she developed a cold and was placed, fully-dressed, on her bed. The following morning she lost consciousness but regained it briefly to murmur the words to the Duke's sister: 'I am tired; it is time for me to go away.' At eight o'clock in the morning of Sunday 11 July 1920, Eugénie died.

The Khedive Ismail

Jechem Afr, Ismail's third wife

Jenan Yar, Ismail's second wife

Louis-Napoleon (Napoleon III)

The Empress Eugénie

The Gezira Palace in the 1870s

The gardens of the Gezira Palace today

The procession of ships at the opening of the Suez Canal

Ferdinand de Lesseps

67   PORT-SAÏD. — General View Harbour. — LL.

The Suez Canal Office in Port Said

Dressed to kill at one of Cairo's fancy-dress balls

The Cairo Opera House, built for the Canal Opening

The tropical gardens of the Shepheard's Hotel

Society gathers on the Shepheard's famous terrace in the 1920s

The Shepheard's Egyptian Hall

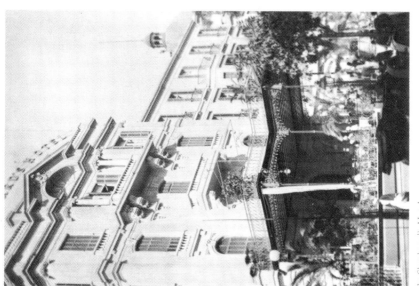

The Shepheard's Hotel

Romance dawns on the terrace of the Shepheard's (by Lance Thakeray)

Tourists mounting the Great Pyramid

British tourists at the Pyramids in the 1920s (Thomas Cook Archive)

The Abdin Palace

Lavish interior of the Abdin Palace

Gardens and pool of the Abdin Palace

The Abdin Palace's 'Byzantine Hall'

Cairo's courtesans obsessed Western visitors

Dancing girls of the 1950s: twilight of the high life

17   The Fall of Ismail

> ... with their interests, their brokerage, their commissions and fictitious payments, and all the tricks of the Paris and London stock exchanges, in a way which would have sent a small man to prison. An Englishman of that day called the big bankers the scum of Europe, for they actually paid over to the cheerful King only sixty per cent of his loans on paper.
>
> (Emile Ludwig, quoted in Raymond Flower:
> *Napoleon to Nasser*)

While the war clouds had been gathering in Europe, Ismail and his dynasty suddenly found themselves faced with financial ruin. Once the celebrations were over and the guests had gone, the Khedive had to count the cost of his extravagance. His European debtors were claiming that he owed them £100 million, while he desperately counter-claimed that he had never borrowed that much. But as his financial situation deteriorated, so did his credit-worthiness and, consequently, the terms on which he was able to borrow. Because of the risk discounts subtracted from loans before he ever received them, he was eventually receiving less than half the amount that he was deemed to have borrowed by the European banks, yet had to pay back the fictitious principal at rates of up to twelve per cent. In hindsight it is possible to feel sympathy for Ismail as one watches the Egypt of the 1980s falling once again into the debtor trap, forced to accept a bitter medicine from the International Monetary Fund and brace itself for the political upheaval that unpopular belt-tightening threatens in its wake.

Even in 1869 there were some who pitied Egypt and accused the Western banks of an unacceptable greed. 'Never,' George Young had commented at the time, 'was there such a spoiling of the Egyptians by the chosen people' – a remark that many must have regarded as anti-Semitic. Between 1862 and 1873 Ismail had borrowed from European banks – Fruhling and Goschen, Bischoffsheim, Oppenheim, Anglo-Egyptian and Banque Impériale Ottomane – £68.5 million, of which Egypt only received £46.8 million after intolerable risk discounts had been subtracted, quite apart from crippling interest payments. State loans for £77 million only saw a receipt of £50 million. On the 1873 Oppenheim loan of £32 million, Egypt was paying an annual charge of £3.5 million and only received a final sum of £18 million. The total cost of transforming Cairo into a replica of Haussmann's Paris, of building the Suez Canal and of building new irrigation canals such as the magnificent Cairo–Ismailiya Canal as well as railways, bridges, telegraphs, lighthouses, harbours, docks and sugar factories appears to have totalled about £25 million.

Between 1865 and 1882 Egypt's population increased from 4.8 million to 5.5 million. The public debt had increased from £3.3 million when Ismail came to power to a staggering £98.5 million when he was forced to abdicate, and imports had increased from £1.99 million to £5.4 million. On the positive side, exports had increased from £4.45 million to £13.81 million, thanks to the advantage Egypt had taken from the cutting off of American cotton supplies during the American Civil War. The number of schools had leapt from 185 to a staggering 4,817, railways from 275 miles to 1,185 miles, telegraphs from 630 miles to 5,820 miles, and canals from 44,000 to 52,400 miles. But this fantastic development was at an equally fantastic cost, and if Ismail was cheated by the bankers, many felt that he deserved it, for he had squeezed the last ounce of ruthlessly imposed toil from his people. Injustice and avarice were rife in Egypt. The Suez Canal had been the jewel in the Khedival crown because the inauguration celebrations had reflected the Khedive's magnificence, but the Canal was to bring wretchedly little to the Egyptian people until it was finally nationalized by President Gamal abd al-Nasser in 1956.

The Canal was the Trojan Horse that led quickly to the British occupation. It neutralized the London–Bombay overland trade route that Waghorn had pioneered in 1845, and Egypt suddenly and unexpectedly found itself of little importance except as a transit route, while Cairo itself became little more than a backwater. The flourishing railway line between Cairo and Suez went out of use and was dismantled. The British had fought tooth and nail against the Canal until the day that it was opened, then found themselves inheriting both the Canal and Egypt soon after it was built. By 1875 Ismail's debts had gone mad. Little remained to him except for his 176,602 shares in the Suez Canal Company, and Stanton, the British Consul in Cairo, was soon reporting home that a group of French financiers were negotiating to buy them. To the British Prime Minister, Disraeli, this was a red rag to a bull, and he remarked to friends in London that if they succeeded 'the whole of the Suez Canal would have belonged to France and they might have shut it up'. He promptly announced that Britain wanted to buy the shares, and was told in November 1875 through Stanton that she could have them for £4 million, but that the offer was only valid for forty-eight hours. The British Parliament was in recess so the credit could not be voted by the government, so Disraeli took the initiative of putting his case to Lord Rothschild who immediately agreed to put up the money against British government security. The shares were bought and British control of the Canal – and therefore of Egypt – quite suddenly became a reality.

Ismail's campaigns in Abyssinia had increased his financial problems. He turned to the British with a request for fiscal reform, and in 1875 Britain sent a Member of Parliament, Steven Cave, to study the Egyptian books. So shocking were the debts that Cave uncovered that, when his report was published in the following year, the European stock exchanges panicked and Egypt's credit was entirely cut off. Ismail was now no longer able to renew his treasury bonds except on utterly hopeless conditions. In response to the chaos Europe sent in the bailiffs. The *Caisse de la Dette Publique*, a commission with a mandate to obtain debt servicing payments and payments due to creditors, was established on 2 May 1876. Two years later Ismail was obliged to hand over his private estates on which a loan of £8.5 million was negotiated with the House of Rothschild. But by then Egypt's credit-worthiness was so low that of this loan less than six million pounds was actually received.

Everything was suddenly going hopelessly awry for Egypt. The

Nile floods of 1878 were below normal, and that year's crops were a failure. The general misery of the population had never been greater at the very time when the state's coffers were being scraped for the last piastre. The commission's report of 1879, declaring the Egyptian government insolvent, was rejected by Ismail. But nothing now could save him. Britain and France moved in and two controllers-general – one British, one French – took Egypt's finances in hand.

On 19 June 1879, the end came. With astonishing contempt, the British and French consuls called at the Abdin Palace and ordered Ismail to abdicate. He could not call upon his people because his taxes and tyranny had made him hated by them. Instead, with a marvellous irony and in a last desperate bid to save his throne, he turned to the Sultan from whom he and his forbears had for so long been trying to free themselves. But the telegram eventually cabled to him from Istanbul was addressed to the 'ex-Khedive Ismail'. The dreadful sheet of paper hung about in the offices of the Abdin Palace as every official who picked it up quickly put it down again and became busy. Eventually Sherif Pasha, the son-in-law of Sulaiman Pasha, bravely took the message to Ismail while a separate message to Ismail's son Tewfik, passing him the succession, was being delivered. Rumours went the rounds of the Palace that Ismail would wreak a horrible revenge on his 'loathed' son, but when Tewfik entered the Long Room of the Abdin Palace and found his father brooding in a corner, Ismail got up at once, raised his son's hand to his lips and said magnificently, 'I salute my Effendina.'[1]

The Sultana Melek, the adopted daughter of the Khedive Ismail's third wife, who was among the visitors come to pay their last respects, remembered Egyptian officials weeping on the Khedival yacht and declaring to Ismail their undying loyalty. But as they went ashore she was astonished to see them rushing to their waiting *calèches*, each one eager to be the first to pay homage to Tewfik, as Ismail, with great dignity, sailed away to Italy on the *Mahroussa*.[2] Almost a century later his descendant King Farouk, the last of the family of Muhammad Ali, was to sail away to exile in Greece on the same yacht, bringing to an ignoble end this great dynasty.

As the guest of King Umberto I, Ismail spent eleven years in the

Palazzo della Favorita near Naples which had been offered to him by the House of Savoy. Ismail would travel in Europe with three of his wives, who lived together in a kind of affectionate sorority. The Khedival flock would frequently visit Milan where they stayed at Milan's Grand Hotel, and where Ismail would receive important guests. Paul Draneht's daughter Despina remembered during this exciting period of the Risorgimento the visit of King Umberto and the crowds lining the Via Manzoni crying '*Viva il Re*', while the hotel manager, Spatz, in his frock coat, ushered the King into the hotel and Draneht escorted him to the first-floor landing where Ismail stood imperially to receive him. Despina remembered King Frederick of Prussia calling on him and stroking her head as he passed her peering at him from behind a pillar. Ismail would stay in the Verdi Apartment which had a full-size portrait of the composer and in which Verdi himself was to die. It was also from the Grand Hotel that Ismail's daughter, Faika, went to London to marry Muhammad Izzet Pasha. Her first marriage had been to Ismail Sadiq, the *muffetish* whom Ismail had had strangled at the Gezira Palace because he knew too much about the Khedival debt.

In 1883 the Khedival family settled for a period in a little hotel in Paris's Rue de Mathurins, where Ismail took a great liking to the six-year-old Despina, whom he teasingly nicknamed Mlle Despinasse, and would order her to his presence where she would sit on his knee and tell fantastic stories and 'scold him galore'. He would ply her with bonbonnières filled with sweets from Boissier or dolls from the Nain Bleu. She would eat off his plate, 'like an impertinent sparrow, his granddaughters standing behind us at attention like a row of shocked ninepins'. When he offered her a half-eaten pear, the truant child pushed it away, saying, 'Not after you, pig!' Her father wanted to punish her for such an insult to a Muslim ex-monarch, but the increasingly sentimental Ismail would reply paternally: 'Come, let the child say what she thinks.' He even took her to the notorious Théâtre des Variétés that represented the heart of Second Empire hedonism. In contrast with Despina, Ismail's own granddaughters were terrified of him. They would stand in a row and intone in obedient fear and trembling: '*Evet, Effendum*' or '*Yok, Effendum*', 'Yes Sir', 'No Sir'.[3]

Edmond de Goncourt came to know Ismail, 'a red-bearded Oriental, looking rather like a Théophile Gautier with a squint', in a far less sentimental light than Despina Draneht. When the ex-Khedive visited Saint-Gratien in September 1882, he was so skilful in his urbane use of French that, as the scathing de Goncourt put it, 'one sometimes forgets that this is an "old Turk" who murdered his ministers'. Ismail portrayed himself as a simple peasant to the French writer but would suddenly shatter the image with a remark like: 'Yes, when my uncle was burnt alive!' As de Goncourt put it, 'And then, willy-nilly, the Europeanized man speaks all of a sudden with the accent of the Nile.'[4]

From La Favorita Ismail wrote to the Sultan begging him to allow him to live in Istanbul:

> I have just spent sixteen well-fulfilled years. Under my administration Egypt has been covered by a network of railways; it has considerably extended the canal system which fertilizes the soil's richness; it has created two big ports, Suez and Alexandria; it has destroyed in Central Africa the sources of slavery and it has made the flag of the Empire fly in countries where it was not known; it has seen the achievement of the canal which joins two seas and, after much resistence, it has organized judicial reform which has prepared for the future the means of establishing harmony of great justice in the contact between the civilizations of the Orient with foreign civilizations.[5]

But permission was refused by a Sultan who had been humiliated quite enough by his independent-thinking vassal and it was not until 1888 that Ismail was to receive the Sultan's consent to move to the Ottoman capital. There, Ismail's last years were to be plagued by ill-health. He would sometimes be seen at the Sultan's table, a subservient figure who – like the Sultan's courtiers — would not touch his food until the Sultan had touched his own. He died a sad man at the Palace of Emirgan on the Bosphorus on 2 March 1895 and his remains were sent to Cairo where he was buried in splendid pomp in the Rifai Mosque beneath the Citadel which his mother had built and in which she, too, was buried.

18   Mr Cook and the Hotel Age

The reign of Tewfiq was to represent the beginning of Britain's 'veiled protectorate'. Under the school-masterly figure of Lord Cromer, whom Edward Prince of Wales described on his 1889 visit to Cairo as 'a very able man but with no manners',[1] Egypt quickly took on all the trappings of colonial rule. British social mores were to follow, although many British institutions were already well established both in Cairo and Alexandria. As early as 1855 the French writer Charles Didier was commenting snidely of Cairo's English-managed hotels that 'the yapping voices of the women formed the soprano of this mercantile concert'. Little love was lost between the British and the French during an era in which the French had, from the time of Napoleon's team of literati and artists, brought education and culture, and in which the British were to bring their debt collectors as a prelude to British soldiery and British order. Indeed, even by the 1830s Cairo had become an important stage in the Grand Tour. Disraeli had found the climate delightful as he sat back in 1831 smoking his *narguileh* pipe cooled in a wet silk bag and sipping spiced coffee or finishing his last *chibuk* with a sherbet or a pomegranate.[2]

The overland route between Cairo and Suez had been opened by Lieutenant Waghorn in 1831–4 with four-horse vans, and in 1840 the Mails were first carried by P & O liners. In 1851 Robert Stephenson, the son of George Stephenson who invented the *Rocket*, had been given the contract to build a line between Cairo and Alexandria, one of the first railway lines in the world and the first in Africa. Three years later, the same year that Egypt was linked to the world by telegraph via Malta, this vital line was opened.

The name mostly closely associated with hotels and tourism in Egypt during the period, and indeed thereafter, was Thomas J. Cook, who paid his first visit to Cairo in 1860. Within a month he had organized a tour for thirty-two ladies and gentlemen and had hired two of the Khedive's steamers which enabled his dignified tourists to sail up the Nile as far as Wadi Halfa. A contemporary English lady, Amelia Edwards, would advise the early tourists on how they should conduct themselves:

> In order to enjoy an overwhelming, ineffaceable first impression of Oriental out-of-doors life, one should begin in Cairo with a day in the native bazaars; neither buying nor sketching nor seeking information, but just taking in scene after scene with its manifold combination of light and shade, colour, costume, and architectural detail.[3]

Cook set up his office in the grounds of the Shepheard's Hotel and from it he quickly ran into competition with Egypt's only local tour operator, Henry Gaze, who soon gave way to bitterness, accusing Cook of filching his dragomans. By 1868 Cook was using the new Egypt created by Ismail as a lure for his tourists, explaining that 'Egypt and Palestine constitute the two greatest features of our present programme . . . After briefly scanning Alexandria, which is a sort of Oriental-European conglomerate with but few attractions, we hasten to modern Egypt – Cairo – which presents a combination of ancient Orientalism with Parisian innovations.'[4]

Cook had a grand tour very much in mind when he attended the Canal celebrations at the personal invitation of Ferdinand de Lesseps one year later: 'Our intention is to leave England on the 3rd of November, and sail from Brindisi on the 8th, in the hope of landing at Alexandria on the 12th . . . The travelling fares from England to Alexandria and back will be about £35 First Class, and £28 Second Class.'[5]

He arranged for his tourists to travel on the Austrian Lloyd's steamer *America* as a floating hotel for fifty guineas. It was to form part of the 'grand Steamboat Procession' through the Canal to Suez, and facilities were afforded for it to join the 'Land Festivities' in the desert and at the Pyramids. His announcement added jovially but directly: 'This is Mr Cook's Programme; and all he now adds is, Send The Money and Secure the Remaining Ten Places. First come, first served.' After the opening Cook was to establish a round-the-world tour which would link up with his new London-Cairo run. One of the early steamers which John Mason Cook was to charter from the government was to be used to spearhead the disastrous expedition to rescue Gordon from Khartoum when he was besieged by the Mahdi and his Ansar.

In 1870 Ismail had appointed Cook official government agent for Nile passenger travel and ten years later he had achieved exclusive control of all Nile tourist traffic. In 1887 he built a luxury hotel at Luxor and by 1900 he was arranging tours to Palestine and Turkey as well as Egypt and advertising himself as sole contractor to the English government for the conveyance of troops and stores up the Nile. Added to the first-class steamers which plied the Nile were luxuriously fitted *dahabiyyas*. In 1873 a three-month excursion around Palestine and up the Nile through Upper Egypt to Aswan cost £120.

The best season for the tourist to visit Egypt was November to May, when Cairo and Alexandria would be one long round of receptions, dinner parties, balls, picnics in the desert, gymkhanas, theatricals and tennis parties. In November the Khedive and his court would return to the capital from the Montaza Palace in Alexandria, returning there when the season ended in May. European visitors would be advised to bring in their wardrobes a woollen travelling and morning suit, an evening dress and a 'smoking'. Silk hats were not considered necessary and gloves were only required for balls. At dinner without ladies guests could appear in a black coat and black cravat, while at dinners with ladies men were required to wear dress coat and white tie. The British Agent in Cairo would give two balls each season.

The British visitors viewed the Egyptians much as they viewed the other races they had colonized. In 1878 *Baedeker* explained without apology to early tourists:

The Egyptians, it must be remembered, occupy a much lower grade in the scale of civilization than most of the Western nations, and cupidity is one of their failings: but if the traveller makes due allowance for their shortcomings, and treats the

127

natives with consistent firmness, he will find that they are by no means destitute of fidelity, honesty and kindliness.

British officials in Egypt, meanwhile, regarded the incoming tourists with a wry humour. At the turn of the century Ronald Storrs remembered an old lady who took a dragoman up the Nile and would constantly ask him to translate the hieroglyphics. The dragoman, who could scarcely read Arabic let alone hieroglyphics, would scan the etchings gravely and reply: 'That, Miladi, means "God very nice".' He also remembered donkey boys who, seeking a reward for piety, would fling themselves at the feet of gullible tourists and cry out: 'Lady, lady, me believe! Gibb it plenty Bibil!'[6]

19 Cairo: the Englishman's Playground

For Cairo Society the golden epoch must have been the later eighties and the nineties. The genius of Lord Cromer had established peace, progress and prosperity. British influence dominated, but had not yet learned to domineer. The social standards and conventions were Continental, on the French model with a faint tinge of the Levant; not yet cosmopolitan.
(Ronald Storrs: *Orientations*, 1937)

Egyptian writers, from the time of the British occupation onwards, were bitterly to satirize the privileged status of the British. Writing at the time of the Arab revolt in 1882, the Cairo newspaper lampoonist Abdullah al-Nadim described a burglar climbing down from a window with his takings. A policeman shouted, asking who he was.

'A *khawaja* [foreigner],' the thief replied.

'Oh, forgive me,' replied the policeman, 'I thought you were an Egyptian.'

Egyptians saw themselves as quite equal to the British, and their exclusion from the elegant lifestyle of the new Cairo was a source of profound humiliation. The Sultan Husayn Kamil told a newspaper in 1906: 'This conservative people is a people of progress. I have followed its development day by day, surprised by the prodigious facility wherewith it assimilates itself to European culture. I have seen in our factories the most intricate machines handled by Egyptians.'

One of the great anglophiles within the Khedival family from the turn of the century was the beautiful Princess Nazli Fazil, the daughter of a Russian mother and of Prince Mustafa Fazil, who was a half-brother of the Khedive Ismail. She spoke perfect Arabic, Turkish, French and English, and reasonable German and Italian. She was morally in a league of her own within her family, although she was no prude, and one of her longest love affairs was said to have been with Zaghloul Pasha, the Egyptian nationalist leader who ran her legal affairs before joining and leading the nationalist cause. According to Lord Lloyd, British High Commissioner from 1925 to 1929, it was at her instigation that Zaghloul learnt French, without which he may never have been able to embark on a political career. Nazli's first marriage was to Khalil Sherif Pasha, the Turkish Minister of Foreign Affairs. She probably acquired her love for the English in Constantinople where the British Ambassador, Sir Henry Layard, had treated her with the love of a father. After Sherif Pasha's death she went to Egypt, where she lived in a large palace behind the Abdin Palace, and married a Tunisian called Si Khalil, with whom she remained happily until her own death in 1913.

Brilliantly intellectual and a socialite throughout her life, she became acquainted with Kitchener, and built up close friendships with Englishmen such as Ronald Storrs, then his secretary. In many ways she remained Turkish in outlook, but with the added sophistication of a European social education. She was immensely well read and would discourse in depth on countries as distant as Japan. She opened a salon in her palace for statesmen, politicians, writers, journalists and intellectuals, both Egyptian and European, although no Egyptian women ever attended it. The first such salon for women was opened by Eugénie Le Brun in the 1890s. Later, May Ziyada, the Lebanese writer and poet, opened her extremely popular literary salon in Cairo, although this too attracted mostly men.

Princess Nazli shared the unfortunate trait, common to the family of Muhammad Ali, of treating things Arab with condescension, and Storrs remembered hearing one of her ministerial visitors casually comment, in her presence, on '*pis arablar*' ('dirty Arabs'). In comparison with her beloved Istanbul, she seems to have regarded Egypt as a land of barbarism. She had no more respect for the new breed of Egyptian than she had for the older generations whom her father had sought to educate and tame. She told de Guerville during one of her merry salon evenings: 'The new generation is not worth the rope to hang itself with. It thinks of nothing but the cut of its clothes, the shape of its boots, or the possession of a European girl for its mistress, who sucks them dry physically and morally, as well as emptying their purses.'[1] She saw the Egyptians as quite unable to govern themselves, assuring him with enthusiasm: 'But, my dear Sir, we are children still, babes in bibs ... Here Lord Cromer does everything, everything. Without him we should have to return to the guardianship of the Powers. Cromer is a great man and Egypt owes him everything, but in the last two years he has become too lenient, too kind.'[2] She inherited the feudal outlook of her family, cherishing its reputation for kindness to its former slaves whom it had treated 'like children', and deplored the abolition of slavery which had broken that feudal relationship and resulted in the creation of thousands of prostitutes.

Storrs was deeply impressed by her personality and by her intellect. Once, when discussing Egyptian politics with Kitchener and Storrs, Kitchener told her that he had failed to understand her point. She replied tartly to the great man: 'You never understand anything.' Kitchener laughed, taking her rebuke with good grace. Nazli came to know most of the statesmen and women of the day, including Queen Victoria, whose Jubilee she had attended in London. In her palace, rich with Egyptian-made Louis XV furniture, she kept pictures of the British royal family as well as those of Cromer and Kitchener. Her palace walls were covered with pages of the illustrated magazines of the day.

Her dinners were famous and were described garishly on the court pages of Cairo's newspapers. She had an amazing capacity for drinking champagne, and was known to drink four bottles one after another without being any the worse for wear. Entertainment in her palace was a curious mixture of Turkish and British, with a servant girl playing the '*ud* (lute) at one moment and a manservant at the piano playing 'God Save the Queen' the next, which she had remembered sung by thousands of voices at the time of Queen Victoria's Jubilee.

A princess who could not have contrasted more strongly with Nazli was Jemileh Hanem, an aunt of the Khedive Abbas II, whom Boyle, perhaps too unkindly, described as 'a most disgusting woman' who looked like an ugly monkey. Although married for

131

society's sake to a Moharrem Pasha, she was a lesbian and he himself had a lover, his Italian groom. One day she insisted that Boyle arbitrate between her and her husband. From this onerous job he heard appalling accounts of her obscenities, which were graphically illustrated in a series of letters she wrote to an Armenian girl with whom she was infatuated.

As Assistant Oriental Secretary to Ronald Storrs after the First World War, Grafftey-Smith also developed friendships with the Turko-Egyptian aristocracy, of whom Princess Iffet was for him the most memorable. She lived in a lovely old palace in Shoubra, where Circassian girls served her and her guests cakes and tea. When he first visited her he demurely averted his eyes, until she, astonished by what she took for lack of interest in young women, encouraged him to look up and admire them. They were slender, bright-eyed sixteen-year-olds in baggy silk pantaloons, babouches on naked feet and scarlet-and-gold boleros over transparent gauze bodices. 'Allow your eyes to enjoy them,' said the jolly woman who acted as an aristocratic marriage broker, importing the damsels from Istanbul to marry them off to suitable spouses after three years' service and 'finishing' with her. Grafftey-Smith had found the effort of averting his gaze from these houris agonizing, noting sadly that 'nothing comparable was visible at the Gezira Sporting Club'.[3]

But the other side of British rule was more practical and far less romantic. 'Khaki, white helmet, Lee-Metford and bayonets, buckles and pipe-clay, swings past Tommy Atkins' was how G.W. Steevens had described his compatriots in Egypt in 1898, complaining already that the lower classes were now filling the positions of the British gentlemanly élite.[4] Like other visitors of the day, Steevens applauded the hi-tech efficiency of the new, British Egypt where even in Port Said and Suez a new telephone system had put that of Turkey into the shade. Already in 1891 William Fullerton had written that 'with the polo, the balls, the races and the riding, Cairo begins to impress itself as an English town'. Cairo had become a fashionable winter resort, attracting 8,000 visitors in every season. The Prince of Wales and Lord Salisbury's sister, Lady Galloway, were regular visitors.

By the end of the century the society cafés of Ezbekiyya read like a list of clubs in Pall Mall. Santini's in the Ezbekiyya Gardens had the air of a Swiss chalet and was the best restaurant in Cairo, while the best place for lunch was the St James's Grill Room, known as 'Jimmy's', in al-Maghreby Street. Allsop's and Bass's ale, as well as newer American drinks, could be had at the Savoy Buffet, the New Bar and the Sphinx, while those who sought a gayer ambience could drink in Ezbekiyya Street with its then forbidden dancing Ghawazee girls or else at the Grand Café Egyptien, also in Ezbekiyya, with its band of Bohemian girls. The aristocratic Turf Club stood in al-Maghreby Street, while the Khedival Club stood in nearby al-Manakh Street. Only the most aristocratic Egyptians were to be seen in Ezbekiyya. The Egyptian writer Muhammad Umar was once surrounded during the Ezbekiyya carnival by a group of 'bright young things' in fancy dress. At first he thought they were Syrians, but then realized that they were the sons of pashas aping the decadent ways of Europe.

The Turf Club, the Shepheard's Hotel, the Khedival Sporting Club – these were the pivots of Britain's effective rule in Egypt. Life's pleasures were cheap for the British at the beginning of the century. You could sit and drink coffee and eat sickly sweets and cakes at Groppi's or, by 1919, see the latest American films at the Metro or the Miami cinemas. In the 1920s Lord Edward Cecil divided British society neatly into sets.

> There is the swagger military set; there is the smug military set. There is the Egyptian army set; there is the smart official set; there is the smug official set. There is the smart professional set; there is the smug professional set, and so on. You may move in two or even several of those sets, but you belong to one.[5]

At the turn of the century the *Sphinx*, an illustrated social magazine, was founded by an American, David Garrick Long-worth. The *Sphinx* was a mixture of the *Tatler* and today's British magazine *Private Eye* and didn't miss an ounce of Cairene gossip. 'Fancy,' it wrote unkindly in one edition, 'Mr and Mrs Shepheard [of Shepheard's Hotel] are staying at the Savoy.' Longworth founded the Sphinx Bar near to the Shepheard's Hotel, and it was in this bar that most of the journal's tittle-tattle was picked up. The *Sphinx* loved sniping at the tourists, alluding on 30 November

1892 to 'the display of English vulgarity, the ladies in their dowdy tourist get-up, with clumsy shoes and yellow veils'.

The Turf Club, formerly the British Agency, stood beside the Sephardi Synagogue. Storrs, who arrived in Cairo in 1906, saw it as the 'fenced city of refuge of the higher British community'. The porter was a gloomy Montenegrin, the head waiter a Greek called Socrates but nicknamed Alphonse. The annual subscription to the club was £7 and a bedroom cost £5 a month with meals for £8 extra. Lord Edward Cecil described it as a 'pot house' and a 'bar' and believed that 'more harm is done in the hall of the Turf Club than in all the other rooms occupied by Englishmen in Cairo'. Scandals were merrily exchanged over drinks. 'It it quite marvellous what stories can be started and believed in Cairo.'[6] Cecil remembered how he and his friends had treated an American gentleman with great respect, believing his tale that he had burnt his entire family to death in his American country house. When it transpired that the man had merely saved his mother from being drowned in a Dutch canal, they treated him 'henceforth with indulgent contempt'. Grafftey-Smith relates the joke circulating in the club about the English member who decided to hide from his mother the fact that he was employed in the Ministry of Public Instruction because, for some perverse reason, he wanted her to believe that he played a piano in a Cairo brothel.

The Khedival Club in neighbouring al-Manakh Street was founded during the early 1870s, under the chairmanship of the British Consul-General, in a group of buildings erected by the Duke of Sutherland. It was Cairo's answer to London's Reform and Travellers' Clubs, and offered reading-rooms that matched the clubs of Pall Mall, as well as excellent billiard-rooms. 'Cayenne' was a popular game although gambling was forbidden at the club. Prince (later) King Fouad was almost murdered in the Khedival Club in 1897. The brother of his wife, Ahmed Saif al-Din, and Prince Ibrahim, lived on stipends of £50,000 a year in a palace beside the British Residency. Their favourite game was to race about taking pot shots at each other with revolvers. Saif al-Din was deeply jealous of Fouad, as he was in love with Fouad's wife who was also his own sister. One day Prince Saif al-Din entered the Khedival Club where Fouad was reading, and began shooting at him, chasing him round and round the room. Two bullets entered the body of the future King, but luckily he survived and Saif al-Din was arrested and sent to the Gezira convict prison.

As the British put down roots, Cairo's hotel registers began to read like pages from Burke's Peerage. On 28 January 1912, the Duke of Westminster and members of his polo team were staying at the Gezira Palace; Lord Aldenham and Lady Victoria Manners were staying at the Semiramis; and Prince Aversperg, the Countess of Albemarle and Lady Elizabeth Keppel were staying at the Continental-Savoy. On 14 February Mrs Harry McCalmont issued invitations for an 'Arabian Nights' ball to be held at the Gezira Casino (in the Gezira Palace).

The 150-acre Gezira Sporting Club was part of the botanical gardens laid out for Ismail by a French landscape gardener, Delchevalerie, and its grounds were presented by the Khedive Tewfik in 1882. The club was founded in that year by Captain Seton-Karr of the Gordon Highlanders with the Khedive's permission. By 1888 golf was the fashionable game, and the golf club numbered among its members erstwhile devotees of tennis and other games. By the 1920s the view took the eye through palm trees and Cairo's pretty white houses across the Nile and towards the Citadel and the Mokattam Hills, although the blackest smoke cloud poured from a factory chimney stack in the middle.

Election was very competitive for foreigners, and almost impossible for Egyptians who were barely welcome at all. Ronald Storrs discovered this to his cost when he took a future Egyptian prime minister to play tennis there in 1904. The first Egyptian admitted to the club was Saif Allah al-Yusri, a cavalry officer and polo-player who was later sent as Ambassador to Washington. By 1909 the Gezira Club had thirteen tennis courts, eight croquet grounds, four polo grounds, hockey, cricket and football grounds, six squash courts, a twelve-hole (soon increased to fifteen-hole) golf links, courses for races and steeplechases and a training track. There were 750 members. A border of tumbling jacaranda surrounded the golf course, prompting Lord Lloyd to joke: 'When I see those jacarandas in bloom, I know it's time to send for a battleship!'

The Winter Race Meetings were the principal event of the year, rivalling in all but size those of England's Epsom and Newmarket. By the 1920s the race days became mini-Ascots with pre-race champagne lunch parties, laughing crowds of men in boaters and elegant women in white cotton dresses and straw summer hats, all murmuring racing tips to each other direct from the stables. The *suffragis* would bring cold beer and fat, foie gras sandwiches to where you sat on wicker chairs under the trees.

The Gezira Club was a lure for romance, and as the humorous writer who wrote in the 1930s under the pseudonym Rameses mused, the cool breezes one felt at the club in autumn were not the north-west wind, but the return of a wife from England who has just been introduced by her frantic husband to the girl who has been 'darning his socks' all summer.

In the early days Lord Cromer 'governed' from the rambling house in Maghreby Street that later became the Turf Club. Soon, however, the Residency was built in Qasr al-Doubbara in Garden City, with gardens that stretched down to the Nile. Contemporaries noted that Cromer had been too involved in state affairs to notice that the building had been set the wrong way round for the prevailing winds. Under Kitchener a ballroom was added to the Residency's north wing. State dinner parties were regularly given at the Residency, and guests would attend in white tie and covered with as many medals as they could lay their hands on. Protocol would be a headache, with officials straining to place British and Egyptian officials in the correct order at table. 'At every dinner party,' wrote Rameses, 'at least fifty per cent of the guests are under the impression that they have been deliberately affronted.'

Garden City had its aristocratic quarter where the Residency, the new Semiramis Hotel, and the splendid new pleasure domes of the great 'resident' British families – the Rolos, the Casdaglises and the Hararises – stood. On the banks of the Nile beside the Semiramis stood the great stone palace of the Khedive's mother. After Garden City came the elegant suburbs of Maadi and Heliopolis laid out in dream patterns, the first like a perfect Raj hill station with all the fantasies of English cottage life, the second as a sort of mad fairyland. In 1900, the five-mile drive from Cairo to Heliopolis was shaded by plane trees and sycamores and ended in broad meadows and cornfields where flocks of ibis hovered. Responding to British encouragement to build on desert land, in 1906 a Belgian company called the Cairo Electric Railways and the Heliopolis Oasis Company began to develop land close to the Greek ruins of Heliopolis (the 'City of the Sun'). Although the building of the new city was headed by the British Sir Reginald Oakes, it was inspired by the Belgian Baron Empain, who matched the elaborate fairytale palaces, towers, arches and balconies of his fantastic new city with a palace he built himself in the style of the Cambodian Ankor Watt temple (or, as some say, of a Saivite temple in South India). This palace still stands today, derelict but intact, on the road from Cairo Airport. On a visit to Heliopolis shortly before the First World War, a US financer commented, awestruck: 'It's splendid, but the shareholders should be in padded cells and the administrators in prison.'

During the years leading up to the First World War, British society in Cairo was fairly informal. The manners of the day were French or Levantine rather than English. Lord Cromer would happily ride to work on a donkey, as would lesser mortals, such as Bimbashi McPherson, who would be seen 'ambling about Cairo on a white mule lost in thought and looking like God the Father'. Entertainment was as much in private villas, those low white-washed villas, a few of which can still be seen in Zamalek, as in the clubs and hotels.

However, as Britian's 'veiled protectorate' matured to virtual colonial status, the early informality waned and the social mixing of the British and the Egyptians decreased. Life became more efficient but less pleasurable. A new caste of lesser British officials appeared and this, combined with the spawning of clubs, English-style sporting activities, and the mass tourist market pioneered by Thomas Cook, took the spice from the old, aristocratic hedonism. The relationship between British and Egyptians was beginning to resemble that of British and Indians under the Raj. The wives of British officials took as little interest in developing contacts with Egyptian or Turkish ladies as the memsahibs did in India. The hard-working new-style English bureaucrat had virtually no contact with his Egyptian counterpart outside office hours, which were 8 a.m. to 1 p.m. Lord Milner saw the devastating riots of 1919 as a reflection of decreasing British dynamism. He saw the British indulging themselves in romanticism in their Egyptian enclaves of the Gezira Club and the Turf Club, where they would spend whole afternoons gossiping and playing golf. English society was dominated by the hotel balls when Lord Edward Cecil served in Cairo, first in the army and then in the Egyptian government service. The smartest, he noted, were held at the Savoy and Semiramis, followed by the 'Ghezira, Shepheard's and Heliopolis, and last of all the Continental, which is much frequented by the *jeunesse dorée* of Pashadom'. Each hotel gave a weekly ball on a different night of the week so that revellers could go out dancing for six nights out of seven for the five-month season. 'We all, or almost all of us dance, and we go on dancing up to any age. Grandmothers and gentlemen with grey hair and a lower chest measurement of fifty inches hop round gravely with the rest.'[7]

In the 1920s and 1930s the Wafdist pashas belonged to the Saadist Club, an Italianate Moorish structure where, writes Magdi Wahba, 'argument, loud rhetoric, and no less loud backgammon reigned supreme'.[8] All the others belonged, 'or tried to belong', to the Muhammad Ali Club in Sulaiman Pasha Street, which aimed to combine the formality of London's St James's Club with the highbrowness of the Paris *Interallie*. According to Wahba, the cuisine at the Muhammad Ali Club was so good that the club's Italian chef, Costi, was spared the misery of a concentration camp during the Second World War. The diplomat and traveller Fitzroy Maclean remembered dining under the stairs of the club during the war under the supervision of Costi, whom he described as 'a truly great *maître d'hôtel*', and enjoying all the foods he had dreamt about during hungry days at the front. He was surrounded by Egyptian pashas, Greek millionaires, exiled princes, high-ranking British officers and cosmopolitan beauties. It was a club where princes, pashas, rich Jews and English aristocrats mingled 'in an environment of hushed splendour'. King Fouad frequently visited it, although his son Farouk, a lover of fast cars, preferred the Royal Automobile Club where his beloved poker was played for very high stakes. When, during the 1946 riots, students tried to burn down the Victoria Club in Sulaiman Pasha Street, members of the Muhammad Ali Club across the street are said to have stood on balconies and cynically applauded.

By the beginning of the century, huge Harrods-style department stores like Hanau, Sednawi and Cirucel had sprung up selling every kind of lingerie. High-class British outfitters were already spawning, and the very word 'British' had become the hallmark of quality. The British-owned 'Ariston' Aerated Water Factory in Cairo – 'purveyors to Lord Cromer and the Leading Residents in Egypt' – warned in advertisements against 'so many unscrupulous firms abroad [who] as a bait to secure custom, use the style "British", when enquiry would discover that neither is the Proprietorship, nor anything concerning the business, of British origin . . .'

Opposite the Café Egyptien in Ezbekiyya, in the Grand Rue de Pera and close to Thomas Cook's offices, stood the Old England Outfitters, while in nearby al-Manakh Street, just off Adly Street, John Collacott, the 'military and mufti' tailor, advertised himself as agent for Stohwasser patent puttee leggings. Davies Bryan and Co., in al-Maghreby Street, meanwhile, specialized in 'helmets, Terai hats, puggarees, mosquito nets and cholera belts'.

By the 1930s Rameses was making light of British attitudes and the growing bureaucratic caste:

> The population of the country is fourteen millions, and consists of seven million *fellahs* or cultivators and seven million Government officials. It is hoped to get this straightened out shortly, and the rulers of the country are striving for an ideal state of affairs where there will only be one million *fellahs* and thirteen million officials. By 1950 it is hoped that the *fellah* will have been completely eliminated, and instead there will be a united nation of black-coated officials and nothing else.[9]

Magdi Wahba's earliest memories of the British in Cairo during the 1930s were parades such as the searchlight tattoo on the polo grounds of the Gezira Club in honour of Edward, Prince of Wales; air shows at Almaza Airport on Armistice Day, 'with poppies raining from the skies'; and church parades in Garden City. He also remembered the changing of the guard outside the Residency when the High Commissioner's black Rolls-Royce slowly emerged through the wrought-iron gates with the monogram of Victoria Regina picked out in gold. On either side of the car moved a detachment of the King's Horse. The high moment of the year was the King's birthday, when the High Commissioner held his reception in the Residency's Regency Ballroom. On the first day of the three-day event came the judges, the ministerial advisers, the knighted residents, the Anglican clergy, visiting celebrities and the diplomatic staff; on the second the irrigation inspectors, the agricultural experts and the higher ranks of the police force; and on the third teachers and university staff. Among these were writers such as Robert Graves, who briefly occupied the post of Professor of English at Cairo University. The British community was somewhat alarmed by the appearance of a certain twenty-four-year-old as lecturer in English, a man who scorned expatriate society and was considered a beatnik ahead of his time. 'We thought,' wrote Grafftey-Smith, 'a spell in Moscow might be good for him – and it was! Today, when Malcolm Muggeridge comes on the screen, I sit at his feet.'[10]

20 Cairo's Sweet-scented Odalisques

> From persons of the best education, expressions are often heard
> so obscene as only to be fit for a brothel; and things are named,
> and subjects talked of, by the most genteel women, without any
> idea of their being indecorous, in the hearing of men, that many
> prostitutes in our country would probably abstain from
> mentioning.
>
> (E.W. Lane: *The Modern Egyptians*)

While the French, almost without exception, appear to have
revelled in the sweetness of Egyptian womanhood, the British
reaction to it was a curious mixture of fascination and revulsion.
Most Egyptian women were not safe, Lane assures us, unless they
were 'under lock and key'. He saw them as being the 'most
licentious in their feelings of all females who lay any claim to be
considered as members of a civilized nation'.[1]

Lane was speaking of ordinary women, while British writers
took a highly moral if hypocrital tone towards the Cairo fleshpots
frequented by the British. A guidebook of the period described in
1901 the notorious fish market behind the Gezira Palace as 'a most
remarkable and revolting sight ... inhabited by the lowest of the
low ... You can hardly call them men and women, they have sunk
to such depravity.' It then goes on to describe men in cafés drunk
with hashish, 'a sort of opium', and women who 'stand or lie about
the dirty, narrow streets, openly plying their horrible trade'. At
eleven the prostitutes would go inside and hide behind iron bars,
inviting clients into their 'dark dens'. They are 'degraded as they
are ugly. It is a wonder,' he adds pompously, 'that such a scene is
possible in a country under British rule.'[2] De Guerville was equally

fascinated, but also somewhat moved by the fish market where he saw beautiful Nubian girls 'with heads and breasts now thrown back, now thrown forwards to within a hand's breadth of my face, their flesh quivering, the scent of their bodies in the air, their harsh cries joined to the wild music. I was completely overcome . . .' Propriety forced him to add, however: 'As to the houses where one can witness incredible orgies, I pass them by in silence, simply remarking that they would not exist a day were it not for the tourists who support them.'[3]

One wonders how writers of such moral standards ever knew what went on in places which clearly played an important role in British life in Egypt. The French had shown no such conflict of conscience. In the 1840s Gustave Flaubert had frequented such houses where he had revelled in girls' flesh 'as hard as bronze'. Staying at the Hotel d'Orient, he had written merrily to his friend Louis Bouilhet: 'Tomorrow we are to have a party on the river, with several whores dancing to the sound of darabukehs and castanets, their hair spangled with gold piastres.' He frequented a brothel behind the hotel where a whore sat 'on the matting: firm flesh, bronze arse, shaven cunt, dry though fatty'.[4] Flaubert revelled in the sordid primitivism he managed to discover wherever he and Maxime du Camp travelled in Egypt.

Gerard de Nerval took a gentler, more aesthetic view of the women he found there. His first experience was disarming. He was mesmerized by the beautiful young Ghawazee girls he saw, their eyes blackened with kohl, until he suddenly noticed the hint of a beard on one of them. The romantic image quickly collapsed as he noted to his disgust that these were all men! Murray, who appears not to have realized that they were sometimes *khawals* (transvestites), cautioned his lady tourists against the Ghawazee girls: 'Many travellers have raved about the beauty of these Ghawazee and the gracefulness of their dance; but the real truth is that nine-tenths of them are ugly and repulsive and their dance inelegant when kept within the bounds of outward decency and disgusting when allowed full swing.'[5]

But de Nerval (best known in Paris for his habit of taking his pet lobster out for walks in the Champs Elysées on a leash of scarlet ribbon) soon came to recognize genuine women, one of whom was an Ethiopian slave girl whom he was offered for £10 with an eight-day guarantee. After careful study he finally selected a Javanese girl. The girls were somewhat disdainful when he approached them in his black gloves, failing to understand how a man with a white face could possibly have black hands. When he briskly took off his golves to explain politely, they leapt back in horror, crying: '*Bismillahi! Enta effrit? Enta shaytan?*' ('In the name of God, are you a spirit? Are you a devil?') Having never seen gloves, they were convinced that he had peeled the black flesh off his hands.[6]

Not all foreigners in Egypt were so charmed by its women. De Guerville met a European physician of twenty-five years' standing in Cairo who explained that whereas Egyptian doctors were obliged to visit women patients in the company of eunuchs, foreign physicians could make their visits quite alone. He explained:

> You see, the temptation is nil. The Egyptian woman as we see her, without her garments, is to us Europeans far from attractive. There is not one good-looking one in a thousand, and, besides, they live in a state of incredible filth. I do not remember having seen the bed of a single woman which did not swarm with vermin.[7]

When de Guerville passed this anecdote on to the widow of one of the most brilliant members of the Khedive Tewfiq's social circle, the Comtessa della Sala, she replied, 'It is a horrible calumny. All the young women I know, princesses or otherwise, are daintiness and refinement personified. They take the greatest care of their persons.'[8] The daughter of the Russian Prince Gagarin, and a clever, witty socialite who was to fascinate Ronald Storrs, the Comtessa knew as much about Egyptian women as any foreigner in Egypt.

When Muhammad Ali became Wali of Egypt, Cairo was a city of narrow lanes. The corbelled balconies of dwellings almost touched each other above, as they had in old, pre-Haussmann Paris. Here, behind windows like bird-cages of delicate *mashrabiya*, the plump, veiled prostitutes ate sweets and cakes and drank from tall glasses of mulberry and liquorice sherbet. Or else they sat, big-breasted mother-goddesses with eyes thickly lined with black or blue kohl, before huge, murmuring *narguileh* pipes, and drank tiny cups of coffee flavoured with cardamom and scented with smoking ambergris. Cairo's Ghawazee girls and *almehs* were on a higher level of society than the prostitutes, although they did not, perhaps, enjoy the status of geisha girls in Japan or the courtesans of Moghul India. Some European travellers found their 'screeching' voices ugly. The Ghawazee girls danced bare-breasted in the streets, using extravagant movements of their arms and revealing brightly hennaed hands. The British writer Sir Francis Henniker noted the erotic movement of their loins, and described them gaily as 'heaven in the eye, and in every gesture not dignity but love'. Their husbands, whom they often dominated and perhaps humiliated, sometimes acted as their musicians or even as their servants. However, when Burckhardt visited Cairo he noted that the Ghawazee girls were not that numerous; 'in a city where among women of every rank chastity is so scarce as Cairo, it could not be expected that prostitution should survive'.[9]

The Ghawazee girls in their *shintians* (billowing trousers) were accompanied by musicians of the same tribe, says Lane, who played the *kemengeh* or the *rabab* while an old woman would play the *tar*. Both *shintian* and *tobe* (long, wide-sleeved gown) were made from semi-transparent, coloured gauze, open almost halfway down the front. 'To extinguish the least spark of modesty which they may yet sometimes affect to retain, they are plentifully supplied with brandy or some other intoxicating liquor. The scenes which ensue cannot be described.'[10] Disapproving as he was, Lane regarded the Ghawazee girls as the most beautiful women in Egypt.

Protest by the *'ulema* (clergy) in 1834 had persuaded Muhammad Ali to ban prostitution and even the *almehs* in Cairo, an act that may well have led to a blurring of the distinction between pure prostitutes and accomplished courtesans. Flaubert's Kuchuk Hanem was clearly one of these latter. She sang and danced and recited like one of the *awalim* of old. Such courtesans responded to the ban with despair, and young men, who as transvestite dancers were known as *khawals*, soon replaced the Ghawazees. Under the reigns of Said and Ismail, however, prostitution returned openly to the streets of Cairo, and in 1866 a tax was imposed on all 'dancing girls'. It was suggested that by instituting the tax, and thereby legalizing prostitution, Ismail had earned the title of

'Pimp Pasha'. The most notorious area under Ismail and under the British was the Wijh al-Birka (the 'Face of the Lake'), an extension of the Wasaah district of which Russell Pasha gives a chilling picture: 'Painted harlots sitting like beasts of prey behind the iron grilles of their ground-floor brothels, while a noisy crowd of low-class natives, interspersed with soldiers in uniform and sight-seeing tourists, made their way along the narrow lanes.'[11]

Until 1916, these wretched women were subject to the terrifying control of the self-proclaimed 'king' of Wasaah, 'Shaikh' Ibrahim al-Gharbi. Russell describes him sitting cross-legged every evening on a bench outside one of his houses in Sharia 'abd al-Khaliq.

Dressed as a woman and veiled in white, this repulsive pervert sat like a silent, ebony idol, occasionally holding out a bejewelled hand to be kissed by some passing admirer, or giving a silent order to one of his attendant servants. This man had an amazing power in the country, his influence extended not only into the world of prostitution, but was also felt in the sphere of politics and high society. The buying and selling of women for the trade both in Cairo and the provinces was entirely in al-Gharbi's hands and no decision of his as to price was ever questioned.[12]

The crowded lanes of the Wasaah, where Nubian and Sudanese women sold themselves for a shilling, reminded Russell of a zoo. During the First World War the Australian and New Zealand Anzac troops were the Shaikh's main clients, and the influence of these battle-scarred men was to lead to bouts of violence. On one of the worst of such nights, mock period sofas were set alight, pianos crashed through windows, and Egyptians and Australians, armed with axehandles, took up their battle positions all around the district. These drunken brawls were not the only dangers, nor were they the worst. Grafftey-Smith was horrified by the scars of syphilis on the arms of the Anzac troops in Cairo on leave from Palestine.

The Wijh al-Birka dated from the time when Ezbekiyya was still a lake, before it was drained by Ibrahim. An officially licensed prostitute quarter by the time of Tewfiq, it housed both Egyptian women and European women of all races except the British, who were forbidden by the British consular authority to practise prostitution in Egypt. While the Wasaah itself housed the lowest class of prostitutes living in squalid one-room shacks, other parts of the Wijh al-Birka housed women of a slightly higher caste who, as Russell noted, 'had no further use for Marseilles, and who would eventually be passed on to the Bombay and Far East markets'.

When Russell's boss, Harvey Pasha, decided unequivocally to track down al-Gharbi and intern him with hundreds of other pimps at the Hilmiya internment camp, Russell was astonished by his boss's courage in confronting this king of the underworld. 'Half an hour later an officer arrived, leading by the hand what looked like a huge negress, clad in white satin, her golden anklets and bracelets clinking as she minced down the corridor.' Harvey 'blew up like a landmine, demanding what the hell everyone meant by bringing that disgusting patchouli-scented sodomite into his presence, and with a bellow of rage sent him below to be stripped of his female finery, put into handcuffs and thrown into the Hilmiya internment camp among his youthful imitators'.[13]

During the two world wars, British soldiers enjoyed the pleasures of the brothels in Alexandria's Seven Sisters Street. One was apparently called 'Combakir', not as one might imagine a Turkish word, but the soldiers' interpretation of the last seductive call of the girls as they left the house: 'When you're in town again, come back 'ere.' In Cairo during the Second World War, British soldiers were housed in one of Ismail's palaces which had been converted into the Qasr al-Nil Barracks where the Hilton stands today. It was notorious among Allied troops as the most bug-ridden barracks in the world. Peering out of its windows at the great bronze lions that still stand on Qasr al-Nil (now Tahrir) Bridge, the soldiers would joke that the lions roared each time a virgin passed by. But, they would add, this hadn't happened for years.

During the Second World War the British Army supplied its troops with an Arabic phrase book. These phrases under the chapter 'In Azbacia' are not without a tragic charm:

British soldier: What is your name?
Girl: My name is Hanem
BS: You are pretty and gentle
BS: I love you so much
G: I love you, too, Sir
BS: You are a liar
BS: You are cunning
BS: You love me for my money
BS: Your cheek is rosy
BS: Let me kiss you for half a millim

While Tommy Atkins frequented the brothels, and holier-than-thou writers decried them, the British authorities tried to stamp them out. One of the *causes célèbres* that the gung-ho Bimbashi McPherson, Russell Pasha's Mamur Zapt (Secret Police Chief), had to unravel was that of the 'beautiful she-devil, Firdus'. An Australian sergeant was the lover of a woman called Firdus, who was said to be the most beautiful woman in Egypt. The sergeant and Firdus would assault and rob the clients of a certain brothel. In a letter to his brother Ja, McPherson described in vivid detail the lengths to which he went to obtain evidence against the sergeant and the 'she-devil'. Dressed as important Turkish civilians, he and his companion visited her residence, no. 14 al-Genina Street. He recognized Firdus by her beauty, and something 'vampire-like in the intense colour of her lips and cheeks'.[14] She lay back in a splendid bed whose covers seemed like cloth of gold. Suspecting him to be a policeman, she offered him lemonade, but the sound of popping champagne bottles and ribald laughter in the next room told him another story and he departed. Delighting in thriller theatricals, McPherson dressed up as an American Jew, returned by night and took up his post in a room in the Eden Palace Hotel on the north side of the Ezbekiyya Gardens, which looked directly into the rooms of Firdus. On his third night of watching there was a row in her salon over a client who had underpaid her, followed by the smashing of glasses and cries of 'murder', and a body came hurtling into the street below. Considering this nothing but 'a side issue', he continued to wait in order to obtain evidence against the Australian whom he saw standing on the balcony 'with the wild terror of a hunted animal in his eyes'. Eventually he saw Firdus

147

undressing him and drawing him into bed, noting with the delicacy of writers of the time, 'they neglected to draw the curtains, but I must'.

Arraigned before the Anzac GOC, Firdus came robed in fine silk with a black veil of shame, and the 'modest quiet air of a vestal virgin'. At the appropriate moment she removed her veil and 'revealed tears of injured innocence flowing from the most lovely eyes one could imagine'. Firdus was banished to Tanta where she was eventually murdered by suffocation in 1921.[15]

A year after McPherson first arrived as a teacher in Cairo in 1902, he noted with relish the social mores of both European lady visitors to Cairo and their Egyptian counterparts. He wondered in a letter to his brother whether the visitors were attracted by the 'antiquities' or 'iniquities' of the city, pointing out that Egyptian ladies preferred European youths to Arabs, and that the local pimps did a good trade in supplying these. A taste for Arab youths was similarly more common among European women than was generally supposed.

21   The Age of the Great Hotels

While Europe's sensualists were fulfilling their fantasies in the haunts of Cairo's underworld, glitzy visitors from Europe's high society were 'being seen' on the terraces of Cairo's great hotels. Large and beautifully furnished, these were the centre of the season for Edwardian tourists, combining the comforts of the West with the luxury of the East. British visitors would compare the Shepheard's with London's Savoy and the Continental with London's Albermarle. One of the first of these great hotels was the Hotel du Nil, later the Bristol, north-east of the Ezbekiyya Gardens. Founded in 1836, it became the favourite haunt of Gustave Flaubert and Maxime du Camp when they made their notorious visit. The entrance of the hotel was through a Moorish horseshoe arch; its back gardens were tropical with orange trees and banana trees and a magnificent wrought-iron kiosk not unlike that of the Gezira Palace or the Salamlik; and the hotel advertized itself as the only hotel in Cairo with an oriental veranda. It was strongly recommended to English travellers, and proudly boasted a 300-foot tower! Its omnibus would meet all trains, and its dragomans would meet steamers at Alexandria.

The Shepheard's Hotel, just off Ezbekiyya on the corner of Alfi Bey and Ibrahim Pasha Streets, was virtually a club in itself, and proudly advertised itself as 'Patronized by Imperial and Royal Families'. On its notice boards would be advertised *dahabiyyas* for hire, meetings at the Turf Club, forthcoming gymkhanas, charity bazaars at the English Agency or fancy-dress balls at the Continental Hotel. The Shepheard's was to become the fulcrum of Cairo life and visitors abandoned their guidebooks as they entered for all of life was there. If you were unlucky, your room would overlook the stable yard at the back, but if you were lucky or knew its charming manager, Mr Baehler, you would be given a room overlooking the sunny gardens where pelicans roamed among the tall palm trees.

On the crowded piazza in front of the hotel, which had all the imagery of a Renoir social view of Parisian high life, noblemen from all over Europe rubbed shoulders with rich London or Marseilles shopkeepers. On arrival at the Shepheard's you would be greeted by a dragoman in his glittering costume embroidered with silver thread, competing for your service. Once you had chosen him he would become something of a college 'scout'. He would sell you antiques, take you snipe shooting at weekends or take you by night to where the wild dervishes whirled and dancers and singers celebrated a wedding or a *moulid* (birthday of a holy man).

When Samuel Shepheard from Northumberland took over the hotel in 1845 he called it the New British Hotel but it and the three hotels which replaced it one after another have always been known as the Shepheard's. The original hotel was built on the site of the Mamluk palace which had been the headquarters of Napoleon's General Kléber. Soon Cairene society was to be glancing up at the Shepheard's flag mast to see which crowned head was visiting. Conversations of state took place in its famous Long Bar.

Sam Shepheard was something of an adventurer and in a letter to his cousins in England in 1851 he described an incident when he had nearly 'been murdered, i.e. - killt outright'. Drinking heavily as they sailed up the Nile, Shepheard and his friends left the boat and somehow found themselves in the seraglio of one of the pashas. Instead of feasting their eyes on beautiful women, they were surrounded by a gang of men who glorified in cracking the head of an 'unoffending Christian dog'. Eventually Shepheard was rescued by the Pasha's chief eunuch, who put them in a dungeon for a few hours until the local police arranged for their release.

Shepheard's was a typical rags-to-riches story. He had started his career in Cairo by helping a certain Mr Hill run the 'British Hotel' near Ezbekiyya in 1841. Shepheard was so conscientious that Hill allowed him to take over the running of the hotel four years later. Although Cook's tours were still a thing of the future, commerce between Europe and the East brought increasing numbers of passengers to Egypt, and many stayed at the Shepheard's with its wonderful veranda and 'big stone baths'. The first Shepheard's, a rectangular building with a flat roof, stood near the Rosetti Gardens. Under Abbas, Shepheard obtained permission to build a new Shepheard's in the former royal palace of Princess Zeinab which overlooked the Ezbekiyya. In 1850, Arnold Bromfield wrote to his sister: 'We landed amidst a confused hubbub of camels, donkeys and vociferous and quarrelsome Arabs and found Mr Shepheard, the proprietor of the hotel at which I am staying, ready, with two or three omnibuses, to whirl us away along an excellent road bordered with thriving acacias to his establishment in this magnificent square, the Ezbekiyya, about a mile and half distance from Boulaq.'[1]

Trollope stayed at the Shepheard's in 1858 while writing *Doctor Thorne*. He had been asked by 'the great men at the General Post Office' to go to Egypt to make a treaty with the Pasha for the conveyance of British mails through Egypt by railway. He found nowhere in his early years as 'delightfully mysterious' as 'Grand Cairo' but lamented the fact that the overland route to India meant that it was now inhabited by 'men wearing coats and waistcoats and by women who are without veils; but the English tongue in Egypt finds its centre in Shepheard's Hotel'.[2] Not everyone liked the Shepheard's, however. Mark Twain had once wryly described it as 'the worst on earth except the one I stopped at once in a small town in the United States'.[3] Théophile Gautier, who stayed there during the Canal celebrations, was disappointed too, saying of it: 'From the outside a large, bare and austere building, more like an English barracks than an Eastern caravanserai, and inside like a great monastery with half-lit stairways and bedrooms like monastic cells.'[4] However, he was clearly charmed by the cuisine and the exotic mixture of diners in the restaurant, remarking on:

> . . . the excellent French cuisine, lightly Anglicized, natural enough in a house whose normal clientele is almost entirely English. No Arab dishes were served by a slave of dusky hue, in white turban and rose-coloured robe ... but we did not regret it too much, local colour being more agreeable to the eye than to the palate. The travellers were grouped at table according to their chosen or professional affinities: there was the corner for

151

painters, the corner for savants, the corner for men of letters and reporters, the corner for men of the world and connoisseurs; but all without strict delineation. One paid visits from one corner to another, and over coffee, which some took Turkish and others European, conversation and cigars blended all ranks and countries; one saw German doctors talking aesthetics with French artists and grave mathematicians listening with smiles to journalists' gossip.[5]

From Cairo Gautier wrote regular letters to Princess Mathilde, whom Louis Napoleon had once hoped to marry. 'I am staying at Shepheard's Hotel, Esbekieh Place, Cairo, Egypt, and I need not tell your highness what I hope by giving you this very detailed, largely written and perfectly legible address.'[6] The Princess's reply contained the news that Gautier's close friend Sainte-Beuve had died. But his sorrow was alleviated to some extent by his meeting in the Shepheard's with the charming poet of his Saint-Gratien circle, Primoli. The meeting helped him out of his constant depressions and killed time before the opening of the Canal, to whose inauguration he was an honoured guest. He had indulged in frantic hypochondria in the hotel, nursing his 'poor left hand, immobilized for so long'.[7]

Gwendoline Mostyn wrote to the authoress of a book on the hotel in 1956, pointing out that she was probably the only person living who could remember the Shepheard's Hotel as far back as 1878 when she was a girl of fourteen. In 1891 a new manager, Mr Phillip Zech, had a new building constructed for the hotel overlooking the Ezbekiyya Gardens. The old building which had, in turn, served as a school, the residence of Princess Kamil and a *waqf* (religious endowment) building, was entirely demolished. In 1896 the new premises were acquired by the Egyptian Hotels Corporation, a company formed to amalgamate the Shepheard's with the Gezira Palace Hotel. The Gezira Palace had been sequestrated by the British after Ismail's forced abdication.

For those who only know today's dull, modern building on the Garden City corniche, Zech's new Shepheard's was a hotel in which it was *de rigueur* for any visitor with social aspirations to stay. Around a spacious hall was distributed a reading-room, a drawing-room and a music room. The 'Renaissance-style' dining-room had seating for up to 500 guests. Over eighty of the bedrooms, a guidebook of the period proudly announced, had private bathrooms. But it was the Shepheard's elegant terraces overlooking bustling el-Kamil Street which were to become for many years the social heart of life for the sybaritic visitors from Europe. During the 1940s and 1950s Mansour's jewellery shop in the hotel's main hall was considered one of the finest in the world. King Farouk bought from Mansour's some limestone figures made in 1376 B.C. during the reign of Akhenaton. Mansour was said to have been particular over whom he sold his treasures to and would lower the price for those he felt would value them, and inflate it outrageously for those he felt would not.

An etching of the period shows an elegant Edwardian couple preparing to descend the steps of the Shepheard's. The pretty lady is leaning forward to lift her copious skirts from brushing the steps, and her husband, plump cigar in hand, is leaning courteously towards her, while at the bottom of the steps a stylized and heavily-veiled Egyptian woman stands demurely with a brass urn on her head. Another etching shows a European woman in heavy, black winter dress gazing in wonder down the steps towards snake-charmers and rollicking monkeys. A third etching shows a chaotic crowd of guests in Cairo for the opening of the Suez Canal being surrounded by every kind of importunate street vendor. A fourth shows Stanley's arrival from darkest Africa. Stanley, in army uniform and white solar topee, is being greeted by Mr Zech in a tight black frock-coat, while pretty European women gaze at what is clearly an historic moment.[8] But Stanley wanted to escape from society after three continuous years in darkest Africa. 'To avoid the lounging critics that sat in judgement upon me at Shepheard's Hotel,' he wrote in his autobiography, 'I sought a retired spot, the Villa Victoria, surrounded by a garden, where, out of sight, I might be out of mind.'[9]

Most of the great writers on Egypt have stories to tell about the Shepheard's. When Harry Boyle was first transferred, as Oriental Secretary, to Lord Cromer's service in 1885, he made straight for the Shepheard's accompanied by his Montenegrin servant and a giant sheepdog. The waiters led him to a dimly–lit table in the gardens. Utterly homesick for his last post in Turkey, he tried to drum up a conversation in Turkish with a splendidly dressed

Turkish officer, but the man at once replied in impeccable English. He turned out to be Colonel Fenwick, the Head of Police. Some years later, according to Clare Boyle in her biography of her husband, Harry was sitting on the hotel veranda at a table near that of Sir Thomas Lipton, who had been nagging him for some time over a post for his nephew. By chance an American tourist, who had been trying to sum up Boyle by his shabby clothing, approached him and asked whether he would introduce him to a 'personable young man' and pressed half a crown into his hand. The man had clearly taken Boyle for the hotel pimp, and was seeking to indulge in the 'fashionable' vice. The witty Boyle at once apologized that he was 'off duty' but that the gentleman at the other table was standing in for him. The grateful American approached the magnificently built and well-dressed Lipton with the same, smutty request as Boyle slipped into the shadows from where he could watch the next act of the drama. And drama it was! Lipton went berserk, pounding the wretched tourist to the ground until the *maître d'hôtel* came running to his rescue, and Boyle slipped away delighted. Ronald Storrs tells the same tale in *Orientations*.[10]

In January 1901, the London journal the *Traveller* wrote:

> The scene from the terrace of Shepheard's is a very moving picture. In the height of the season the crowd of hotel visitors, sitting placidly enjoying their coffee under the shady palms and verandas, is itself a sight; the 'beauty and fashion' of travelling Americans, Britishers, Germans, Russians, are assorted with Japanese, Indians, Australians, South Africans – well-to-do, well-dressed and handsome specimens of what we call civilization.

In a series of delightful watercolour cartoons published in 1908 called *The Light Side of Egypt*, Lance Thackery portrayed the dandy in double-breasted suit, swagger stick, green bow tie and green velvet hat, simpering down the steps of the Shepheard's terrace. At the bottom stand the 'vultures', the dragomans in their red *tarboushes* rubbing their hands as they embark on their favourite hobby – collecting baksheesh. 'He [the dragoman] is always prepared to like you and, if you are spending money, he gets to love you ... Oh, he is a cheerful humbug is the dragoman.' 'Romeo and Juliet' is a picture of a dandy in white suit and shoes, and green hat and tie, smoking as he gazes at a pretty English woman in white dress and white, veiled hat reading a romance on the terrace. Behind the railings the dragomans are congregated, waiting for their spoils. The arrival of some new beauty, Thackery explains, sends a flutter through the hearts of the male visitors, and when she boards her train and breaks away from the 'twisted heart-strings of her admirers, a sigh of relief goes up from the mothers of rival daughters, a groan or two from the bent heart of some ancient warrior, and the pulse of the Turf Club drops to normal'.[11]

In 1903, despite chronic ill health, Theodor Herzl, the founder of World Zionism, visited Cairo to pút his case for a Jewish homeland in Palestine to Lord Cromer and the Egyptian Government headed by Butros Ghali. He stayed at the Shepheard's. Peering at the 'masked ball' of Cairo from the famous veranda he spoke with the melancholy of the sick man he was:

> You sit on the terrace with a fly whisk and let things come to you, pass you. Colours and cries. A hundred different pro-positions from guides and traders. The childishness, the squalour of the East. But in its midst a few stern, watchful, first-class policemen. A platoon of Highlanders march past in tartan trousers, jaunty young men – the 'Occupation'. Other English gentlemen, officers, wear the *tarboush*, which is higher than the Turkish fez. It is wonderful how they know how to keep order, without brutality, without tropical frenzy.[12]

Although he admired the British as the first occupiers not to oppress the Egyptians, he found Lord Cromer 'the most disagree-able Englishman I have ever faced'.

By the time of the First World War, the Shepheard's had taken on a mythical aura. In a letter to Lord Lloyd, T.E. Lawrence wrote: 'My statement, when they offered me the succession to Allenby, was that I'd shut up the Residency, except as offices, take a room at the Shepheard's and ride about Cairo and the Delta on my motorbike; and yet "run" the Government from underneath.'[13] After the horrific evacuation of the Dardenelles, there were said to have been some 200 Allied generals staying at the Shepheard's.

After the war, many of those who attended the 1921 Cairo Conference headed by Winston Churchill, the founder of the Jordanian Arab Legion, Peake Pasha, for one, stayed at the Shepheard's. Evelyn Waugh was so intrigued by the hotel when he visited it in the 1930s on his honeymoon, that he transferred it to London's Dover Street as the haunt of his 'bright young things' in *Vile Bodies*. 'There is a good deal too much furniture at the Shepheard's,' he writes of his Mayfair Shepheard's, 'some of it rare, some of it hideous beyond description; there is plenty of red plush and red morocco and innumerable wedding presents of the 'eighties . . .'[14]

During the Second World War, the Shepheard's became the centre of political intrigue. A doll's house mock-up of the Shepheard's at the military museum at El Alamein is captioned: 'The Shepheard's Hotel was a meeting place for spies.' As Rommel's Africa Corps prepared to advance on Alexandria in 1942, the Shepheard's became, in Cecil Beaton's words, 'lousy with generals; General Messervy in the telephone booth, General Le Gentilhomme standing by the revolving doors with General Catroux and General Ritchie coming out of the washroom'.[15] Rommel had earmarked the Shepheard's as his future head-quarters, and it was even rumoured shortly before the Battle of El Alamein that he had sent a radio message to Cairo to book a suite at the great hotel. One humorous young Commonwealth officer is said to have approached one of the porters and casually asked whether 'Herr Rommel has arrived'. The astonished clerk thumbed through his book before calmly replying: 'No, sir, he hasn't arrived.' 'He soon will,' replied the officer as he sauntered off. Some believed that Rommel had actually stayed at the hotel disguised as a British officer.

The hotels during the halcyon days of the turn of the century were crammed with high-society clientele who came from every corner of the earth to winter in Cairo, and enjoy an uninterrupted succession of balls and fêtes. By the 1920s this ambience appears to have been in decline, or was it just in vogue by then to disparage it? Evelyn Waugh for one had little time for Egypt's hotels, writing in *When the Going was Good*:

All the hotels in Egypt are bad but they excuse themselves upon two contrary principles. Some maintain, legitimately, that it does not really matter how bad they are if they are cheap enough; the others, that it does not really matter how bad they are if they are expensive enough. Both classes do pretty well. We sought out one of the former, a large, old-fashioned establishment under Greek management in the Midan el-Khaznedar, called the Hotel Bristol et du Nil, where rooms even in the high season are only eighty piastres a night. My room had three double beds in it under high canopies of dusty mosquito netting, and two derelict rocking chairs. The windows opened on a tram terminus. None of the servants spoke a word of any European language, but this was a negligible defect since they never answered the bell.[16]

In 1898, shortly after the rebuilding of the Shepheard's, George Nungovich Bey took over the Savoy Hotel, now known as the Continental-Savoy, in Kamel Street on Opera Square. The Savoy looked a bit like London's Harrods with a dome under which the hotel's name was inscribed in stone. It had the best restaurant in Cairo and was frequented by the élite. During the First World War, neighbouring Ezbekiyya became the heart of Cairo's brothels, adding a downtown colour to the atmosphere of the hotel. The streets glittered with coloured electric lights and honkytonk piano music came from every little café. The prostitutes, mostly Italian women, operated in the alleys, in the fish market and under the Italianate arches.

Hardly a European prince or princess passed through Cairo without being honoured by the tireless Nungovich who had become a millionaire through a curious incident, to which he owed his fame. He had started work as hall porter in a small hotel when some British officers, impressed by his honesty, placed the management of their mess in his hands. From these beginnings he soon became director of the Hôtel d'Angleterre. When an English regiment arrived unexpectedly in Cairo, they were greeted at the station by M. Nungovich who informed them that he had prepared rooms in his hotel for all the officers. They were royally entertained at the Hôtel d'Angleterre and when, well fed and merry on M. Nungovich's plentiful wines, they called for the bill,

157

the wily Nungovich promptly replied: 'Sirs, there is none. M. Nungovich is only too happy to have the honour of entertaining Her Majesty's [Queen Victoria's] officers.' There and then M. Nungovich was appointed hotel-keeper by appointment to Her Britannic Majesty's officers.

By 1901, the *Traveller* magazine was describing the Savoy as the 'most exotic hotel in the East', but today's Continental-Savoy is a gloomy place and the renovations underway seem likely to sever forever its connections with an era when outside it you could buy anything from a panther in a cage to a boa-constrictor. Originally called the New Hotel, it was taken over by the Khedive Ismail to house further guests for the Canal opening, and was later sold to a French company. It was eventually renamed the Continental-Savoy and became the rival, and then the ally, of Shepheard's as the giddy centre of the city's seasonal social life. During the First World War it became the Allied army's headquarters, while Australian regiments such the Australian Light Horse established themselves in camps behind the Mena House. T.E. Lawrence would stay at the Shepheard's, but often escape to the Continental for a cool drink away from publicity. Once, when he was sitting at the Continental bar with Ronald Storrs, an elderly woman rushed up to him, longing to introduce herself, and cried out as she fanned herself nervously: 'Just think, Colonel Lawrence, ninety-two – ninety-two!' With his sharp wit Lawrence replied gravely: 'Many happy returns!'[17]

When Storrs arrived in Cairo in 1904 on a salary of £20, he couldn't afford the glamorous Continental so put up at the nearby Italian-run Pension Tewfik, which was housed in the upper storey of the New Hotel. Deeply lonely in Cairo and hoping, as he admitted, to better himself, he soon moved to the Metropolitan Hotel in Boursa al-Gadid Street, a hotel in central Cairo which few had heard of and no cabman could find. For five pounds a month he was given a bedroom, bath, light and a hearty breakfast at seven-thirty. The more sordid Cairo's pensions were, it seemed, the more English they sounded. Among the best known were Madame Frizell's Drummond Pension, Madame Rosenfeld's Britannia and the 'Houses' – Gresham House, Albion House, Osborne House, Killiney House, Warwick House.

The Mena House Hotel, which stands across the road from the

untidy little village of Nazlat as-Saman at the foot of the Giza Pyramids, was originally a Khedival lodge. Today it is owned by the Oberoi Hotels chain, and what is now the dining-room was the core of the lodge which Ismail used as a rest-house for himself and his guests when they wanted to hunt in the desert or visit the Pyramids. During the building boom of 1869 several rooms were added to the rest-house; the small library became the entrance and the dining-room was turned into a 'breakfast' room. In the early 1880s it was bought by an English couple, Frederick Head and his wife. They named the hotel after Mena, the first name of the seventy-six kings on the Tablet of Abydos. After the death of Frederick Head, the Mena House was sold to another English couple, the Locke-Kings. They installed English log fireplaces and other furnishings which contrasted with the heavy *fin-de-siècle* furniture of the great Cairene houses. Most characteristic of the hotel were the imposing *mashrabiya* balconies which still cover most of the hotel's façade on the Pyramids Road. *Mashrabiya* – interlocking screens of knotted wood – was the traditional Ottoman and Mamluk method of ventilation (hot air cooled as it passed through the lattices) and, at the same time, of allowing the women of the harem to peer at the outside world without being seen by menfolk.

Evelyn Waugh stayed at the Mena House with his wife Evelyn during part of a convalescent Grand Tour in 1928. The hotel was terribly expensive and the gardens' garish flowers and 'improbable insects' reminded her of 'the final scene of a Paris review'. The eccentricities of the other guests, 'demi-mondaines' in picture frocks, and jovial Australian tourists wearing sun helmets and wielding fly whisks, made it all worthwhile, however. One of the young women had a pet monkey in a silver harness. Evelyn confessed that as she waited for her husband's recovery she spent most of the day in the pool, as much as anything else to admire the antics of a splendid negro swimming instructor.[18]

22 Cairo's Last Flame

> From the London newspapers it is clear that Cairo is imagined
> to be in a state of tense and bellicose anxiety but . . . yesterday
> there was a race meeting numerously attended, the tennis courts
> are overcrowded; you cannot get a table at the Club, bazaars are
> open and doing a certain amount of business.
>
> (Ronald Storrs, 1914)

The First World War saw Egypt occupied not only by British
troops but by colonial Australian troops, whose rough-and-ready
ways militated against any human understanding of the Egyptians,
particularly at a time of crisis. Storrs noted with revulsion that they
fired their pistols into cafés they favoured and overturned donkey-
drawn buses that refused to stop for them.

Egypt was already heavily exposed to Western ideas, which
included the concepts of freedom and democracy, and the war was
that final catalyst for the Egyptian nationalists led by Saad
Zaghloul. 'I have no quarrel with them personally,' he said of the
British, '. . . but I want to see an independent Egypt.' The image of
the tricky 'Gyppo', however, dominated the imagination of the
British Tommy and the Aussie, some of whom were catatonic
from the horrors of the Somme and Passchendaele, and oblivious
to the suffering and indescribable squalor in which the average
dweller of Cairo's Boulaq or Shoubra lived.

The US President Wilson gave Egyptians the hope of independence at the end of the war, and the British listened politely to Saad
Zaghloul's request for independence on the basis of his 'fourteen
points'. A month later, however, they arrested Saad and deported
him to Malta. This was the cue for a massive uprising throughout

160

the country, an uprising that was as important a threat in Egypt to British colonial rule as the massacre at Amritsar the same year in India. The Egyptian nationalists believed that independence was imminent, and the flame of their enthusiasm was carried by the mob whose rule has always been Egypt's most regular and most gruesome way of expressing itself. The Dominion troops in Cairo had just emerged from the trenches. They were battle-trained, spoiling for a fight, and unwilling to brook any nuisance from a native mob.

The uprising of 1919 was to be a bitter foretaste of the 1952 riots, in which a good deal of Ismail's Cairo and England's Cairo were destroyed. In March 1919 life in Egypt came to an abrupt halt. Nobody went to work, and trains and trams ceased to function. On 18 March eight British soldiers were murdered on their way to Cairo, and during the weeks that followed such incidents became commonplace. Writing to his father from the Savoy Hotel, then Britain's military headquarters, Thomas Russell (Russell Pasha), Cairo's English Chief of Police, wrote on 9 April that 'a native mob is looting and murdering in Sharia Bustan'. Four days later he was writing of the 'ghastly murders' of British soldiers by the mob, and of his own detective being 'stabbed to pieces by a crowd, while others danced around his body'. Russell had to exert himself to prevent the unruly Australian Common-wealth soldiers setting on the mob, an action that would have sparked off a far greater uprising and got the Australians killed in the process.

The city lay behind barricades, and students from al-Azhar built trenches to prevent troops and Russell's police from operating. Russell persuaded the British authorities not to use the Egyptian soldiery which was on the point of mutiny and would most likely have joined the mob, which was 'several thousand of the roughest elements of Cairo' who 'had knives, spear heads, chisels, adzes, tree trunks' and jagged pieces of cast-iron grating and were 'shrieking, yelling and waving weapons in the air', he told his father. Russell described the events as a mixture of Dante's *Inferno*, the French Revolution and oriental fanaticism, but still wanted the troops kept out at all cost. 'Allenby is getting angry and woe betide this town if he starts roaring.' If more Europeans were attacked, he wrote, 'he'll put troops on them and there will be one of the bloodiest scenes in history'. Russell's wife Dorothea, writing to her own father, told him that Wilson Pasha of the Hijaz Army had seen the riot from the Continental Hotel and that his 'heart was in his mouth'.[1]

Egyptian women played a major role in the demonstrations, throwing off their *hijabs*, creating picket lines and haranguing the mob. When 150 of what Dorothea called the 'harem' ladies set off on their march, Russell blocked them 'gently' with his troops where, he wrote, 'the dear things had to remain for an hour and a half in the hot sun'. Dorothea had written that they were kept in the sun for three hours until 'they were burnt scarlet', but that Russell had been so charming when he addressed them that they had come away delighted with his treatment of them.

Much of the real trouble, Russell pointed out, was started by 'low-class Europeans losing their heads and firing at the demonstrators from their houses'. On 9 April, thirty Egyptians were executed for murdering British officers. However, Britain had by now read the signs and sent Allenby to replace Wingate as Resident, while Saad Zaghloul was released from his confinement in Malta. His party was now called the Wafd after the 'Delegation' he had sent to the Residency in 1919.

In 1912, Britain had given Egypt her 'sovereignty' and the Khedive Fouad automatically became 'King Fouad'. But it did not alter the tenor of British rule nor the activities of the nationalists. Between 1922 and 1924, seventeen British officials were assassinated and twenty were viciously attacked in broad daylight. In 1924 Sir Lee Stack, the Sirdar (Commander-in-Chief) of the Egyptian Army and Governor General of the Sudan, was shot dead by a well-organized gang of seven young Egyptians as he drove through Cairo. After a much publicized trial, six of the seven were executed.

But notwithstanding the underlying violence, British influence was beginning to make enormous social and architectural inroads on Cairo as a city. By the early 1930s the new 'little England' garden cities of Heliopolis, Zamalek, Garden City and Giza began to replace Ezbekiyya and Abbasiyya as the homes of foreign officialdom and Egypt's new bourgeoisie. The splendid half-Italian and half-Ottoman houses of Ismail's time, elaborate with stucco gone mad, were converted into flats and office buildings.

The modern styles of Paris and Marseilles began to set the tone for the new houses built by French, Italian and Jewish architects, for whom the twenties were boom years not unlike those of Saudi Arabia in the 1970s. These new buildings were grand and spacious, but sacrificed the splendid gardens that Cairenes had always valued so much. Extending on to the tree-lined pavements, they lacked the privacy of the private houses of Haussmann's Paris and opulent London town houses.

Meanwhile, to furnish these gaudy buildings, cabinet-makers were pouring into Cairo from all over Europe to compete with each other to fill spacious halls with 'imitation Sheraton, Jansen, Maple's and Heal's'.[2] The emphasis was on furniture and statues, especially bronze, the walls remaining bare except for occasional Flemish tapestries. In the little side streets of what remains of Ismail's Cairo, this flamboyant, gleamingly gilded furniture, cruelly labelled 'Louis Farouk' by Cairenes, can still be seen being carved and hammered out in the little warehouses and on the pavements. Even in modern high-rise buildings, opulent drawing-rooms are filled with a mixture of 'Louis-Farouk' and genuine imitation Louis XIV furniture from the 1870s.

The new commercial centre consisted of a triangle of tree-lined streets – Qasr al-Nil, Sulaiman Pasha and Fouad. Here were the department stores guarded by Albanian doormen in their exotic, flowing costumes and high boots. Here also were the French and English bookshops, the tearooms and Parisian-style cafés such as Groppi's with its delicious cakes and sugar-coated almonds, fashionable designer window displays, art galleries filled with classical French and English collections, and imposing gentlemen's clubs closely modelled on such London clubs as the Travellers' and the Athenaeum. Europeans and Cairo's other wealthy ethnic groups – Levantines, Jews and Greeks – did their shopping here or sipped capuccino coffee in the marble-pillared, high-stucco-ceilinged rooms of the great cafés.

Between the new quarter and the old stood the opera house with its winter season of Italian opera and Comédie Française repertory, one of the few areas where shared culture drew Europeans, Levantines and Egyptians together. In severe contrast, stretching from the alleys between the Citadel, al-Azhar and Abbasiyya to the outskirts of Shoubra, Zeitun, Roda Island and Giza behind the zoo, lay the sprawling areas of the lower-middle class as well as of the shop-keeper class who were gradually being dispossessed by the growing Levantine commercial houses, the impoverished *'ulema* of al-Azhar and the lowly paid clerks of the ministries.

To the south lay the British dream-world of Maadi, which was somewhere halfway between London suburbia and an Indian hill-station, while to the north, on the edge of Shoubra where Muhammad Ali had built his Shoubra Palace, was a very gloomy shantytown where one of the few entertainments was the annual visit of an Algerian circus patronized by the Prince of Upper Egypt, Farouk, and his four young and beautiful sisters. To the east lay the City of the Dead, where the poor millions had not yet dared to penetrate for fear of the 'evil eye'.

Although the Greeks of Cairo were an extremely important community, they did not reflect the brilliant hedonism of their cousins in Alexandria. They were a self-sufficient society with their own clubs, services and political persuasions. When war came, the Greek government in exile was established in Cairo, and the community enjoyed its moment of glory when Cairo became the exile of George Seferis, Elli Papadimitriou, Sophocles Venizelos, the pianist Gina Bachauer and the novelist Stratis Tsirkas. During the pre-war and the war years, the Egypt–Greece Friendship Society published a weekly magazine in French. It contained some of the earliest poetry of poets such as Cavafy, as well as short stories by writers such as Forster, Graves and Maurois. When the Greek King Paul came to live in exile in Cairo during the war, he gave new glitter to the social rounds. Magdi Wahba remembered the mute, German-trained philologist who wandered from café to café writing his grammatical commentary on Dickens, and the classical guitarist Avlonitis who changed his name to Alboniz to give the impression that he was as Spanish as Segovia.

The most important community of all was the French-speaking community which, wrote Wahba, encompassed the banks and cotton houses, most foreign schools, the Catholic missions, most of the royal family, Egypt's Muslim and Coptic plutocracy, the Masonic lodges, the great department stores, the Suez Canal Company, most of the press, the eligible young girls of all the foreign communities who expected brilliant marriages, the *habitués* of the tearooms and restaurants, the young cinema industry, the legal profession, the better-class brothels, the hotels, the tram and metro inspectors and the learned societies. To all these, of course, had to be added the large French community itself.

The largest European group was that of the Italians, who were concentrated in Cairo, Alexandria and the Canal Zone, unlike the Greeks who filtered into the provincial cities and villages. For the Italians in Egypt the 1930s were a Golden Age. Their class structure embraced garage mechanic and intellectual aristocrat alike. Many of Egypt's Italians were fascist during the 1930s, and Wahba remembered Italian schoolchildren singing 'Giovinezza' as they marched to school. Some of the supporters of fascism at the time were Italian Jews. The Party established magnificent sports clubs and stadiums, homes for the old, summer-holiday camps in Italy and winter excursions to Libya and Somalia. He remembered a box at the opera filled with black-shirted, opulent Italian lawyers, and Egyptian peasant children outside the Ala Littorio Club near the Pyramids singing '*Duce, Duce*' in unison with the Italian children inside. In 1940 the community collapsed, with the men taken to camps in Fayed and Ismailiya and the women making do in the cities.[3]

For the first three years of the war Cairo was the pivot of all Allied attention. Everyone passed through Cairo, and every language but German could be heard in the streets. 'They would,' noted Freya Stark, 'come from Scandinavia or Chungking, and salute you unexpectedly on the terrace of Shepheard's or the Continental.' They were, 'like diamonds on velvet', times set in danger 'in the orbit of advancing armies, the drama of existence or death'. Yet, she adds that 'no one can forget the gaiety and the glitter of Cairo while the desert war went on'.[4] On the whole the war seemed, if anything, to have enhanced the atmosphere of fun for the Allies, apart from those few days of the Great Flap in 1942 when Rommel's march on Alexandria seemed inevitable. When Cecil Beaton was posted to Cairo earlier in the year, the city still presented 'a luxurious façade with ultrafashionable Egyptian, Greek and Syrian women giving lavish entertainments, servants without number and none of the usual restrictions'.[5] As part of Britain's policy of giving heart to the Egyptians, Cairo's local press presented a picture of the war that was so optimistic that many English expatriates believed in March that it would be over in two months. Even Churchill's speeches were censored if they were not encouraging enough. Englishwomen still went about the great shops of Qasr al-Nil with jasmine-scented wrists and glimmering ear-rings and pearls, and there was no slackening of the dance-crazy parties on the Nile houseboats around Gezira or on the roofs of the great villas of Qasr al-Doubbara. Freya Stark remembered lingering conversations beneath Cairo's blue lamps as an operatic version of the Parisian reality. Olivia Manning saw Cairo as 'the final bolt-hole of European refugees'. She described them as 'existing on credit, or the British Government, they moved in a café society of crowded emptiness, seething with rivalries, petty scandals, squabbles, hurt feelings and exhibitions of self-importance'.

Staying at the Mena House during the early part of the war, when Mussolini's armies made their initial but quickly countered attempt to invade Egypt, Freya Stark had summed up the continuing festive atmosphere. She wrote:

> Sometimes it would be the Mena House, round the swimming pool in the open with lights dimmed so that men late from their offices would peer among bare jewelled shoulders and mess uniforms that still existed (given up when the Dominion troops arrived with only the more austere luggage of war . . .) to find their party at the little tables.[6]

The Mena House was to win kudos as host for the crucial talks held in November 1943 between Winston Churchill, President Roosevelt and General Chiang Kai-Chek. In his history of the Second World War, Churchill wrote:

> The headquarters of the conference and the venue of all British and American Chiefs of Staff was at the Mena House Hotel . . . The whole place bristled with troops and anti-aircraft guns, and the strictest cordons guarded all approaches. Everyone set to work at their various levels upon the immense mass of business which had to be decided or adjusted.[7]

Towards the end of the conference Churchill remembered taking Roosevelt to see the Sphinx: 'Roosevelt and I gazed at her for some minutes in silence as the evening shadows fell. She told us nothing and maintained her inscrutable smile.'[8]

23   Setting Fire to Ismail's City

By early 1952 Egypt was heading for breakdown. The Canal Zone saw constant battle between Egyptian guerrillas and British forces, who took severe reprisals against attack. On 1 January the British Ambassador, Sir Ralph Stevenson, protested to the Egyptian Foreign Ministry against the offer of £E1,000 reward to any Egyptian killing General Sir George Erskine, the British GOC in the Canal Zone. The chilling offer had been made the previous day by the Egyptian newspaper *Gumhour al-Misri*. On 25 January, General Erskine announced that he was going to disarm and expel from the Canal Zone all Egyptian auxiliary police who were suspected of supporting the guerrillas. British troops and tanks surrounded the Ismailiya police barracks, but the Egyptian commander rejected the British demand to surrender. Soon there was an exchange of small-arms fire, then British tanks opened up on the barracks at point-blank range. After three hours of heroic resistance, the Egyptian police surrendered. Forty-one had been killed and seventy-two were wounded. Three British soldiers had been killed.

The following day the country exploded in anger against the British. Cairo newspapers called it the Egyptian Stalingrad. At seven o'clock on that Black Saturday, units of the auxiliary police (the *Buluk Nizam*) marched from their barracks in Abbasiyya to Fouad University, where supporters of the Wafd Party, Communists and *Ikhwan al-Muslimun* (Muslim Brethren) had gathered for a huge demonstration. The enormous march moved across the bridges to gather in front of the Parliament building, formerly Princess Shevikiar's pink-and-grey baroque palace. Out stepped Abdel Fattah Hassan, the Minister for Social Affairs, who immediately promised vengeance in the hope that the crowds would disperse and leave the government to kick the British out of the Canal Zone. But the mob, realizing that the government was making no attempt to keep order, and that the police were eager to join the demonstrators, merely increased its anger, swelled, and moved howling towards the Abdin Palace. Having shouted slogans at Farouk and the British, and accused them of responsibility for the Canal massacre, the mob continued towards Opera Square.

The desperate Stevenson, loath to call out British troops and risk a political disaster, tried to contact Serag al-Din, the Interior Minister, but was informed that he was bargaining for property in Cairo. Nahas Pasha, the Prime Minister, was having his feet pedicured. The King was entertaining senior army officers at a great feast at the Abdin Palace. According to one witness of that ghastly day, the mobs raced to the palace shouting 'Long live the King' but when he came out on to his balcony the slogans changed to 'Where is your mother? How many teeth has your son got?' The King then ordered the palace gates to be shut and, according to one witness, ordered his guards to machine-gun the crowd. Having watched the slaughter, he saluted and went back indoors. While he was on the balcony, it was also rumoured, extremists had entered the palace and threatened him from behind. In any case, the King would not bring out the army. Nobody moved. Each party was waiting for the other to take the decision to confront the rebellion, and each party intended to exploit it for its own goals. Moreover, Haidar Pasha, the Egyptian Army Commander, is believed to have warned the King that he could not depend upon the loyalty of his army. Even among the 500 officers he had invited to the feast, a third appear to have been hostile to him.

At midday the crowd reached the Badia Cabaret, where a policeman was lazily drinking and fondling a pretty dancing girl who sat on his knee. The angry mob heckled the policeman for enjoying himself while his brothers were being slaughtered at Ismailiya. The policeman jeered back and the dancer giggled, but then, quite suddenly, the mob which had been peaceful until that moment, went berserk. The cabaret was smashed, kerosene was poured over the broken furniture and within minutes it was ablaze. The next target of the now blooded mob was the Rivoli Cinema in

Fouad street. Men from jeeps, armed with crowbars and petrol cans, ran in and within minutes the cinema was an inferno. Then they set alight the Metro Cinema. Later that morning Barclays Bank was aflame. Witnesses said that tank lorries brought petrol which the mob poured into drums and passed from hand to hand. Children lit bonfires. When the mob reached the Adès Store it plundered it before soaking long strips of material in petrol and setting fire to them. This was how the other great Jewish stores, Cicurel and Robert Hughes, were burnt down. The police rode about in lorries aiding the mobs.

Then the mob made for that most hallowed of British institutions, the Turf Club. Eighteen British men and women were sitting in the club. Some had, indeed, taken refuge there, believing that it was too obscure to be noticed. But it was actually one of the mob's main targets. British members tried to rush for the garden but were caught in the foyer where they were attacked brutally with crowbars. The crowds doused the furniture and the paintings of Cromer, Kitchener, Gorst and Lloyd with paraffin and the building was soon blazing. British corpses were flung into the flames and several Britishers who tried to rush from the foyer were grabbed by the crowd and flung into the fire to burn alive. One tried to climb out of a window by tied sheets but when he reached the pavement he was trampled to death by the crowd. Within about half an hour twelve people were dead, including nine British civilians. Among them were James Craig, a British official and scholar, and the Canadian Trade Commissioner.

The crowd, now full of 'a passionate intensity', moved down the Khedive Ismail's two great boulevards, Qasr al-Nil Street and Sulaiman Pasha Street, smashing and burning even shops whose grilles had been pulled firmly down. Flames leapt up everywhere from cinemas decorated with hoardings of the half-naked women that the mob associated with the British and with the corrupt King Farouk. Then they made for the British and French social centres, the St James's Club (which was destroyed solely by the police, said witnesses), the Cecil Bar, the Ritz Café and Groppi's Coffee House, which they failed to burn (it still stands today). Soon the TWA building was blazing, then came the turn of the Weinstein Stationary Shop, Chryslers and the great department stores.

To begin with they ignored the Shepheard's Hotel, perhaps

reserving this ultimate symbol of the *belle époque* until last. It was as if the Shepheard's was off limits and some said that it had the protection of the Muslim Brotherhood. But, having passed it by several times, at 2.30 p.m. the ghastly mob stopped ominously before it. The splendidly dressed dragomans who had, until then, stood their ground in front of the magnificent building, soon realized what was happening and fled, while the *shawish* (policeman) on duty is said to have been the first to rush in with his drum of petrol. The now-well-practised arsonists poured through those great terraces and into the imposing hall of the hotel, piled up the Louis Farouk furniture and doused it in petrol. Guests, including King Farouk's European mistress of the moment, raced through every door they could find as the flames swept the building and its graceful dome began to crumble. Two young girl singers with the Italian Opera Company fled in their underwear, clutching their jewellery in their hands. Another panicked and flung herself from a fourth-storey window to her death. By now, Ismail's Cairo, European Cairo, lay beneath a thick pall of black smoke. Broken glass spattered with blood and scattered with trampled debris from the great shops covered Cairo's pavements. By the end of the day seventeen Europeans and fifty Egyptians were reported to have been killed. *The Times* correspondent described the streets 'as though they had been attacked by a fleet of bombers'.

According to one witness, the King cried like a child at the end of that night as he saw his burnt-out city, and two days later walked unescorted to the ruins of the Shepheard's and Fouad Street. A few days later he went to his favourite club, the Automobile Club, where he burst into tears, moaning over and over again: 'They shall see, they shall see!'

Epilogue: Ismail's Cairo Today

Cairo's transformation into the Paris of Africa had made it the heart of a *belle époque* which lasted until the 1950s, when European socialites might give their balls in Ismail's palaces with their oriental charm rather than in the demure surroundings of European stately homes. But what survives today of that extra-ordinary city that so fascinated the Empress Eugénie in 1869? The answer, sadly, is that Ismail's city was a chimera that has virtually disappeared; the few traces that do remain are under constant threat of destruction. The struggle for space and the explosion of land prices in Cairo today have left little compassion among the modern Cairenes for a city which is considered a European grafting.

What Ismail had begun was a process that continued until the 1930s. The Art Nouveau era in the Europe of the 1900s can be seen in many of the Viennese and Italian villas of Cairo, but many were demolished between 1920 and 1930 to make way for the great department stores such as Cicurel and Adès. One of the few palaces to remain is the Gezira Palace on the banks of the Nile in Zamalek. Villas such as those of the Boghoz Pasha Ghali, Charaoui, Mosseri, Batigelli, Bakhoum and Rafi families have all been demolished. Even the palazzo of the adored singer Umm Kulthum, on the western side of Zamalek, was torn down one night shortly after her death and several days before Parliament was to place a conservation order on it. One of the few mansions from the period that do survive is that of a cousin of King Farouk, the late Adel Bey Sabet, which stands as a curiously Cairene anachronism beside a heavily-guarded US embassy and among the concrete blocks and roaring traffic of Garden City. Adel Sabet was one of Cairo's charismatic figures and entering the mansion now owned by his son Mahmoud, is like entering a tiny island of a lyrical past. On the walls of his marble hall hangs a painting of a Sabet forebear, Ismail's prime minister Sherif Pasha, and in the drawing-room filled with memorabilia of the century are photographs of a Sabet cousin, beautiful Queen Nazli, and her children, among them Farouk.

The palaces and buildings of Ismail's city were being constantly demolished until lobbying helped slow the trend, but if you drive at dawn through the city's great arterial boulevards from Ezbekiyya to Sulaiman Pasha Square (now Talaat Harb Square), you can still just conjure up that extraordinary period. A few buildings such as the Cosmopolitan Hotel off Qasr al-Nil Street, for many years the home of Madame Farida Galassi, have been restored to their original Art Deco splendour, but others such as the great stone palace behind the multi-storey car park which stands in place of the opera house have been demolished. Many Egyptians mourn the loss of Ismail's Cairo as they sip gin-and-tonics in lavish penthouse apartments of the city's ubiquitous high-rise monsters. But at a time when a highly unstable economy reminds modern Egyptians of the chaos following Ismail's bankruptcy, few have the time or energy to rescue architecture which represents only one small layer of Egypt's many-layered history.

Egypt, with only four per cent of its land mass cultivated, is essentially a man-made country. To call it 'the gift of the Nile' has become a platitude, but when you fly over the Nile Delta to Cairo you quickly realize that the country's fifty million people are restricted to the Delta itself with its apex at Cairo, and the slim, brilliantly fertile Nile Valley, man-made and man-preserved, is rarely more than a few miles across and extends like the stem of a tulip down to Aswan and the High Dam.

At the turn of the century, Cairo's population was barely half a million; today it is fifteen million and increasing by about one million a year. Since the revolution in 1952, the government has concentrated on building new high-rise residential cities in the desert, such as Nasser, Sadat and Ten Ramadan cities, but this has done little to relieve the crisis-point congestion of the city itself. Basic facilities in these new cities tend to be primitive, sometimes totally defunct. Meanwhile, the poor have poured into the splendid houses and courtyards of the City of the Dead, the northern cemetery north of al-Azhar. This immense area, in which the dead appear to have been offered vastly better housing than the living, is a newly emerging city. Afraid of the 'evil eye', many Egyptians, including the police, fear to enter it, making it an ideal haven for criminals evading the strong arm of the law.

Over the centuries various cities were built on Cairo: Fustat by the Arab invaders, then the Islamic city (Fatamid, Ayyubid, Mamluk) around al-Azhar University and Mosque, then Ismail's city linked by what are today's Tahrir, Talaat Harb, Mustapha Kemal and Opera Squares. Today new quarters such as Mohande-seen and garden suburbs such as Maadi are being massively redeveloped in order not to interfere with the classical, Islamic parts of Cairo. Meanwhile, new flyovers and ring roads and a metro system reflect plans to relieve urban strain.

Sitting in Groppi's once elegant coffee house, with its high ceilings and yellowing walls, in Talaat Harb Square, formerly Sulaiman Pasha Square, in the heart of rococo nineteenth-century Cairo, you can breathe an era which began with the building of the New Cairo in the 1870s and ended with the revolution. Until the late 1960s you could still see the old pashas in their fezzes and Savile Row suits sipping coffee by the windows, but today you are more likely to see Islamic couples drinking lemonade, or businessmen discussing opportunities offered by Egypt's new, American-oriental economy.

The structure of Ismail's Cairo can still be seen in the boulevards that radiate from Talaat Harb Square, Talaat Harb Street, Qasr al-Nil Street and Sabri abu Alam Street. If you drive through these streets at dawn you can visualize the horse-drawn *calèches* and the throbbing nightlife which drew the sybarites of Europe to stop in this city before ascending the Nile to Luxor and Aswan. By day the cacophony of honking cars, the milling crowds and the ubiquitous pollution dispel much of the romance of old Cairo, but shortly after dawn the stenching soapbox carts and the donkeys of the little Coptic *zabbaleen* girls clatter through the streets to collect the daily rubbish. Later the drinks bars crammed with the fruit of the season – mangoes, guavas, oranges – entice you in with their delicious fragrances.

Where Fasciotti and Rossi's lovely opera house stood is now a huge multi-storey car park. In the 1950s and 1960s foreign companies occupied the opera house from November to the end of April. In one season alone there were visits from the Great Opera in Peking, the Comédie Française, a French ballet company with its prima ballerina Tamara Toumanova, the Dublin Gate Theatre and a German opera company celebrating the bicentenary of Mozart. But all was to end with the tragic destruction of the opera house in 1972.

Attempts to bring *Aida* back to Cairo in 1984 failed because the Egyptian Ministry of Culture was unwilling to interfere with its tourism-oriented performances of *son et lumière* at the Pyramids. However in May 1987, during the ill-chosen Muslim fasting month of Ramadan, the opera was performed with a tremendous fanfare, and at a cost of $10 million, at the 3,200-year-old Temple of Ammon at Luxor by the Verona Opera Company, who hired the American choreographer Dennis Wayne to create the *Aida* Ballet especially for the occasion. Placido Domingo played Radames, although only for one performance 'because of the heat and dust', and Maria Chiara played Aida. Added to the opera and ballet companies of the Arena di Verona were 350 Egyptian soldiers from the Luxor barracks, a chorus of 200 real Nubians and sixty horses.

In 1983 the Marriott Hotel Corporation opened in Cairo what was both its biggest hotel worldwide and the biggest hotel in the Middle East. The Gezira Palace is the heart of this great complex. After the Khedive Ismail's abdication in 1879, the palace and its sixty *feddans* of private gardens were sequestrated by the British. After a short period when it was owned by the ancestors of a scion of the Egyptian royal family, Prince Hassan Hassan, it was bought by the Swiss-owned Egyptian Hotels Corporation. During the First World War it was used by the British as a military hospital, and in 1922 it was bought by Prince Habib Lutfallah. For forty years the palace was shared by the Lutfallahs and their in-laws, the Sursocs, until it was sequestrated in 1962 by Colonel Nasser's regime and became the still fondly remembered Omar Khayyam Hotel which, albeit somewhat seedily, retained the decadent air of its exotic past.

When I visited Princess Lodi Lutfallah in her palace in

Alexandria's élite Bulkly quarter to learn more about the period between 1922 and 1962, when Colonel Nasser's sequestrators abruptly ordered her family and that of the Sursocs to quit the Gezira Palace, I realized that the Salamlik Kiosk and the Palace were constantly confused by writers of the period. The Salamlik was burnt down when plastic flowers caught alight during a splendid charity ball given by the charity *Petits Lits Blancs* in 1967.

The project to convert the Gezira Palace into the five-star Marriott Hotel was controversial, but what has remained gives the visitor an exotic glimpse of Cairo's *belle époque*. You cross a large courtyard of white and brown marble flagstones shadowed by the once dark, now gilded Moorish arches of Carl Von Diebitch. At dawn and dusk the sun throws geometrical shadows across the flagstones, and the atmosphere of light and shadow is so delicate that the arches seem about to take flight. In front of the arches where the *shawish* (the white-uniformed policeman) guides guests to their taxis, are two dozing marble lions. One is sleeping luxuriously on one paw, while the other reveals fine, white teeth and alert, greedy eyes. Two rampant lions bearing shields inscribed with the ubiquitous IP (Ismail Pasha) guard the hotel's main door. In the completely remodelled front lobby are the heavily wrought, gilded chairs that were so much in vogue during the *belle époque*, but are now produced as 'Louis Farouk' in Cairo's back streets. In the centre of the front lounge are two pretty marble statues that came from another palace. The nude slave girl on the left was probably sculpted in 1872, like the statue in the centre, by the Italian G. Strazza. The girl has a calm, beautiful, despairing face. Rope is tied loosely around her wrists and an identity locket hangs around her neck. In the centre is Strazza's mischievous and almost winking Pan chasing an irritated goat around a prickly palm trunk.

If you take the Corniche road along the front of the Palace, you follow the pretty turn-of-the-century buildings after the hotel called Saray al-Gezira, the 'Seraglio of the Island'. Here the flame trees, with their decaying black branches from which great blood-red flowers grow in spring, run along the banks of the Nile. When you reach the end of these buildings whose names – Dorchester House, Park Lane, Nile View – evoke the days of British hegemony, you look to your right at the entrance to the Gezira Club whose lawns and fields take up a large part of the island. The 150-acre Gezira Club is the largest remaining part of the magnificent botanical gardens laid out by Delchevalerie in the 1860s as part of Ismail's vision of a perfect city.

Until the revolution in 1952, election to the club was restricted to the élite, but since then it has been open to all and nowadays there are several thousand members. There are twenty tennis courts with a centre-court stadium, an Olympic-size swimming pool, playing fields for everything from cricket to javelin-throwing, and other activities ranging from saunas to a riding school. Membership is comparatively inexpensive and on ordinary days it can be pleasant to dine al fresco on one of the clubhouse verandas, although alcohol has been banned since a fight in the early 1980s in which one person was seriously wounded. On Fridays, Sundays and feast days the club becomes very crowded and the streets around it are jammed with cars. At dawn you can see elegant horsemen and women trotting around the racetrack, and during the season there are races on Fridays and Sundays.

Zamalek is the part of the island north of the Gezira Club, and the little streets bordered by the club, the western and eastern sides of the Nile and 26 July Street contain embassy residences and apartment buildings with great marble halls and penthouse apartments where the rich give fashionable parties among period French and Ottoman furniture. Despite the traffic, these streets can be very pretty during the periods of the blossoming of Cairo's myriad flowering trees, and they still retain some of the peace which reflects the island's original ethos as a bucolic retreat. After the British occupation, residences were built throughout the northern end of the island. The entire island is now built over, apart from the club which is Cairo's last surviving lung. Since the building of the flyover, however, some of the pressure has been taken off Gezira, and some of its former tranquillity has been restored.

Few care about Ismail's great city any more, despised as it is by many nationalist Egyptians as a European intrusion. Crumbling stone veneer betrays the clumsy haste in which much of it was built, and it is only if you stand in Sulaiman Pasha Square and gaze at the elegant domes and rooftops that you can truly understand the vision of a ruler whose charisma may one day be recognized by his people.

Notes

Introduction
1. Russell Pasha, Sir Thomas: *Egyptian Service 1902-1946*, p. 179
2. Ibid.

Chapter 1: Chibuks and Lice in Ismail's Harem
1. Boyle, Clare: *Boyle of Cairo*, p. 138
2. Lott, Emmeline: *Harem Life in Egypt and Constantinople*, p. 50
3. Chennells, Ellen: *Recollections of an Egyptian Princess*, p. 279
4. Lott: op. cit., p. 167
5. Much of the background to this chapter can be found in Chennells's and Lott's accounts of their sojourns in Ismail's harem in the 1860s

Chapter 2: Obsession for an Empress
1. Sencourt, Robert: *The Life of the Empress Eugénie*, p. 37
2. Blunt, Wilfrid: *My Diaries – being a Personal Narrative of Events 1888-1914*, p. 176
3. C. de B.: *Letters from Paris 1870-1875*, p. 23
4. Ludwig, Emil: *Bismarck*, p. 209
5. Maurois, Simone: *Miss Howard and the Emperor*, p. 112

Chapter 3: Napoleon's Hated 'Mission Civilizatrice'
1. Gabarti (Jabarti), Abd al-Rahman ibn Hasan al-: *Merveilles Biographiques et Historiques*, quoted in Aldridge: *Cairo*, p. 196
2. Quoted in Herold, J. C.: *Bonaparte in Egypt*, p. 15
3. Richardson, Frank: *Napoleon, Bisexual Emperor*, p. 126
4. Ibid., p. 175
5. Gabarti, quoted in Stewart: *Great Cairo*, p. 180

6. Hourani, Albert: *Arab Thought in the Liberal Age*, p. 50

7. Blanch, Lesley: *The Wilder Shores of Love*, p. 209

8. Stewart: *Great Cairo*, p. 173

9. Richardson, Frank: op. cit., pp. 127–9

10. Stewart: op. cit., p. 176

11. Gabarti, quoted in Aldridge: *Cairo*, p. 169

12. Aldridge: *Cairo*, p. 171

Chapter 4: Muhammad Ali – a Brutal Age of Development

1. Ninet, John: *Lettres d'Egypte 1879–1882*, p. 234

2. Lane, E.W.: *Manners and Customs of the Modern Egyptians*, p. 113

3. Ninet, John: op. cit., p. 234

4. Various descriptions of the massacre, notably J. A. St John: *Egypt and Nubia*, pp. 120–4

5. Ibid.

6. Ibid.

7. Webster, James: *Travels through the Crimea, Turkey and Egypt*, quoted in Stewart: *Great Cairo*, p. 185

8. Duff Gordon, Lucie: *Letters from Egypt*, p. xiii

9. Blake, Robert: *Disraeli*, p. 68

10. Steegmuller, Francis: *Flaubert in Egypt*, p. 28

Chapter 5: A Cruel Princess

1. There are several versions of the story. One is told by Tugay in her *Three Centuries* (p. 117), another is told in an unpublished manuscript in Cairo by Jean Papasian.

2. Ghali, M.B.: *Mémoires de Nubar Pacha*, p. 49

3. Ibid., p. 49

4. Lott: *Harem Life in Egypt and Constantinople*, pp. 63–115

5. Chennells: *Recollections of an Egyptian Princess*, pp. 288–90

Chapter 6: Rulers of the New Renaissance

1. Ninet, John: *Lettres d'Egypte*, P. 236

2. Ghali: *Mémoires de Nubar Pacha*, p. 44

3. Ibid., p. 51

4. Boyle: *Boyle of Cairo*, p. 35

5. MacCoan, James Carlile: *Egypt under Ismail*, p. 9

6. de Leon, Edwin: *The Khedive's Egypt*, p. 81

7. Landes, D.S.: *Bankers and Pashas*, p. 99

8. Cromer, Earl of: *Modern Egypt*, p. 16
9. MacCoan: op. cit., p. 19

Chapter 7: Ismail – a Ruler Obsessed
1. Ghali: *Mémoires de Nubar Pacha*, p. 311
2. Draneht, Despina: *Twilight Memories*, p. 93
3. Boyle: *Boyle of Cairo*. p. 38
4. Lott: *Harem Life in Egypt and Constantinople*, p. 284
5. MacCoan: *Egypt under Ismail*, p. 81
6. Milner, Alfred: *England in Egypt*, p. 176
7. MacCoan: *Egypt as It is . . .*, p. 92
8. Ibid., p. 93
9. Ibid., p. 93
10. de Leon, Edwin: *The Khedive's Egypt*, p. 171

Chapter 8: Paris's Belle Epoque and the Great Exhibition
1. Ghali: *Mémoires de Nubar Pacha*, p. 312
2. Baldick, Robert (ed.): *Pages from the Goncourt Journal*, p. 130
3. Draneht, Despina: *Twilight Memories*, p. 94
4. Knepler, Henry (ed. and transl.): *Man about Paris: The Confessions of Arsène Houssaye*, p. 289
5. Zola, Emile: *Nana*, Introduction, p. 9
6. Ibid., p. 7
7. Baldick, Robert (ed.): op. cit., p. 343
8. Fulford, Roger (ed.): *Your Dear Letter: Private correspondence of Queen Victoria and the Crown Princess of Prussia 1865–71*, p. 142
9. Ibid., p. 140
10. Ibid., p. 141
11. Ibid., p. 142
12. Ibid., p. 143
13. Duff, David: *Eugénie and Napoleon III*, p. 183
14. Ibid., p. 117

Chapter 9: Ismail's Cairo – a Glitzy Age
1. MacCoan: *Egypt as It is . . .*, p. 48
2. Ibn Battuta, Muhammad ibn Abd Allah: *The Travels of Ibn Battuta AD 1325–54*, quoted in Aldridge: *Cairo*, p. 115
3. Crabitès, Pierre: *American Officers in the Egyptian Army*, p. 43
4. Lane-Poole, Stanley: *The Story of Cairo*, p. 27

5. Mardaga, Pierre: 'Alger 1830-60' in the journal *Urbi, Villes Coloniales*, p. 23, October 1982, Liège, Belgium
6. MacCoan: op. cit., p. 57
7. de Guerville: *New Egypt*, p. 116
8. Gabarti, quoted in Aldridge: *Cairo*, p. 142-4
9. Steegmuller, Francis (ed.): *Flaubert in Egypt*, p. 67
10. MacCoan: op. cit., p. 48

Chapter 10: The Finest Opera House in the World
1. Ghali: *Mémoires de Nubar Pacha*, p. 366
2. Osborne, Charles: *Verdi: A Life in the Theatre*, p. 209
3. Draneht, Despina: *Twilight Memories*, p. 86
4. Osborne, Charles: op. cit., p. 214
5. Ibid., p. 217
6. Walker, Frank: *The Man Verdi*, p. 368
7. Draneht, Despina: op. cit., p. 78
8. *Letters of Giuseppe Verdi*, p. 184, 8 December 1871 (quoted in Osborne, Charles: *Verdi: A Life in the Theatre*, p. 222)
9. *La Perseveranza*, Milan, 27 December 1871, quoted in Osborne: op. cit.

Chapter 11: The Palace of the Empress
1. Chennells: *Recollections of an Egyptian Princess*, p. 217
2. Magnus, Philip: *King Edward the Seventh*, p. 102
3. Ghali: *Mémoires de Nubar Pacha*, p. 365
4. Article in the French journal *L'Illustration*, Journal Universelle, 1869
5. Chennells: *Recollections of an English Governess*, p. 217

Chapter 12: The Cousin of the Empress
1. Herold: *Bonaparte in Egypt*, p. 377
2. Ferdinand de Lesseps in a speech given in Paris to the Société des Gens de Lettres in April 1870.
3. Quoted in Beatty, Charles: *Ferdinand de Lesseps: A Biographical Study*, p. 51
4. Ferdinand de Lesseps in a speech given in Paris to the Société des Gens de Lettres in April 1870
5. Pudney: *Suez: de Lesseps' Canal*, p. 33
6. Beatty, Charles: op. cit., p. 139

Chapter 13: La Belle Eugénie
1. Baldick: *Pages from the Goncourt Journal*, p. 155
2. des Garets, Comtesse: *The Tragic Empress*, p. 36
3. Ibid., p. 48
4. Ibid., p. 48
5. Ibid., p. 49

Chapter 14: The Opening of the Accursed Canal
1. Ghali: *Mémoires de Nubar Pacha*, p. 361
2. Fulford Roger (ed.): *Your Dear Letter: Private Correspondence of Queen Victoria and the Crown Princess of Prussia 1865-71*, p. 245
3. Ibid., p. 246
4. *Punch*, 29 November 1869
5. Magnus: *Edward the Seventh*, pp. 102–3
6. *Pall Mall Gazette*, 18 November 1869
7. Kinross, Lord: *Between Two Seas, the Creation of the Suez Canal*, p. 239
8. Tugay, Emine Foat: *Three Centuries, Family Chronicles of Turkey and Egypt*, p. 136

Chapter 15: A Week of Hedonism
1. Quoted in Pudney: *Suez: de Lesseps' Canal*, p. 149
2. Ibid., p. 152
3. Ibid., p. 152
4. Ibid., p. 153
5. Paléologue: *The Tragic Empress*, p. 32
6. Quoted in Pudney: op. cit., p. 157

Chapter 16: The Fall of Eugénie
1. des Garets: *The Tragic Empress*, p. 105
2. Fulford, Roger (ed.): *Your Dear Letter: Private Correspondence of Queen Victoria and the Crown Princess of Prussia 1865-71*, p. 301
3. de Guerville: *New Egypt*, p. 239
4. Duff: *Eugénie and Napoleon III*, p. 284

Chapter 17: The Fall of Ismail
1. MacCoan: *Egypt under Ismail*, p. 273
2. Tugay: *Three Centuries, Family Chronicles of Turkey and Egypt*, p. 141

3. Draneht, Despina: *Twilight Memories*, p. 91
4. Baldick: *Pages from the Goncourt Journal*, p. 277
5. Draneht, Despina: op. cit., p. 122

Chapter 18: Mr Cook and the Hotel Age
1. Magnus: *King Edward the Seventh*, p. 216
2. Blake, Robert: *Disraeli*, p. 681
3. Edwards, Amelia: *A Thousand Miles up the Nile*
4. Quoted in Nelson, Nina: *Shepheard's Hotel*, p. 28
5. Thomas Cook's Guidebook to Egypt, 1869
6. Quoted in Storrs, Ronald: *Orientations*, p. 22

Chapter 19: Cairo: The Englishman's Playground
1. de Guerville: *New Egypt*, pp. 137–8
2. Ibid., pp. 139–40
3. Grafftey-Smith, Laurence: *Bright Levant*, p. 78
4. Steevens, G.W.: *Egypt in 1898*, p. 59
5. Cecil, Lord Edward: *The Leisure of an Egyptian Official*, p. 89
6. Ibid., p. 116
7. Ibid., p. 142
8. Wahba, Magdi: 'Cairo Memories' published in *Encounter*, May 1984
9. Rameses: *Oriental Spotlight*, p. 6
10. Grafftey-Smith, Laurence: op. cit., p. 123

Chapter 20: Cairo's Sweet-scented Odalisques
1. Lane, E.W.: *Manners and Customs of the Modern Egyptians*, p. 303
2. *Cairo and Egypt* (guidebook), 4th edition, 1900–1901, p. 166
3. de Guerville: *New Egypt*, p. 79
4. Steegmuller: *Flaubert in Egypt*, p. 40
5. Murray: *A Handbook for Travellers in Lower and Upper Egypt*
6. de Nerval, Gerard: *The Women of Cairo*, p. 152
7. de Guerville: op. cit., p. 149
8. Ibid., p. 150
9. Sim, Katharine: *Jean Louis Burckhardt*, p. 161
10. Lane: op. cit., p. 386
11. Russell Pasha, Sir Thomas: *Egyptian Service 1902–1946*, p. 179
12. Ibid., p. 179
13. Ibid., p. 180

14. Carman, Barry and McPherson, John: *Bimbashi McPherson – A Life in Egypt*, p. 211
15. Ibid., p. 214

Chapter 21: The Age of the Great Hotels
1. Bird, Michael: *Samuel Shepheard of Cairo*, p. 130
2. Ibid., p. 160
3. Twain, Mark: *Innocents Abroad*
4. Letter of 1869, quoted in Richardson, Joanna: *Théophile Gautier*, p. 233
5. Ibid., p. 233
6. Ibid., p. 233
7. Ibid., p. 234
8. These prints are reproduced in Nelson: *Shepheard's Hotel*
9. Autobiography of Henry M. Stanley quoted in Nelson: *Shepheard's Hotel*, p. 53
10. Boyle: *Boyle of Cairo*, p. 24
11. Thackery, Lance: *The Light Side of Egypt* ('Romeo and Juliet')
12. Stewart, Desmond: *Theodor Herzl*, p. 311
13. Garnett, David: *The Letters of T. E. Lawrence*, p. 820
14. Waugh, Evelyn: *Vile Bodies*, p. 36
15. Buckle, Richard: *Self-portrait with Friends: The Selected Diaries of Cecil Beaton 1926–1974*, p. 101
16. Waugh: *When the Going was Good*, p. 33
17. Aldington, Richard: *Lawrence of Arabia*, p. 382
18. Amory: *The Letters of Evelyn Waugh*, pp. 32–3

Chapter 22: Cairo's Last Flame
1. Russell Pasha, Sir Thomas: Papers in St Antony's College, Oxford, March 1966
2. Wahba: 'Cairo Memories' published in *Encounter*, May 1984
3. Ibid.
4. Stark, Freya: *Dust in the Lion's Paw*, p. 56
5. Buckle: *Self-portrait with Friends: The Selected Diaries of Cecil Beaton 1926–1974*, p. 94
6. Stark, Freya: op. cit., p. 57
7. Churchill, Winston: *History of the Second World War*, Volume 5, p. 289
8. Ibid., p. 371

Bibliography

Aldington, Richard: *Lawrence of Arabia, A Biographical Enquiry* (Collins, London 1955)

Aldridge, James: *Cairo* (Macmillan and Co., London 1969)

Amory, Mark (ed.): *The Letters of Evelyn Waugh* (Weidenfeld and Nicolson, London 1980)

Baedeker, Karl: *Egypt and the Sudan: Handbook for Travellers*, 5th edition (K. Baedeker, Leipzig 1929, reprint David and Charles, Newton Abbot 1974)

Baldick, Robert (ed.): *Pages from the Goncourt Journal* (Oxford University Press, Oxford 1962)

Baring, Evelyn, 1st Earl of Cromer: *Modern Egypt*, 2 vols (Macmillan and Co., London 1908)

Beatty, Charles: *Ferdinand de Lesseps, A Biographical Study* (Eyre and Spottiswoode, London 1956)

Berque, Jacques: *Egypt: Imperialism and Revolution*, translated by Jean Stewart (Faber and Faber, London 1972)

Bird, Michael: *Samuel Shepheard of Cairo* (Michael Joseph, London 1957)

Blake, Robert: *Disraeli* (Eyre and Spottiswoode, London 1966)

Blanch, Lesley: *The Wilder Shores of Love* (John Murray, London 1954)

Blunt, Wilfrid Scawen: *My Diaries – being a Personal Narrative of Events 1888-1914* (Martin Secker, London 1932)

Blyth, Henry: *Skittles: The Last Victorian Courtesan. The Life and Times of Catherine Walters* (Rupert Hart-Davis, London 1970)

Boyle, Clara: *Boyle of Cairo, A Diplomat's Adventures in the Middle East* (Titus Wilson Kendal, London 1965)

Buckle, Richard: *Self-portrait with Friends: The Selected Diaries of Cecil Beaton 1926-1974* (Weidenfeld and Nicolson, London 1979)

Burke's Royal Families of the World, Volume II - Africa and the Middle East (Burke's Peerage Limited, London 1980)

Butcher, Ellen L.: *Egypt as We Knew It* (Mills and Boon, London 1911)

Butler, Alfred Joshua: *Court Life in Egypt* (Chapman and Hall, London 1887)

Cairo and Egypt 1900-1901 (guidebook), 4th edition (Simpkin, Marshall and Co., London)

C. de B., a political informant to the head of the London House of Rothschild: *Letters from Paris 1870-1875*, translated by Robert Henrey (J.M. Dent & Sons Ltd, London 1942)

Cameron, Donald Andreas: *Egypt in the Nineteenth Century, or Mehemet Ali and his Successors until the British Occupation in 1882* (Smith, Elder and Co., London 1898)

Carman, Barry and McPherson, John: *Bimbashi McPherson - A Life in Egypt* (British Broadcasting Corporation, London 1983)

Cecil, Lord Edward: *The Leisure of an Egyptian Official* (Century Publishing, London 1984)

Chapman, Brian: *The Life and Times of Baron Haussmann* (Weidenfeld and Nicolson, London 1957)

Chennells, Ellen: *Recollections of an Egyptian Princess* (William Blackwood, London 1893)

Churchill, Winston S.: *The Second World War*, 6 vols (Cassell, London 1948-54)

Thomas Cook and Son: *Tourist's Handbook for Egypt, the Nile and the Desert* (Thos. Cook and Son/Simpkin, Marshall and Co., London 1876, later editions 1888, 1892, 1897)

Thomas Cook and Son: *Cook's Handbook for Egypt and the Sudan*. By E.A. Wallis Budge (Thos. Cook and Son, London 1905, 1906, 1911, 1921, 1929)

Thomas Cook and Son: *The Business of Travel: a Fifty Years' Record of Progress*. By W. Fraser Rae and others (Thos. Cook and Son, London 1891)

Crabitès, Pierre: *American Officers in the Egyptian Army* (George Routledge, London 1938)

Didier, Charles: *Les Nuits du Caire* (Paris 1860)

Draneht, Despina (née Zavudachis): *Twilight Memories*, privately printed in Lausanne, Switzerland, under the initials D.Z.D. (no date)

Duff, David: *Eugénie & Napoleon III* (Collins, London 1978)

Ebers, Georg Moritz: *Egypt, Descriptive, Historical and Picturesque*, 2 vols (Cassell & Co., London 1881, 1883)

Edwards, Amelia Blandford: *A Thousand Miles up the Nile* (Longmans, London 1889 and Century Publishing, London 1982)

Flower, Raymond: *Napoleon to Nasser: The Story of Modern Egypt* (Tom Stacey, London 1972)

Fulford, Roger (ed.): *Your Dear Letter: Private Correspondence of Queen Victoria and the Crown Princess of Prussia 1865-1871* (Evans Brothers, London 1971)

Fullerton, William Morton: *In Cairo* (Macmillan and Co., London 1891)

Gabarti (Jabarti) Abd al-Rahman ibn Hasan al-: *Merveilles Biographiques et Historiques du Cheikh Abdel-Rahman el Djabarti*, translated by Chefik Mansour Bey and others, 9 vols (Imprimerie Nationale, Cairo 1888-96)

des Garets, Comtesse: *The Tragic Empress*, translated by Helene Graeme (Skeffington & Son Ltd, London, no date)

Garnett, David: *The Letters of T.E. Lawrence* (Spring Books, London 1964)

Gautier, Théophile: *L'Orient* (Charpentier, Paris 1893)

Ghali, Mirrit Boutros (ed.): *Memoires de Nubar Pasha* (Librairie du Liban, Beirut 1983)

Gordon, Lucie Duff: *Letters from Egypt* (Virago, London 1983)

Grafftey-Smith, Laurence: *Bright Levant* (John Murray, London 1970)

Guedalla, Philip: *The Second Empire* (Hodder and Stoughton, London 1922)

de Guerville, B.: *New Egypt* (William Heinemann, London 1905/1906)

Herold, J.C.: *Bonaparte in Egypt* (Hamish Hamilton, London 1962)

Horne, Alistair: *The Fall of Paris - The Siege and the Commune 1870-71* (Macmillan and Co., London 1965; Penguin, London 1981)

Hourani, Albert: *Arabic Thought in the Liberal Age* (Cambridge University Press, Cambridge 1983 rpt)

Hughes, Pennethorne: *While Shepheard's Watched* (Chatto and Windus, London 1949)

Ibn Battuta, Muhammad ibn Abd Allah: *The Travels of Ibn Battuta AD 1325-1354*, translated by H.A.R. Gibb (Cambridge University Press, Cambridge 1958)

Kinross, John P.D. Balfour, Lord: *Between Two Seas, The Creation of the Suez Canal* (John Murray, London 1968)

Knepler, Henry (ed. and transl.): *Man about Paris: The Confessions of Arsène Houssaye* (Victor Gollancz, London 1972)

Landes, David S.: *Bankers and Pashas* (Heinemann, London 1958)

Lane, E.W.: *An Account of the Manners and Customs of the Modern Egyptians* (Gardner, London 1985)

Lane-Poole, Stanley: *The Story of Cairo* (J.M. Dent and Sons, London 1902)

de Leon, Edwin: *The Khedive's Egypt* (Sampson Low, Marston, Searle & Rivington, London 1877)

de Lesseps, Ferdinand: *The Suez Canal, a Personal Narrative by M. Ferdinand de Lesseps*, translated by Sir Henry Drummond Wolff (William Blackwood and Sons, London 1876)

Lloyd, Lord: *Egypt since Cromer* (Macmillan and Co., London 1933)

Lott, Emmeline: *Harem Life in Egypt and Constantinople* (Richard Bentley, London 1865)

Ludwig, Emil: *Bismarck: The Story of a Fighter*, translated by Eden and Cedar Paul (Allen and Unwin, London 1927)

MacCoan, James Carlile: *Egypt as It is . . .* (Cassell Petter and Galpin, London 1877)

MacCoan, James Carlile: *Egypt under Ismail, a Romance of History* (Chapman and Hall, London 1889)

Maclean, Fitzroy: *Eastern Approaches* (Jonathan Cape, London 1949)

Magnus, Philip: *King Edward the Seventh* (John Murray, London 1964)

Mardaga, Pierre: 'Alger 1830-60' in *Urbi, Villes Coloniales*, 6 October 1982, Liège, Belgium

Maurois, Simone André: *Miss Howard and the Emperor* (Collins, London 1957)

Meyer, Michael: *Henrik Ibsen, The Farewell to Poetry 1864–1882* (Rupert Hart-Davies, London 1967, 1971)

Milner, Alfred: *England in Egypt*, 7th edition (Edward Arnold, London 1899)

Moorehead, Alan: *The Blue Nile* (Penguin, London 1983)

Moorehead, Alan: *The White Nile* (Penguin, London 1973)

Murray: *A Handbook for Travellers in Lower and Upper Egypt*, 8th edition (John Murray, London 1981)

Nelson, Nina: *The Mena House* (London 1979)

Nelson, Nina: *Shepheard's Hotel* (Barrie and Rockliff, London 1960)

de Nerval, Gerard: *The Women of Cairo* (translation of *Voyages en Orient*) (Routledge, London 1929)

Ninet, John: *Lettres d'Egypte 1879–1882* (Editions du CNRS, Paris 1979)

Osborne, Charles: *Verdi: A Life in the Theatre* (Weidenfeld and Nicolson, London 1987)

Paléologue, Maurice: *The Tragic Empress: Intimate Conversations with the Empress Eugénie* (Saturn Press, London 1928)

Pudney, John: *Suez: de Lesseps' Canal* (J.M. Dent, London 1969)

Rameses (pseudonym of Clarence Scudamore Jarvis): *Oriental Spotlight* (John Murray, London 1937)

Richardson, Frank: *Napoleon: Bisexual Emperor* (William Kimber, London 1972)

Richardson, Joanna: *Théophile Gautier* (Max Reinhardt, London 1958)

Ridley, Jasper: *Napoleon III and Eugénie* (Constable, London 1979)

Rowlatt, Mary: *A Family in Egypt* (Robert Hale Ltd, London 1956)

Russell Pasha, Sir Thomas: *Egyptian Service 1902–1946* (John Murray, London 1949)

The Thomas Russell Pasha Papers, on loan to St Antony's College, Oxford (March 1966)

Russell, William Howard: *The Prince of Wales' Tour: a diary in India, with some acount of the Visits . . . to the Courts of Greece, Egypt, Spain and Portugal* (London 1877)

Shaarawi, Huda: *Harem Years, the Memoirs of an Egyptian Feminist*, edited and translated with an introduction by Margot Badran (Virago, London 1987)

Sim, Katharine: *Jean Louis Burckhardt: A Biography* (Quartet Books, London 1981)

Stark, Freya: *Dust in the Lion's Paw* (John Murray, London 1961)

Stark, Freya: *East is West* (John Murray, London 1945)

Steegmuller, Francis (ed.): *Flaubert in Egypt* (Michale Haag Ltd, London 1983)

Steevens, G.W.: *Egypt in 1898* (William Blackwood, London 1898)

Stewart, Desmond: *Cairo* (Rupert Hart-Davis, London 1969)

Stewart, Desmond: Theodor Herzl (Hamish Hamilton, London 1974)

St John, J.A.: *Egypt and Nubia* (Chapman and Hall, London 1835)

Storrs, Ronald: *Orientations* (Ivor Nicholson & Watson, London 1937)

Strage, Mark: *Cape to Cairo* (Jonathan Cape, London 1973)

Swinglehurst, Edward: *Cook's Tours - The Story of Popular Travel* (Blandford Press, Poole, Dorset 1982)

Thackery, Lance: *The Light Side of Egypt* (Adam and Charles Black, London 1912)

Toye, Francis: *Giuseppe Verdi* (Victor Gollancz, London 1962)

Tucker, Judith E.: *Women in Nineteenth-Century Egypt* (Cambridge University Press, Cambridge 1985)

Tugay, Emine Foat: *Three Centuries, Family Chronicles of Turkey and Egypt* (Oxford University Press, Oxford 1963)

Twain, Mark: *Innocents Abroad* (Collins, London 1985)

Twentieth-Century Impressions of Egypt (Lloyd's Greater Britain Publishing Company, London 1909)

Vickers, Hugo: *Cecil Beaton* (Weidenfeld and Nicolson, London 1985)

Walker, Frank: *The Man Verdi* (J.M. Dent, London 1962)

Waugh, Evelyn: *Vile Bodies* (Penguin, London 1938)

Waugh, Evelyn: *When the Going was Good* (Penguin, London 1951)

Webster, James: *Travels through the Crimea, Turkey and Egypt, Performed during the Years 1825-1828*, 2 vols (London 1830)

Zola, Emile: *Nana*, translated by George Holden (Penguin, London 1972)

Index

Abbas I, Khedive, 37-8, 39
Abbas Hilmi, Khedive, 66-7, 92, 101
Abbasiyya, 62, 66, 162, 167
Abdin Palace, 3, 10, 45, 64, 66, 67, 122, 168
Abdul-Aziz, Sultan, 52-3, 57-8, 98-100, 103-4, 122, 124
Abdul Hamid I, Sultan, 16-17, 53, 57
Abu Kir, 19
Abu Kir, Battle of, 21
Abu Simbel, 117
Abyssinia, 121
Adès Store, 169, 171
Africa Corps, 156
Aguado, Marquis d', 11
Ahmed (Said's son), 41
Aida, 28, 72, 74-82, 101, 174
L'Aigle, 98, 100, 104, 109, 112
El Alamein, Battle of, 156
Alba, Duke of, 118
Albemarle, Countess of, 135
Albert, Prince Consort, 11, 59, 93
Albert I, King of Belgium, 67
Alboniz, 164
Aldenham, Lord, 135
Alexander II, Tsar, 55, 56, 58
Alexandra, Princess of Wales, 83, 85, 86, 105, 106

Alexandria, 16, 19, 25, 36, 40, 65, 90, 125, 126, 165
Alfonso III, King of Spain, 118
Algiers, 65
Ali Pasha, 99-100
Allenby, Viscount, 161, 162
Almaza Airport, 139
America, 126
American Civil War, 63, 120
Ammon, Temple of, 174
Anderson, Arthur, 89
Andrassy, Count Jules, 108
Anglo-Egyptian Bank, 120
Annapolis Naval Academy, 63
Antigny, Blanche d', 54
Aosta, Duke of, 106
Arab revolt (1882), 129
Arabia, 26
'Ariston' Aerated Water Factory, 139
Art Deco, 172
Art Nouveau, 171
Aswan, 127, 172
Atatürk, Mustafa Kemal, 43
Australia, 160, 161
Austrian Lloyd, 126
Automobile Club, 170
Aversperg, Prince, 135
al-Azhar University, 173

191

Bab Zouela, 24
Bachauer, Gina, 164
Badia Cabaret, 168
Baedeker, 127-8
Baehler, Mr, 150
Bagier, 74, 76
al-Bakri, Shaikh, 18
Banque Arabe d'Investissements
   Internationaux, 10
Banque Impériale Ottomane, 120
Barclays Bank, 169
Barillet-Deschamps, Jean-Pierre,
   69-70
Baron, Delphine, 80
Barron, Henri, 44-5
Bartholdi, Frederic Auguste, 102
Baudelaire, Charles, 54
al-Bawwab, Sulaiman Bey, 23-4
Beaton, Cecil, 2, 156, 165
Behidja Toussoun, Princess, 27
Bekir Bey, 28
Bellanger, Marguerite, 13
Bellefonds, Linant de, 89
Belliard, General, 19
Bellisle, Marguerite Pauline
   (Bellilote), 18, 19
Belzoni, Giovanni, 25, 35
Benedetti, 114
Benha Palace, 38
Beust, Baron Frederick de, 108
Beyer, 59
Beylerbey Palace, Istanbul, 1,
   98-9
Bischoffsheim Bank, 120
Bismarck, Count Otto von, 9,
   12-13, 56, 58, 77, 96, 110,
   114-15
Bitter Lakes, 88
Blacque Bey, 63
Blanch, Lesley, 17
Blunt, Wilfrid, 11, 13, 115
Blythe, 117-18

Bottesini, Giovanni, 79
Bouilhet, Louis, 142
Boulaq, 3, 64, 74, 151, 160
Boulaq Museum, 56
Boyle, Clare, 117, 154
Boyle, Henry, 5, 37, 38, 117,
   131-2, 153-4
Bravay, 39
Brissac, Comte de, 97
Bristol Hotel, 149
Britain, 15, 38, 89; French
   withdrawal from Egypt, 19-
   20; and the Suez Canal, 94,
   104-5; Eugénie in exile in,
   116-17; occupation of Egypt,
   120-2, 125, 129-40; tourism
   in Egypt, 126-8; and Egyptian
   nationalism, 160-2, 167-70
British Army, 64, 146-7
Bromfield, Arthur, 151
Bruce, Sir Frederick, 38
Buluk Nizam, 167
Bulwer, Sir Henry, 40
Burckhardt, Johann Ludwig, 144
Burgoyne, Sir John, 116
Butcher, Mrs E.L., 85
Butler, Alfred Joshua, 49-50
Butler, E.M., 91

Cairo-Alexandria railway, 38, 39-
   40, 125
Cairo Conference (1921), 156
Cairo Electric Railways, 137
Cairo-Ismailiya Canal, 120
Caisse de la Dette Publique, 121
Cambridge, Duke of, 56
Canal Zone, 167-8
'Carlos Bey', 19-20
Carr, John, 65
Casdaglise family, 136
Catroux, General, 156
Cavafy, Constantin, 164

Cavala, 21
Cave, Steven, 121
Cavour, Count Camillo, 96, 98
Cecil, Lord Edward, 133, 134, 138
Cerisy, 37
Cézanne, Paul, 54
Chaillé-Long, 63
Chakrian, Artin Bey, 37
Champolian, Jean François, 37
Charles, Hippolyte, 15
Chasseriau, Frederic, 65
Chennells, Ellen, 33, 83, 85, 86
Chiang Kai-Chek, General, 166
Chiara, Maria, 174
Chirin Bey, 36
Chopin, Frédéric, 10
Churchill, Sir Winston, 156, 166
Cicurel, 169, 171
Citadel, 22, 24-5, 26, 37, 38, 61, 67, 124
City of the Dead, 164, 172-3
Clarendon, Lord, 10-11
Clary, Comte, 97
Cleopatra's Needle, 25
Clot, Antoine (Clot Bey), 23, 28, 37, 107
Club Méditerranée, 37
Colet, Louise, 106
Collacott, John, 139
Communists, 167
Compagnie Universelle du Canal Maritime de Suez, 10, 40
Connaught, Duke of, 117
Constantinople, 130
Continental Hotel, 138, 149
Continental-Savoy Hotel, 157-8
Cook, John Mason, 127
Cook, Thomas, 107, 125-6, 137
Cooper, Duff, 2-3
Coquelin, 73
Cordier, Charles, 66

Cosmopolitan Hotel, 172
Cosse-Brissac, Count of, 108
Costi, 138
Courier de L'Egypte, 14-15
Craig, James, 169
Crane, 116
Cromer, Lord, 5, 40, 44, 117, 125, 129, 131, 136, 137, 139, 153, 155, 169

al-Darawalli, Muhammad Bey Khusraw, 29
Daudet, Alphonse, 93
Davies Bryan and Co., 139
Davillier, Comte, 97
Degas, Edgar, 54
Delamalle, Madame, 92
Delchevalerie, 83, 86, 135, 175
Della Sala, Comtessa, 143
Denderah, Temple of, 16
Desaix, General Louis, 15-16
Description d'Egypte, 16
Didier, Charles, 125
Diebitch, Carl Wilhelm Valentin von, 64, 84, 85, 175
al-Din, Serag, 168
Disraeli, Benjamin, 2, 27, 103, 121, 125
Dolphin, 112
Domingo, Placido, 174
Douay, General, 97
Draneht, Despina, 46, 53, 123-4
Draneht, Paul (Paul Pavlides), 23, 28, 73-5, 77-8, 79-80, 123
Du Camp, Maxime, 107, 142, 149
Du Locle, Camille, 75-6
Duff, David, 118
Dumas, Alexandre, 106
Duveau, Georges, 59

Edward, Prince of Wales, 2, 39, 56, 57, 74, 83, 85, 105, 106, 125, 132, 139

Edwards, Amelia, 126

Egypt-Greece Friendship Society, 164

Egyptian Hotels Corporation, 152, 174

Eiffel, Gustave, 102

al-Elfi, Muhammad Bey, 16, 38, 69

Elliot, Sir Henry, 108

Emine (Muhammad Ali's wife), 22, 29

Empain, Baron, 137

Ems Telegram, 115

Ena, Queen of Spain, 118

Enfantin, Prosper, 89-90, 91

Ernest-Auguste, Prince of Hanover, 108

Erskine, General Sir George, 167

Eugène, Prince of Savoy, 70

Eugénie, Empress, 44, 45, 58, 67, 72; background, 10-13; unpopularity, 96-7; journey to Egypt, 1, 3, 97-100; Ismail's love for, 5, 9; in Egypt, 101-2, 106, 109-13; in exile, 110, 115-18; Franco-Prussian War, 114-15; last visit to Egypt, 117; death, 116, 118

Evans, Doctor, 100, 116

Exposition Universelle, Paris (1847), 8, 44, 52, 54, 56, 58, 101-2, 110

Ezbek, Emir, 68

Ezbekiyya, 2, 14, 62, 64, 65, 66, 68-71, 72, 132-3, 157, 162

Ezbekiyya lake, 16

Faika, Princess (Ismail's daughter), 47, 123

al-Falaky Bey, Mahmoud, 62

Farouk, King, 2, 3, 25, 28, 67, 122, 138, 153, 164, 168, 169, 170

Fasciottoi, 72

Fatma, Princess, 84

Fawzia, Princess, 67

Fenwick, Colonel, 154

Feuillant, Xavier, 55

Filippi, Filippo, 80, 81-2

Firdus, 147-8

First World War, 145, 146, 155-6, 157, 158, 160, 174

Flaubert, Gustave, 2, 27, 54, 69, 106, 107, 142, 144, 149

Flower, Raymond, 119

Forbin, Comte A. de, 25

Forster, E.M., 164

Fouad, King, 28, 67, 134-5, 138, 162

Fouad University, 167

Fourès, Lieutenant, 18

France, 9-13; Napoleon I's invasion of Egypt, 14-20, 21; influence in Egypt, 1, 27, 44-5; rebuilding of Paris, 58-60; and the Suez Canal, 88-95; Franco-Prussian war, 13, 77, 79, 96, 110, 114-15; Eugénie's escape into exile, 115-16

Franz, Julius (Franz Bey), 64-5, 84, 86

Franz-Joseph, Emperor of Austria, 105, 108, 110-13

Frederick, King of Prussia, 55, 104, 108, 110, 112, 114, 123

Fromentin, Eugène, 109, 113

Fruhling and Goschen, 120

Fullerton, William, 132

Fustat, 173

Gabarti, 14, 16, 69
Gagarin, Prince, 143
Galassi, Farida, 172
Galis Bey, 28
Galleti-Gianoli, Isabella, 78
Galloway, Lady, 132
Garden City, 3, 70, 136, 139, 162
Garden City movement, 65
Garets, Comtesse des, 98, 99, 114
Gautier, Théophile, 10, 106, 151-2
Gaze, Henry, 126
General Postal Union, 63
George V, King of England, 27
Gezira, 3, 166
Gezira Club, 9, 87, 132, 135-6, 138, 139, 175-6
Gezira Palace, 3, 47, 64, 65, 70, 83-7, 101, 135, 141, 171
Gezira Palace Hotel, 152, 174-5
Ghali, Butros, 155
al-Gharbi, 'Shaikh' Ibrahim, 145-6
Ghawazee girls, 2, 133, 142, 144
Ghislanzoni, Antonio, 76
Giza, 23, 65, 87, 162
Giza Palace, 39, 68, 85
Goldsmith, Lewis, 15
Goncourt, Edmond de, 53, 55-6, 97, 123-4
Gordon, General, 44, 127
Gordon, Lucie Duff, 25, 48-9
Gorst, Lord, 169
Gounod, Charles François, 75
Grafftey-Smith, Laurence, 132, 134, 140, 145
Gramont, Duc de, 114
Grand Continental Hotel, 66
Grand Tour, 2, 125
Granger, Lublin, 80

Grant, General, 105
Grassini, Ms, 15
Graves, Robert, 140, 164
Great Flap (1942), 165
Greece, 164
Grille, 112
Grivegnée, Catherine de, 11
Groppi's Coffee House, 163, 169, 173
Grossi, Eleonora, 78
Guerville, B. de, 66, 117, 130-1, 141-2, 143
Gumhour al-Misri, 167

Haidar Pasha, 168
al-Halabi, Sulaiman, 19
Halévy, Ludovic, 74
Halim, Prince, 41
Hanem, Kuchuk, 144
Hanki Bey, Aziz, 46
Haramlik Palace, 8
Hararise family, 136
Hardy, 65
Harris, Selina, 33-4
Harvey Pasha, 146
Hasan (Ismail's son), 84
Hassan, Abdel Fattah, 167-8
Hassan Hassan, Prince, 174
Haussmann, Baron George, 1, 4, 44, 52, 53, 58, 59-60, 61, 64, 65
Head, Frederick, 159
Heliopolis, 66, 136-7, 138, 162
Heliopolis Oasis Company, 137
Helwan, 64
Henniker, Sir Francis, 144
Henry, Prince of the Netherlands, 105, 108, 110, 112
Herzl, Theodor, 2, 155
Hill, Mr, 150
Hilmiya internment camp, 146

Hitler, Adolf, 2
Hortense, Queen, 12, 112
Hôtel d'Angleterre, 157–8
Hôtel Baudard de Saint James, Paris, 10
Hôtel du Nil, 66, 149
Hôtel d'Orient, 66, 107
Houssaye, Arsène, 54
Howard, Ebenezer, 65
Howard, Miss, 13
Huescar, Duke of, 108
Hughes, Robert, 169
Hugo, Victor, 106
Husain (Ismail's son), 84
Husayn Kamil, Sultan, 129

Ibn Battuta, 62
Ibrahim, Hafiz, 68
Ibrahim Pasha (Ismail's son), 6, 48, 66, 92, 134
Ibrahim Pasha (Muhammad Ali's son), 22, 26, 27, 30, 35–7, 69
Iffet Hasan, Princess, 27, 132
Ignatieff, General, 105, 108, 112
Ikhwan al-Muslimun, 167
Ilhami (Abbas I's son), 38
L'Illustration, 84–5
India, 38, 63, 89, 120, 137, 161
Ingee Khanum, 39
Insha Palace, 67
Institut d'Egypte, 16, 88, 106
International Monetary Fund, 119
Iran, 43
Islamic City, 173
Ismail, Khedive of Egypt, 1–2, 22, 25, 39; accession, 41, 42; reforms, 43–4; character, 45, 46–7, 49–51; harem, 5–8, 46; visits France, 52–6; rebuilds Cairo, 44–5, 52, 62–71; in England, 57; Opera House,

72–4; and the Suez Canal, 94, 97, 98, 102–6, 107–13; Empress Eugénie's visit, 5, 9–10, 101–2; tours European capitals, 103–4, 106; legalizes prostitution, 144–5; fall of, 103, 119–24; death, 124
Ismail (Muhammad Ali's son), 22
Ismailiya, 66, 112
Ismailiya Palace, 68
Istanbul, 26, 35–6, 42
Italy, 96, 122–3, 165
Izzet Pasha, Muhammad, 123

Jawhar Palace, 26
Jemileh Hanem, Princess, 131–2
Jerome, King of Westphalia, 10, 11, 54
Joinville, Prince de, 116
Josephine, Empress, 12, 15, 16, 17, 53

Kamil, Princess, 152
Kashif, Amir Hasan, 16
Keppel, Lady Elizabeth, 135
Khalil, Si, 130
Khartoum, 127
Khedival Club, 133, 134–5
Khoshyar Hanem, Paramount Princess, 47–8
Kinross, John P.D., 106
Kirkpatrick, Dona Maria Manuela, 10–11, 13
Kirkpatrick, William, 10
Kitchener, Lord, 130, 131, 136, 169
Kléber, General, 19, 150
Koubbeh Palace, 66–7
Krupp, 55, 56, 110
Kulthum, Umm, 3, 171

Lamartine, Alphonse Marie de, 28
Lambert, Charles, 28
Lampugnani, 79
Landes, David, 39
Lane, E.W., 22, 141, 144
Lane-Poole, Stanley, 64
Latif, 111
Lawrence, T.E., 155, 158
Layard, Sir Henry, 130
Le Brun, Eugénie, 130
Le Gentilhomme, General, 156
Le Pére, Jean-Baptiste, 88-9
Lebreton, Madame, 116
Lefèbre, Edouard, 102
Leon, Edwin de, 38, 40, 51, 89
Leopold, King of Belgium, 11
Lesseps, Charles de, 109
Lesseps, Ferdinand de, 10, 11, 39, 40, 88, 90-4, 103, 107, 108, 111, 115-16, 126
Lesseps, Jules de, 109
Lesseps, Mathieu de, 11, 90, 91
Letessier, Caroline, 54
Lipton, Sir Thomas, 154
Lloyd, Lord, 130, 135, 155, 169
Locke-King, Mr and Mrs, 159
Longworth, David Garrick, 133
Lott, Emmeline, 6, 30, 48
Louis, Prince of Battenberg, 105
Louis XIV, King of France, 42, 89
'Louis-Farouk' furniture, 163, 175
Louis Philippe, King of France, 11, 25, 27
Lubbert Bey, 28
Ludwig, Emile, 119
Luigi, Count, 30-3
Lutfallah, Prince Habib, 174
Lutfallah, Princess Lodi, 174-5
Luxor, 127, 173, 174

Maadi, 136, 164, 173
McCalmont, Mrs Harry, 135
MacCoan, James Carlile, 37, 39, 41, 50, 61, 66, 70-1
McKillop, Captain, 111
Maclean, Fitzroy, 138
McPherson, Bimbashi, 137, 147-8
Maffei, Comtesse de, 77
Magdi, Salih, 46
Maguè's, 12
Mahdi, 127
Mahroussa, 52, 108, 122
Maillart, 67
Malcolm, Sir Ian, 109-10
Malta, 125
Mamluk Palace, 150
Mamluks, 21-2, 23-5
Manet, Edouard, 54
Manial Palace, 37
Manners, Lady Victoria, 135
Manning, Olivia, 166
Mansour's jewellery shop, 153
Mariam Hanim, 27
Mariani, Angelo, 78-9
Marie Antoinette, Queen, 9-10
Mariette, Alfred, 80
Mariette, Auguste Ferdinand François, 74, 75-6, 77, 80, 101-2, 107, 109
Mariette, Claude, 28, 56
Marriott Hotel, 3, 87, 174, 175
Marseilles, 163
Mary, Princess Royal, 27
Maspero, Sir Gaston, 98
Mathilde, Princess, 10, 11, 13, 46, 97, 152
Maurois, André, 164
Maximilian, Emperor of Mexico, 58
Mayloum Pasha, 39
Mecca, 23

Medina, 23
Medini, Paolo, 78
Meilhac, Henri, 74
Melek, Sultana, 122
Memphis, 74
Mena House Hotel, 158-9, 166
Mendrici, 25
Menou, General, 19
Menzaleh, Lake, 40
Mérimée, Prosper, 13, 56
Messervy, General, 156
Metro Cinema, 169
Metropolitan Hotel, 158
Michael, Grand Duke, 110
Milan, 123
Milner, Lord, 49, 137-8
Mimaut, 90
Mohandeseen, 173
Moharrem Pasha, 132
Monet, Claude, 54
Monge, Gaspard, 15, 16
Mongini, Pietro, 78
Montaza Palace, 127
Montijo, Count of, 10
Morny, Duc de, 94
Mosque of Al-Azhar, 18-19
Mostyn, Gwendoline, 152
Mott, Colonel Thaddeus P., 63
Mougel Bey, 28
Mubarak, Ali Pasha, 62
Mugama'a Building, 68
Muggeridge, Malcolm, 2-3, 140
Muhammad Ali, 10, 20, 29, 31,
    35, 37, 43, 61, 62, 67, 144;
    background, 21-3; cruelty, 22;
    slaughters Mamluks, 21, 23-5;
    as ruler of Egypt, 25-6, 66;
    palaces, 26-7, 83; and French
    in Egypt, 27-8, 89; and
    Ferdinand de Lesseps, 90, 92;
    surveys Suez isthmus, 91
Muhammad Ali Club, 138

Muhammad Ali Mosque, 3, 67
Muqattam Hill, 3, 26, 67
Murad, 57
Murat, Prince Joachim, 97, 108
Murray, 142
Musk, Izz ad-Din, 69
Muslim Brethren, 167, 170
Musset, Alfred de, 109
Mussolini, Benito, 166
Mustafa Fazil, Prince, 129-30
Muzio, Emanuele, 74, 76

Nadaillac, Madame de, 97
Nadar, 54
al-Nadim, Abdullah, 129
Nahas Pasha, 168
Napoleon I (Bonaparte),
    Emperor, 2, 10, 12, 14, 15-
    20, 21, 27, 61, 62, 69, 88-9,
    97
Napoleon III (Louis Napoleon),
    Emperor, 55, 101; and
    Eugénie, 10-13; Ismail visits in
    Paris, 52-3; rebuilds Paris, 58-
    9; and the Suez Canal, 93, 94,
    97; political naïvety, 96;
    Franco-Prussian War, 114-15;
    forced into exile, 9-10
Napoleon Joseph, Prince (Plon
    Plon), 54, 93, 115
Narriman, Queen, 67
Nasiriya quarter, 16
al-Nasser, Gamal abd, 2, 68, 120,
    174
Nazlat as-Saman, 159
Nazli, Princess (Muhammad Ali's
    daughter), 1, 22, 29-34, 47
Nazli, Queen, 172
Nazli Fazil, Princess, 129-31
Nazli Hanem, 27
Nazli Sabri, 28
Nelson, Admiral, 19

Nerval, Gerard de, 89, 142–3
New Hotel, 66
Nezib, Battle of (1839), 27
Niccolini, 78
Nile, River, 21, 25, 41, 122, 126, 127, 172
Ninet, John, 22, 35
Northern Cemetery, 40
Nubar Pasha, 30, 31, 35, 36–7, 42, 43, 45, 52, 73, 84, 94, 102–3, 108
Nungovich Bey, George, 157–8

Oakes, Sir Reginald, 137
Oberoi Hotels, 159
Offenbach, Jacques, 54–5, 74
Omar Khayyam Hotel, 174
Omar Pasha Sultan, 65
Opera House, 28, 72–82, 163, 173–4
Oppenheim Bank, 120
Orloff, Princess, 13
Ottoman Empire, 21–2, 26, 35–6, 42, 62, 103–4

P & O, 108, 125
Palestine, 126, 127, 155
Pall Mall Gazette, 106
Palmerston, Lord, 10–11, 89, 93, 94
Panama Canal, 89
Pantanelli, 65
Papadimitriou, Elli, 164
Parcq, 65
Paris, 2, 12, 44–5, 49, 52–5, 58–60, 115–16, 123, 163
Patti, Adelina, 82
Paul, King of the Hellenes, 164
Paul I, Tsar, 88
Pavlides, Paul *see* Draneht Bey
Peake Pasha, 156
Pearl, Cora, 54

Pension Tewfik, 158
Perier, Casimir, 59
Persigny, 96–7
Petits Lits Blancs, 175
Pissarro, Camille, 54
Poëze, Comtesse de la, 97
Polytechnic School, 23
Porkosh-Osten, Baron, 108
Port Said, 94, 101, 107, 109–11, 132
Potocka, Delphine, 10
Pourtales, Comtesse de, 12
Pozzoni, Antonietta, 78
Primoli, 152
Princeteau Bey, 28
Prokesch, Baron de, 84
Prussia, 9–10, 12–13, 114–15
Psyche, 112
Pückler-Muskau, Prince, 86
Punch, 104–5
Pyramids, 64, 66, 67, 86, 105

abd al-Qader, Amir, 108
Qait Bey, Sultan, 68
Qasr al-Doubbara, 136, 166
Qasr al-Nil, 166
Qasr al-Nil Barracks, 146
Qasr al-Nil Palace, 109

Rainbeaux, Monsieur, 97
Rameses, 136, 139
Rameses II, Pharoah, 25
Raouf Pasha, 98
Ras al-Tin Palace, 26, 41
Ravaisse, Paul, 44
Recamier, Madame, 106
Red Sea, 88–9
Redon-Stuckle, 65
Reffye, Commander de, 97
Renoir, Pierre Auguste, 54
Repton, Humphery, 86
Reyer, 80–1

Reza Khan, 43
Rhodes, 36
Ricordi, Giulio, 76, 80
Rifai Mosque, 124
Ritchie, General, 156
Rivery, Aimée Dubucq de, 17, 53
Rivoli Cinema, 168-9
Roda Island, 37
Rolo family, 136
Rommel, Field-Marshal, 3, 156, 165
Roosevelt, Franklin D., 166
Rosetta, 19
Rosetti, 69
Ross, Janet, 45
Rossi, 72
Rossini, Gioacchino, 78
Rothschild, Lord, 12, 121
Rotli, Lake, 68-9
Rowlatt, Arthur, 70
Rowlatt family, 87
Royal Automobile Club, 138
Russell, Dorothea, 162
Russell, Thomas (Russell Pasha), 2, 145-6, 147, 161-2
Ruyssenaers, M., 103

Saadist Club, 138
Sabet, Adel Beg, 3, 171-2
Sabil Kuttab, 64
Sabry, Muhammed, 42
Sadat, Anwar, 173
Sadiq, Ismail, 45, 47, 62, 123
Said, Khedive, 38-41, 42, 44, 62-3, 85, 92-4
Saif al-Din, Ahmed, 134-5
St James's Club, 169
Saint-Simon, Comte de, 10, 22, 89
Saint-Simon, Louis, Duc de, 89
Saint-Simonians, 22, 90, 91
Sainte-Beuve, Charles Augustin, 152

Sakakini Palace, 65
Salamlik kiosk, 64, 65, 83-4, 85-6, 174-5
Saleh Kosh, 23
Salt, Consul-General, 49
Sand, George, 10
Saudi Arabia, 23, 163
Savoy Hotel, 66, 138, 157-8, 161
Schneider, Hortense, 2, 53-4, 55
Second World War, 138, 146-7, 156, 165-6
Sedan, Battle of (1870), 115
Saferis, George, 164
Selim, Sultan, 17, 53
Semiramis Hotel, 135, 136, 138
Sencourt, Robert, 11
Sesto, Duke of, 11
Seton-Kerr, Captain, 135
Sèves, Colonel (Sulaiman Pasha), 23, 27, 37, 107-8
Shahin, 24
Shaarawi, Huda, 65
Shaw, Norman, 65
Shepheard, Samuel, 150-1
Shepheard's Hotel, 2, 16, 19, 66, 126, 133, 138, 149-56, 169-70
Sherif Pasha, Khahil, 130
Sherif Pasha, Muhammad, 27, 45, 108, 122, 172
Shevikiar, Princess, 167
Shoubra, 26, 61, 164
Shoubra Palace, 26-7
Sisley, Alfred, 54
Spain, 114, 116, 118
Spatz, 123
Sphinx, 166
Sphinx, 133-4
Stack, Sir Lee, 162
Stanhope, Lady Hester, 91
Stanley, Henry Morton, 153

Stanton, 121
Stark, Freya, 3, 165, 166
Statue of Liberty, 102
Steevens, G.W., 132
Steinschneider, Luigi, 85
Steller, Francesco, 78
Stephenson, Robert, 38, 39, 94, 125
Stevenson, Sir Ralph, 167, 168
Stolz, Teresa, 78, 79, 82
Storrs, Ronald, 73, 128, 129, 130, 131, 132, 134, 135, 143, 154, 158, 160
Strauss, Johann, 58
Strazza, G., 175
Sublime Porte, 21, 42, 103-4
Sudan, 26, 45, 63
Suez, 43, 132
Suez Canal, 44, 48, 62-3; Le Père surveys, 88-9; Saint-Simonian interest in, 89-91; de Lesseps wins concession, 40, 91-5; opening celebrations, 1, 2, 5, 74-5, 97, 102-6, 107-13, 126-7; Disraeli buys shares in, 103; value to British, 120-1
Suez Canal Company, 121, 164
Sulaiman Pasha (Colonel Sèves), 23, 27, 37, 107-8
Sursoc family, 174
Sutherland, Duke of, 105, 134
Syria, 26

Tawhida (Muhammad Ali's son), 22
Teba, Count of, 10
Teghetoff, Admiral, 108-9
Tewfik, Khedive, 49-50, 84, 85, 122, 125, 135
Thackery, Lance, 154-5
Théâtre des Variétés, Paris, 53, 55, 123

Thénard, Baron, 28
Thiers, Louis Adolphe, 15
The Times, 47, 57, 93, 104, 106, 108, 111, 170
Le Tivoli, 14-15
Toulon, 52
Toumanova, Tamara, 174
Tourah, 23
Toussoun (Muhammad Ali's son), 22, 23
Traveller, 154, 158
Trollope, Anthony, 2, 151
Tsirkas, Stratis, 164
Tugay, 106
Tuileries Palace, Paris, 9-10, 12, 27, 52-3, 115-16
Turf Club, 2, 133, 134, 136, 138, 169
Turkey, 43, 127
Twain, Mark, 2, 151

Umar, Muhammad, 133
Umberto I, King of Italy, 122-3
United States of America, 102
Uzoun-Ali, 23

Valide, Sultana, 99, 100
Venizelos, Sophocles, 164
Verdi, Giuseppe, 28, 72, 74-82, 123
Verona Opera Company, 174
Victor-Emmanuel, King of Italy, 96, 98, 105-6
Victoria, Crown Princess of Prussia, 57, 104, 116
Victoria, Queen, 11, 24, 45, 56-8, 93, 100, 104, 105, 106, 116, 131
Victoria Club, 138
Villa St Maurice, 65
Vivant Denon, 15, 16

Wadi Halfa, 126
Wafd Party, 167
Waghorn, Lieutenant, 120, 125
Wagner, Richard, 75, 79, 82
Wahba, Magdi, 138, 139, 164, 165
Wahhabis, 23
Walk, 112
Walpole, 24
Wasaah, 145-6
Wasah, 2
Washington, George, 70
Waugh, Evelyn, 156-7, 159
Waugh, Mrs Evelyn, 2, 159
Wayne, Dennis, 174
Webster, James, 24-5
West Point Naval Academy, 63
Westminster, Duke of, 135
Wijh al-Birka, 145-6
William, King of Prussia, 55, 56, 105, 114, 116
Wilson, Woodrow, 160

Wilson Pasha, 162
Wingate, Sir Reginald, 162
Winter Race Meetings, 135-6
Winterhalter, Franz Xaver, 12
Wolff, Sir Henry Drummond, 44
Worth, 97

Yachut, 112
Young, George, 119-20
Youssoufian, Boghoz Bey, 35
al-Yusri, Saif Allah, 135

Zaaferan Palace, 68
Zaghloul, Saad, 130, 160-1, 162
Zamalek, 70, 87, 137, 162, 171, 176
Zech, Phillip, 152, 153
Zeinab, Princess, 6, 151
Ziyada, May, 130
Zola, Emile, 1, 53, 54-5, 106